The debate about the expansion of the regional integration of Europe is set to dominate the European Union's (EU's) policy agenda in the coming years. While the countries of Central and Eastern Europe may aspire to EU membership only in the longer term, Austria, Finland and Sweden have all recently achieved membership status. This volume, derived from the proceedings of a conference run jointly by the Centre for Economic Policy Research and the Yrjö Jahnsson Foundation, examines the discussion surrounding both actual and possible future expansion of the EU. The contributors address the key issues in the debate, including: the implications of expansion of the EU for the global trading system; the pressure any imminent expansion might put on the EU to reform its political and decision making processes; the theoretical motivation behind the clamour for entry to the EU; the economic consequences of membership for new entrants; and the effect on the location of economic activity and on migration in a larger EU. Using new trade theory, game theory, empirical assessment and simulation to report new results and insights, the contributors not only shed light on the consequences of Austria, Finland and Sweden joining the EU, but also discuss and evaluate the possible membership of Central European ex-socialist countries. This is an important book not only for students and scholars interested in regional integration, but also for policy-makers in the new EU member countries and in applicant countries. Many of the issues addressed in this volume will be relevant for the EU's inter-governmental conference in 1996.

G000056819

Expanding membership of the European Union

Yrjö Jahnsson Foundation

The purpose of the Foundation is to promote Finnish research in economics and medical science and to support Finnish institutions of research and education. The Foundation supports scientific research by financing research projects and the work of individual scholars, as well as by giving scholarships for graduate studies, both in Finland and abroad. In addition, the Foundation organises workshops, lectures and symposia on topics considered to be important. The Yrjö Jahnsson Foundation was established in 1954.

In the field of economics, the Yrjö Jahnsson Foundation is clearly the most important source of private research funding in Finland. In 1963 the Foundation started the series of Yrjö Jahnsson Lectures, given biannually by distinguished economists. Four of the contributors to the Jahnsson Lectures later received the Nobel Prize in Economics: Kenneth Arrow, Lawrence Klein, Sir John Hicks and James Tobin. The lectures have also been published and distributed internationally. Since the late 1980s, the Yrjö Jahnsson Foundation has placed more emphasis on European integration as a challenge to research, and in 1991 a lecture series on integration issues was launched. These lectures have also been published. In 1992, the Board of the Foundation decided to establish a European prize called the 'Yrjö Jahnsson Award in Economics', to be awarded biannually to a distinguished young economist.

In medical science, the Foundation aims to focus its support on a few well-defined fields of research. Priority is given to research projects in preventative medicine, which may also have economic importance.

The Board

Jaakko Honko	(Chairman)
Timo Laatunen	(Vice-chairman)
Veikko Kallio	
Pentti Talonen	
Pentti Vartia	

Scientific Committee

Jaakko Honko	Marianne Stenius
Veikko Kallio	Antti Tanskanen
Mikko Salaspuro	Pentti Vartia

Officers

Arto Alho	Managing Director
Mika Widgrén	Research Director

Centre for Economic Policy Research

The Centre for Economic Policy Research is a network of over 250 Research Fellows, based primarily in European universities. The Centre coordinates its Fellows' research activities and communicates their results to the public and private sectors. CEPR is an entrepreneur, developing research initiatives with the producers, consumers and sponsors of research. Established in 1983, CEPR is a European economics research organisation with uniquely wide-ranging scope and activities.

CEPR is a registered educational charity. Institutional (core) finance for the Centre is provided through major grants from the Economic and Social Research Council, under which an ESRC Resource Centre operates within CEPR; the Esmée Fairbairn Charitable Trust; the Bank of England; 15 other central banks and 30 companies. None of these organisations gives prior review to the Centre's publications, nor do they necessarily endorse the views expressed therein.

The Centre is pluralist and non-partisan, bringing economic research to bear on the analysis of medium- and long-run policy questions. CEPR research may include views on policy, but the Executive Committee of the Centre does not give prior review to its publications, and the Centre takes no institutional policy positions. The opinions expressed in this volume are those of the authors and not those of the Centre for Economic Policy Research.

1 March 1995

Expanding membership of the European Union

Edited by

RICHARD BALDWIN

PERTTI HAAPARANTA

and

JAAKKO KIANDER

CAMBRIDGE
UNIVERSITY PRESS

CAMBRIDGE UNIVERSITY PRESS
Cambridge, New York, Melbourne, Madrid, Cape Town, Singapore, São Paulo

Cambridge University Press
The Edinburgh Building, Cambridge CB2 8RU, UK

Published in the United States of America by Cambridge University Press, New York

www.cambridge.org
Information on this title: www.cambridge.org/9780521481342

First published 1995
This digitally printed version 2008

A catalogue record for this publication is available from the British Library

Library of Congress Cataloguing in Publication data
Expanding membership of the European Union / edited by Richard Baldwin,
Pertti Haaparanta, and Jaakko Klander.
        p.   cm.
Proceedings of a conference held in Sannäs, Finland, in May 1993,
organized jointly by the Centre for Economic Policy Research and
the Yrjö Jahnsson Foundation.
Includes index.
ISBN 0 521 48134 1
1. European Union – Congresses.
2. European federation – Congresses.
3. Europe – Economic integration – Congresses.
I. Baldwin, Richard.   II. Haaparanta, Pertti.   III. Kiander, Jaakko.
IV. Centre for Economic Policy Research (Great Britain).
V. Yrjö Jahnssonin säätiö.
JN30.E96   1995
341.24′2–dc20   95–9286   CIP

ISBN 978-0-521-48134-2 hardback
ISBN 978-0-521-05785-1 paperback

Contents

Figures

Tables

Preface

This volume contains the proceedings of the conference 'Expanding Membership of the European Union' held in Sannäs, Finland (14–15 May 1993). The conference was organised jointly by the Centre for Economic Policy Research and the Yrjö Jahnsson Foundation, and it was financed by the Jahnsson Foundation, to whom we wish to express our gratitude.

A joint conference on the enlargement of the EC was initiated by Jaakko Honko, the President of the Foundation, in December 1991 when Richard Portes was visiting Helsinki. At that time the discussion on the possible EC membership of the EFTA countries was about to begin. It was this prospect of future membership which dictated the programme of the conference. Although Austria, Finland and Sweden are now members of the EU, the themes of the conference are still relevant; the adjustment to the membership and its obligations is still ahead.

The editors would like to thank CEPR's permanent staff for their support; especially Richard Portes and Peter Johns for their contribution to the preparation of the conference programme, and Lisa Dowling and Jennifer Jones for their help in administrative tasks. Kate Millward and David Guthrie have skilfully organised the volume's production. We also thank Barbara Docherty for editorial assistance.

March 1995

Richard Baldwin
Graduate Institute of International Studies, University of Geneva
Pertti Haaparanta
Helsinki School of Economics
Jaakko Kiander
Labour Institute for Economic Research, Helsinki

Acknowledgements

The publisher and editors thank the following for permission to reproduce copyright material.

Cambridge University Press, for data in table 2.1, from J. de Melo and A. Panagariya (eds.), *New Dimensions in Regional Integration* (1993).

Quarterly Journal of Economics, for data in table 6.6, from R. Summers and P. Heston, 'The Penn World Table (Mark 5)' (1991).

Office for Official Publications of the European Communities, for data in tables 7.1 and 7.3, from D. Biehl (ed.), *The Contribution of Infrastructure to Regional Development* (1986).

Goethe-Institut, Frankfurt-am-Main, for data in table 7.1, from D. Biehl and P. Ungar, 'Kapazitätsaussatattung und Kapazitätsengpässe an Grossräumig Bedeutsamer Infrastruktur' (1991).

Commission of the European Communities, for data in table 7.5, from 'Community structural policies: assessment and outlook' (1992), and in table 7.6, from 'The Community's structural interventions', *Statistical Bulletin*, 3 (1992).

CEPR, for data in table 7.7, from 'Is bigger better? The economics of EC enlargement' (1992).

OECD, for data in table 8.3, from *Economic Outlook*, 54 (1993).

IFPRI, for data in table 9.1, from R. Tyers, 'Economic reform in Europe and the former Soviet Union: implications for international food markets', *Research Report*, 99 (1994).

USDA, for data in table 9.2, from *Western Europe Agriculture and Trade Report* (1992).

List of conference participants

Pekka Ahtiala (*University of Tampere*)
Kari Alho (*Research Institute of the Finnish Economy*)
Kym Anderson (*University of Adelaide and CEPR*)
Richard Baldwin (*Graduate Institute of International Studies, Geneva, and CEPR*)
Riccardo Faini (*Università degli Studi di Brescia and CEPR*)
Harry Flam (*Institute for International Economic Studies, Stockholm, and CEPR*)
Thorvaldur Gylfason (*University of Iceland and CEPR*)
Jan Haaland (*Norwegian School of Economics and Business Administration, Bergen, and CEPR*)
Pertti Haaparanta (*Helsinki School of Economics and Business Administration and CEPR*)
Carl B. Hamilton (*Institute for International Economic Studies, Stockholm, and CEPR*)
Heather Hazard (*Copenhagen Business School*)
Eduard Hochreiter (*Österreichische Nationalbank*)
Bernard Hoekman (*GATT Secretariat, Geneva, and CEPR*)
Seppo Honkapohja (*University of Helsinki and CEPR*)
Ilkka Kajaste (*Ministry of Finance, Helsinki*)
Jaakko Kiander (*Labour Institute for Economic Research, Helsinki*)
Seppo Leppänen (*Economic Council, Helsinki*)
Yngve Lindh (*Sveriges Riksbank*)
Philippe Martin (*Graduate School of International Studies, Geneva*)
Håkan Nordström (*Institute for International Economic Studies, Stockholm*)
Guido Tabellini (*Università di Brescia, IGIER, and CEPR*)
Hannu Törmä (*University of Jyväskylä*)
Risto Vaittinen (*Consumer Research Unit, Helsinki*)
Pentti Vartia (*Research Institute of the Finnish Economy*)

Mika Widgrén (*Research Institute of the Finnish Economy*)
Andreas Wörgötter (*Institut für Höhere Studien, Wien, and CEPR*)
Stephen Yeo (*CEPR*)

1 Introduction

RICHARD BALDWIN, PERTTI
HAAPARANTA and JAAKKO KIANDER

1 Resurgent European integration

In 1985, an unkind observer could have referred to the European
Economic Community as a glorified customs union held together by a
protectionist agriculture policy. Just 10 years later, the depth and
breadth of the Union's economic integration goes far beyond anything
seen in modern times. EU membership rose from nine to 15 members,
expanding the number of EU citizens by 25 per cent. Concomitantly,
microeconomic integration has been radically deepened and further
macroeconomic integration is in the works. The European Union is now
the vanguard of regional integration.

Deeper and wider European integration cannot be considered a
parochial affair, given Europe's economic size. The nations now
participating in European integration account for half of world trade and
a quarter of world GDP. Indeed since the EU's trade rules directly
govern one-third of world trade, they rival the importance of the General
Agreement on Tariffs and Trade (GATT). The economic weight of
Europe also means that European integration has an unavoidable impact
on the global trading system. Moreover, the factors that foster
preferential market opening in Europe also operate in the rest of the
world, so regional integration is on the rise world-wide. Because
European integration has gone much further and faster than the other
regional arrangements, the problems facing Europeans today are likely
to reappear in other regions in the future.

This volume focuses on the issues raised by expanding EU membership.
While the economics of deeper integration cannot be completely
separated from that of wider integration, EU expansion has brought to
the forefront three new issues. These are (1) European integration,
regionalism and the global trading system, (2) enlargement-created
pressures to reform EU institutions and policies, and (3) the location of

economic activity in a wider Europe. The final issue addressed in this volume is more standard, namely, the economic consequences of membership for the entrants.

Before turning to the key issues raised in this volume, we set the stage with a brief precis of recent integration.

1.1   Deeper Europe

European integration has been characterised by two concentric circles since the mid-1970s. The larger circle is a plurilateral duty-free zone for industrial trade supported by four sets of agreements: the Treaty of Rome (which removed tariffs on intra-EU trade), EFTA (which removed them on intra-EFTA trade), the EC–EFTA free-trade agreements (which removed duties on trade between the groups) and a set of ad hoc, bilateral free-trade agreements with non-EFTA, non-EU European nations. The smaller, inner circle (known successively as the EEC, the EC and the EU) has always been more integrated, including labour-market integration and supranational economic policies. The extent of economic integration in both circles has greatly deepened since 1985.

Jacques Delors' Single European Act (SEA) was the initiative that kicked off the recent resurgence of Europe integration. Proposed in 1985, signed in 1986 and ratified by member states in 1987, it is best thought of as a massive liberalisation of the EU economy. Before the Single European Act, firms based in member states enjoyed duty-free access to each other's markets; however, they certainly did not enjoy free trade. Trade was obstructed by a maze of differing national standards, regulations and practices, differing VAT and excise tax rates, capital controls, preferential public procurement, and administrative and frontier formalities. Although most of these barriers seem negligible individually, the confluence of their effects served to substantially fragment the European market. In industry after industry, local firms enjoyed dominant positions that allowed them to charge high prices and operate at inefficient scales of production. The Single Market programme was aimed at sweeping away all these remaining barriers by ensuring the free movement of goods, people, capital and services. In a sense, the so-called '1992' programme finally made good the promise implied by the EEC's popular name, the Common Market.

The Treaty on European Union was the second deepening. Beyond several cosmetic changes, institutional fine-tuning and a handful of vague promises about common foreign, security and defence policies, the so-called Maastricht Treaty committed the EU to a monetary union by the year 1999.

Both deepening phases have been extensively studied. For instance, the CEPR has produced two conference volumes on the Single Market programme – Winters (1992) and Winters and Venables (1991) – and several studies, e.g. Begg *et al.* (1991), on the European monetary union. These studies present state-of-the-art analysis; however they can also be thought of as updates of older literatures. The main issues addressed in the Single Market literature are the same as those examined in the 1970s' literature on trade creation and diversion. The core concern is the microeconomic impact of tighter integration on the member states. The principal issues in the recent EMU literature are also akin to those in a 1970s' literature. The questions of optimal currency areas, linkages between monetary autonomy and macroeconomic stabilisation and the mechanics of exchange rate management were all addressed in the famous Werner Report (1970). As we shall see below, the key issues raised by widening European integration have been subject to much less formal analysis.

1.2   Wider Europe

In 1986, the Iberian accessions to the EU shifted almost 50 million Europeans from the outer to the inner circle (Portugal came from EFTA and Spain already had a bilateral free-trade agreement with the EU). This greatly increased the economic diversity of the EU since these new members were much poorer than the average incumbent. Moreover, this enlargement boosted the EU's political–economy diversity because the entrants' powerful special-interest groups were concerned with issues that differed from those in incumbent nations. For example, compared to incumbents Iberian farmers specialise in different crops (fruits and vegetables rather than cereals, meat and dairy), their fishing industries are important, and the manufacturers focus more on labour-intensive goods.

The next step was to expand the outer circle eastward. In the early 1990s, the EU and EFTA signed bilateral free-trade agreements with several Central and Eastern European countries (CEECs). These were of two types, the Partnership and Cooperation Agreements and the Association Agreements (also known as Europe Agreements). Both establish duty-free trade in industrial goods. The Europe Agreements also contain political cooperation elements and evolutionary clauses that promise closer integration of the single-market type. As of early 1995, Europe Agreements had been signed with six Central and Eastern European nations (whose combined population is 96 million). It is likely that Europe Agreements will have also been signed with the three Baltic states by summer 1995, bringing to 104 million the total number of citizens in the outer circle of European integration. EFTA agreements with the Easterners are essentially limited to reciprocal liberalisation of import duties on industrial products.

This eastern expansion has profoundly increased the diversity of the outer circle. The new nations are much poorer and much more agricultural than most EU and EFTA members. Moreover, the Easterners are in the throes of massive and painful economic transitions. It is important to note, however, that the outer circle involves virtually no supranational decision making. Political and economic diversity thus does little to hinder operation of the Agreements – at least as compared to how diversity complicates the functioning of the EU.

Just as the outer circle expanded eastward, a new intermediate circle was created via the European Economic Area (EEA) Agreement. While this is a complicated arrangement (and the nuances are important), the EEA should be thought of as an attempt to extend the Single Market to non-EU countries. This attempt, however, was short-lived. First, Swiss voters refused to join it, and then Austria, Finland and Sweden joined the EU. The EFTA side had a population of 26 million when the EEA was set up on 1 January 1994, but just one year later it had a total population of only 4.6 million (4.3 million of them Norwegians). To a first order of approximation, the EEA is now an EU–Norway bilateral arrangement.

The most recent phase is a widening of the inner circle – what we might call the northeast enlargement of the EU. Since 1 January 1995, Austria, Finland and Sweden have become EU members. While small in terms of augmenting the EU population (only +6 per cent) and GDP (only +8 per cent), this enlargement increases the economic and political diversity of the EU. The nominal *per capita* income of the entrants is almost 40 per cent higher than that of the incumbents, all three are militarily neutral and have strong traditions of social equality.

An eastern enlargement of the EU is the next stage. At the Copenhagen summit in June 1993, EU heads of state promised to eventually admit all Central and Eastern European nations that have Europe Agreements. At the same time, they informally assented to negotiating Europe Agreements with the Baltic States and Slovenia. The Baltic talks are already under way. Italy, however, continues to veto negotiations with Slovenia. Due entirely to Italian obstructionism, Slovenia is now the only peaceful European nation to be excluded from the resurgence in European integration. Be that as it may, the Copenhagen promise portends an enlargement that would bring in nine or 10 new members with a combined population of over 100 million. Shifting these countries from the outer to the inner circle would dramatically increase the degree of economic diversity in the EU.

2 European integration, regionalism and the global trading system

Chapters 2 and 3 in this volume address 'big-think' issues raised by regionalism and its impact on the global trading system. Broadly speaking, chapter 2 looks at the causes of expanding regionalism and chapter 3 looks at the consequences.

2.1 The causes of expanding membership

In chapter 2, Richard Baldwin looks at the political economy forces behind the expansion of EU membership. He sets up the problem by asking a question: 'Why did regional integration spread like wildfire, while the GATT talks proceeded at a glacial pace?' For instance, the agenda setting negotiations for the Uruguay Round began in 1985 with the Round itself concluding in 1994. During this period, the EU negotiated, signed and largely implemented a radical market-opening initiative (the '1992' programme), agreed to adopt a common currency, signed a half dozen bilateral free-trade agreements, established the EEA, and accepted five new members with a total population of 70 million. In North America, the US and Canada signed and largely implemented the Canada–US Free-Trade Agreement (CUSTA), and the US, Canada and Mexico negotiated and ratified the North American Free-Trade Agreement (NAFTA).

Baldwin's answer is simple; deeper European integration caused wider European integration. A single idiosyncratic shock – such as the '1992' programme – can trigger membership requests from countries that were previously happy to be non-members. To trace through the reasoning, note that the stance of a country's government concerning membership is the result of a political equilibrium that balances anti- and pro-membership forces. Among the pro-EU forces are the firms that export to the regional bloc. Since closer integration within a bloc is detrimental to the profits of non-member firms, deeper integration stimulates the exporters to engage in greater pro-EU political activity. If their government was previously indifferent (politically) to membership, the extra activity may tilt the balance and cause the country to put in an application. Enlarging the bloc, however, raises the costs of non-membership and raises the benefits of membership. This second-round effect will bring forth more pro-EU activity in non-members, and thus may lead to further enlargement. The new political equilibrium will involve an enlarged EU. Meanwhile, it would appear that regional liberalisation is spreading like wildfire. In North America the triggering, idiosyncratic event was announcement of the US-Mexico free-trade talks.

If this explanation is correct, it is clear that shortcomings of the world trade system are not responsible for resurgent regionalism throughout the world. This is an important conclusion when pondering reform of the world trading system. Baldwin argues that GATT was not to blame for the stark contrast between regional and multilateral liberalisation, so one should not search for ways to fix this aspect of GATT.

2.2   The global consequences of expanding membership

In chapter 3, Håkan Nordström looks at the consequences that expanding regionalism has for the global trading system. To do this, he sets up a stylised computable trade model (of the monopolistic competition type) with a large number of fairly small nations. With this model on-line, he simulates formation and expansion of a single customs union under a variety of assumptions regarding the bloc's common external tariff (CET). (Tariffs are the only type of trade policy considered.) The two most relevant assumptions are that (1) the bloc's external tariff remains unchanged on average (as required by GATT, Article 24), and (2) the external tariff is set to fully exploit non-member countries (optimal tariff).[1] This formulation of the model is right on the money when it comes to considering recent regionalism. Although the EU is not the only preferential trading area, it is the only customs union of an appreciable size. In particular, NAFTA and most of the other regional arrangements have no coordination of external tariffs.

Nordström arrives at a rich array of interesting results concerning the consequences of expanding EU membership. Here we review only those that mesh most closely with the general theme of this volume. First, enlarging a customs union such as the EU always harms non-members, even if the bloc's average external tariffs are unchanged. To phrase it more colloquially, even without raising the ramparts of 'Fortress Europe', deeper European integration poses problems for non-Europeans. This result seems to be quite robust and the economics of it are straightforward. Under imperfect competition, the profit of one firm depends upon the marginal costs of all firms; anything that lowers the costs of one's rivals harms one's own profits.

Of course, Nordström's model is stylised, so his quantitative results should not be viewed as estimates; his aim is to use simulation to do theory that is too difficult to do analytically. In an earlier paper (Haaland

and Norman, 1992) the authors of chapter 8 in this volume simulate the impact of enlarging the EU's Single Market to include EFTAns. Like Nordström, they find that the US and Japan lose, but that the losses are quite small – of the order of 5 hundredths of 1 per cent of GDP.

Nordström's second result concerns the welfare maximising number of EU members. He finds that even in the unchanged external tariffs case, total EU welfare reaches its highest level when its members account for about half of world trade. Interestingly enough, this is the position that Europe will be in once it admits the Central and Eastern European nations.

It may seem strange to some readers that global free trade is not the best position. Again, this is a quite robust result, presuming only that external barriers consist only of tariffs.[2] Enlarging the customs union leads to two contradictory welfare effects. Lower tariffs tend to boost welfare by reducing resource allocation distortions, but they tend to lower welfare by worsening the bloc's terms of trade against non-members. Of course, the sign of the terms of trade effect can be reversed for non-tariff barriers such as voluntary export restraints (VERs) and price undertakings. For non-tariff barriers, liberalisation – via expansion of bloc membership, or other means – actually improves the bloc's terms of trade. Thus, to the extent that non-tariff barriers are the major form of external protection in the modern world, the optimal bloc size is the whole world.

Nordström's next set of results deal with Europe's temptation to abuse its market power via beggar-thy-neighbour external trade policy. The received wisdom on the 'optimal' tariff is that it might be a good idea, if foreigners were passive, but because foreigners are likely to retaliate, imposing optimal tariffs could end up making everyone worse off. While well accepted, this argument is not airtight; a sufficiently large country might gain despite retaliation.

Here is where Nordström's contribution fits in. With this model, Nordström can numerically calculate the retaliation that other countries would actually impose in a bilateral (Nash) tariff war with the customs union. He shows that as long as the customs union accounts for less than three-quarters of world trade, such retaliation is sufficiently painful to make beggar-thy-neighbour tariffs unattractive. As Nordström puts it, the fact that GATT sanctions retaliation for Article 24 violations makes Article 24 'incentive compatible' for blocs even as large as the EU. Indeed, it would even be incentive compatible for a super-bloc consisting of NAFTA and EU (this would account for about two-thirds of world trade).

Finally, Nordström turns to the debate concerning trade blocs and global free trade. The key question is: 'Are regional trading arrangements "building blocs" or "stumbling blocs" when it comes to facilitating global free trade?' Nordström's contribution on this point may be controversial, but seems quite sensible. If the world breaks into two trading blocs and these are close enough in size, then the two blocs would find it optimal to negotiate a bilateral free-trade agreement which would bring about global free trade. Again, Nordström performs his analysis using the concepts of cooperative game theory. Each bloc would prefer to keep its tariffs and have the other bloc remove its tariffs, but fear of the prisoners' dilemma outcome makes reciprocal liberalisation incentive compatible.

It seems that Nordström's simulation approach is very fruitful and helps us get a feel for many important issues. The point here is that 'big-think' questions concerning regionalism and the global economy are far too complicated to settle with models simple enough to solve with paper and pencil. Nordström's findings are not definitive; they point the way towards more comprehensive future research.

3   Implications for current policies and institutions

The addition of five new members and 70 million new citizens has brought many EU institutions and policies to breaking point. Even a modest eastern enlargement, consisting only of the Visegrad-nations and their 64 million citizens, would push many EU institutions and status quo policies over the edge. As a consequence, expanding membership has forced the EU to consider a whole set of issues that had hitherto been ignored. Put simply, the EU must rethink its policies and institutions if it is to continue expanding its membership. The 1996 intergovernmental conference (IGC96) is where policy makers will address such issues. Two chapters in this volume constitute seminal contributions on the topic. In chapter 5, Mika Widgrén uses a specialised branch of game theory to formally analyse the impact of enlargement on voting in the Council of Ministers. In chapter 9, Kym Anderson and Rod Tyers use a computable model of world food production and consumption to work out the impact of the 1995 enlargement and the future eastern enlargement, presuming that the Common Agricultural Policy (CAP) is unreformed.

3.1   Voting, power and EU enlargement

The public debates on the 1995 enlargement and the prospective eastern enlargement demonstrate that one of the most sensitive issues surrounding expanding membership is that of power in EU institutions. In the Nordic countries much discussion was devoted to the question: 'How much power can a small country like mine have in the EU?' A major question in the minds of incumbents was: 'What will the new members do to the balance of power in EU institutions?' Lastly, a vital question facing policy makers at IGC96 will be: 'How must EU decision making procedures be streamlined so that the eastern enlargement will not create gridlock in the Council of Ministers?' In chapter 5, Widgrén explains and then uses formal measures of power to investigate the impact of expanding membership on the EU's decision making process.

Before turning to Widgrén's results, it is worth justifying his basic approach. His chapter is rich in material and as such demands much work from the reader. This work will be amply rewarded. In fact, this chapter is one of a series of papers by Widgrén on this subject (see chapter 5 for references). Although not all will accept his findings as relevant, it seems likely that this approach will become a standard instrument in every first class policy analyst's toolkit.

The Shapley–Shubik index of power and EU spending priorities
Perhaps the most intuitive measure Widgrén uses is the so-called Shapley–Shubik index (SSI). The SSI measures how likely it is for a particular country's vote to switch a losing coalition into a winning coalition. Specifically, it is the ratio of the number of times a particular country can play this pivotal role divided by the total number of times that any country is pivotal. It may be helpful to think of the SSI in the following way: suppose that each time a country is pivotal, it asks for and may be granted a special gift. In this light, a country's SSI equals its expected fraction of all special gifts awarded.

This latter interpretation suggests that EU member states' SSIs should be closely correlated with their net receipts, since those that have the power should get a lot of cash. Let us look at the data to see whether the SSI is a useful tool.

In figure 1.1, the dark bars show the *per capita* net receipts in 1992 for the EU-12. Countries with negative receipts (Germany, France, the UK and the Netherlands) are net contributors. The light bars show the *per capita* SSI (the index is multiplied by 50 for scaling purposes). The line shows *per capita* GDP. It is quite clear that *per capita* GDP has absolutely nothing to do with net receipts; a simple regression of it on *per capita* receipts has an R^2 of 3 per cent. It is just as clear that net receipts line up exceedingly well with the SSI power index; a simple regression of the two yields an R^2 of 87 per cent. In fact even the raw number of *per capita* Council votes does a pretty good job of accounting for EU spending priorities (the simple regression has an R^2 of 76 per cent). What

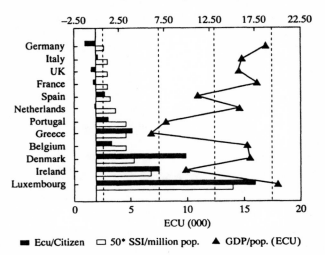

Figure 1.1   Explaining EU spending with *per capita* SSI v. *per capita* income

all this goes to show is that EU spending seems to be dictated by power in the Council of Ministers. More importantly, the power indices calculated by Widgrén seem to be a useful measure of this power.

Be sure to note that this constitutes a radical way of thinking about EU spending priorities. If you read politicians' speeches and media reports, you might be under the impression that the EU spending is directed mainly by high-minded ideals: rich countries pay more to help poorer members. Figure 1.1 shows that this standard notion of EU spending priorities is nonsense. Members with the most *per capita* power get the most *per capita* money.

Widgrén's results fall into two broad categories: backward-looking and forward-looking results. The first set deals with the impact of expanding membership on the power of incumbents and entrants. The second set deals with the power implications of the institutional reform that are now widely recognised as a precondition for enlargement beyond the EU-15.

Granting power to entrants, diluting power of incumbents
Under current EU rules, small countries receive far more votes per citizen than large countries. For instance, Sweden has about 1/2 Council of Minister votes per million Swedes while Germany has only about 1/8 votes per million Germans. Widgrén finds that the newest EU members should consequently have a good deal of power in the Council.

Figure 1.2 shows Widgrén's results. The light bars indicate the national power indices and the dark bars show the same index per million citizens.

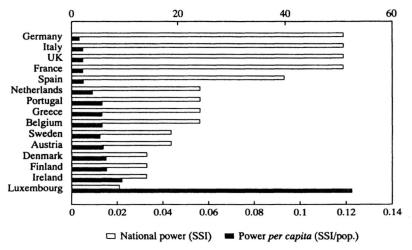

Figure 1.2   Power and *per capita* power in the EU-15

What this shows is that Austria and Sweden (which received 4 votes each) should have about a third of the power of the 'big-4' EU countries (Germany, France, Italy and the UK) and Finland should have about 1/4 of Germany's power.

When a club grants votes to new members, the power of incumbents tends to be diluted. Widgrén calculates the extent to which the northeast enlargement (i.e. the admission of Austria, Finland and Sweden) reduces the power of the 12 incumbents. He finds that the power of the big and medium-sized incumbents (i.e. countries with populations at least as large as Belgium's) is reduced by 10–15 per cent. The power of Denmark and Ireland is reduced about 20 per cent (as measured by changes in their SSIs), while Luxembourg actually experiences a significant increase in its power.

Interestingly, Widgrén finds that the northeast enlargement reduces the power of incumbents by much less than the southern enlargement did. Giving Council votes to Greece, Spain and Portugal lowered the SSI of the big and medium-sized incumbents by 25–30 per cent, lowered that of the small incumbents by 26 per cent and raised the power of the 380,000 Luxembourgers about 20 per cent.

Reforms of EU voting
It is fairly easy to see that voting rules in the EU must be changed before the eastern enlargement occurs. For instance, Baldwin (1994) projects the

number of Council votes that the Visegrad-4 countries (Hungary, the Czech Republic, Slovakia and Poland) would have under current rules and then looks at the possibility of blocking coalitions. Under the current EU rules governing the so-called qualified majority, countries with only 30 per cent of the total votes can block any measure. On many issues, there would be a clear alignment of interest between the old poor-4 (Spain, Portugal, Greece and Ireland) and the new poor-4 (Hungary, the Czech Republic, Poland and Slovakia). Since these eight countries would have 43 votes where a blocking minority would require only 32, it seems manifest that decision making would become difficult. After all, recall how the current poor-4 agreed to the Treaty on European Union only after the EU doubled the amount of transfers to poor regions by creating the Cohesion Fund.

Widgrén's next set of results deal with the implications of two commonly proposed voting reforms. The first is the so-called double majority, which would require a qualified majority of countries both in terms of Council votes (as before) but also in terms of population (see figure 1.3). The second would be to reduce the majority threshold from 71 per cent to 50 per cent in order to make proposals easier to pass. Most of the writers who propose the first rule change presume that they would tend to give more power to the medium-sized and large countries. Using the SSI measure, Widgrén's results show that the double majority would increase the power of Germany, which has by far the largest population, but that it would weaken the other big and medium-sized countries. Apart from Germany, the only other countries projected to gain are the three newest members (Austria, Finland and Sweden) and two other small countries (Denmark and Ireland), and tiny Luxembourg (the city of Lyons has three times the population of Luxembourg). Widgrén finds that the proposal to switch from the 71 per cent to a 50 per cent majority rule would have very little impact on the power of any country.

3.2   Enlarging membership and the Common Agricultural Policy

The EU currently spends about half its budget on the CAP. The budgetary impact of new members depends in consequence very much on their agricultural sectors. In chapter 9, Anderson and Tyers estimate the impact on EU food markets and the CAP of admitting EFTA nations into the Union and of admitting the Visegrad-5.

Anderson and Tyers use a multicommodity dynamic simulation model of world food markets that is based on 1990 data. The model distinguishes seven commodity groups: wheat, coarse grain, rice, sugar, dairy products, meat of ruminants and meat of non-ruminants. These

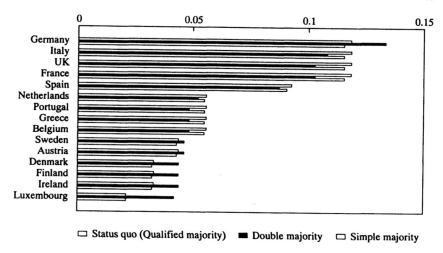

Figure 1.3   SSI under current rules and two types of reform

seven commodity groups exclude edible oils and beverages. This disaggregation provides a big payoff because the distortionary effects of the CAP vary greatly between products. The output composition of various nations' agricultural production also varies greatly. The model is global in coverage, so changes in Europe feed into world prices. It also allows production and consumption cross-effects in the interdependent markets for grains, livestock products and sugar. It is dynamic in the sense that it incorporates effects of income, population and productivity changes for each year through to 2010. The model was developed as part of an IFPRI project, Tyers (1993).

Although it is well known that the CAP has lifted EU food prices far above world prices, it is less well known that the EFTA nations have even more protectionist policies in food. For instance, while EU producer prices for food are on average 2.5 times higher than world prices, EFTA producers enjoy prices that are twice as high as EU prices (taking 1990 as the base year).

Membership for EFTAns would mean adopting the CAP and to be concrete, Anderson and Tyers assume no change in CAP support prices. There are exceptions to this. For instance, Finland has managed to negotiate a five-year adjustment period for agriculture during which she is allowed to hand out subsidies in excess of CAP. It remains to be seen whether she can continue this beyond the adjustment period. Since CAP prices are substantially lower than EFTA prices for most foods, this implies a substantial liberalisation of EFTA agriculture. As a result,

EFTAns produce less and consume more food. This turns the EFTAns into net food importers and increases world food prices by an average of 1.7 per cent. The biggest impact, however, is on the CAP budget. Due to increased EFTA consumption of food from the EU-12, the EU food surplus falls. This directly reduces one major CAP cost, namely the volume of the CAP-created EU food surplus that must be dumped on the world market. Since world food prices also rise, the cost per tonne dumped falls along with the number of tonnes to be dumped. The total savings to the CAP budget is estimated to be $31 billion. To summarise, the EFTA enlargement makes the CAP easier to maintain. Of course, Norway and Switzerland did not accede to the EU, so the exact Anderson–Tyers numbers are somewhat overstated as far as the actual northeast enlargement is concerned.

Anderson and Tyers generate a second set of results concerning the cost of allowing the Visegrad-4 access to the CAP. In particular, they consider the effects on farm trade and welfare of a Visegrad enlargement, assuming that the McSharry reforms are fully implemented. The results reported are for the year 2000. The scenario undertaken by the authors supposes that there are no changes in the CAP beyond the McSharry reforms, so that farmers and consumers in the incumbent EU nations are unaffected. Eastern consumers would face higher prices, which would cost them an extra $15.9 billion annually. This loss, however, would be more than offset by the gain to Visegrad farmers since the Visegrad nations would be important exporters at CAP prices. Anderson and Tyers find that Visegrad farmers would be better off to the tune of $52.5 billion. Taken together, allowing the Visegrad countries into the CAP would involve a massive transfer from incumbent EU taxpayers and Visegrad consumers to Visegrad farmers.

Absorbing Visegrad food production into the CAP would be costly to the EU budget for several reasons. First, the CAP food prices and production subsidies would stimulate Visegrad agricultural production. The Visegrad group's combined output of farm products would be almost $10 billion higher than under the non-membership scenario, with the production increase concentrated largely in the livestock sectors. After full adjustment, the annual Visegrad output of pig and poultry meat would rise by one-third, that of beef by a half and that of dairy products by two-thirds.

There are two main reasons for this massive food-production response. First, the CAP is heavily biased towards northern European farm products. For instance, while it raises the average producer prices to about 2.5 times the world level, it raises dairy prices by 4 times. Second, the Visegrad countries are large and blessed with farmland that is well suited to northern European farm products. In fact there are 320,800 km^2 of arable land in the Visegrad-4 (the comparable figure for France is 177,500 km^2). All of this Visegrad land is north of Lyons.

To maintain CAP prices after a Visegrad enlargement, all of the surplus Visegrad output would have to be dumped on the world market. Thus besides production subsidies, the EU would have to provide large export subsidies for the excess food. Of course, dumping this extra food on the world market would further depress world food prices. Apart from any international trade ramifications, the lower prices would make it also more expensive to subsidise the export of EU incumbents' surplus food. Anderson and Tyers estimate that the total extra cost to the EU budget would amount to $47 billion each year, or 37.6 billion ECU using an exchange rate of 1.25. This would more than double the current CAP budget.

4 Implications for the location of economic activity

Expanding EU membership has enormously increased the geographic range of Europe, and increased the dispersion of industrial structure. Partially in response to this widening of Europe, and partially in response to political developments, issues surrounding the location of economic activity have come to centre stage. German trade unions, for instance, fear that their jobs will flee to lower-priced southern or eastern labourers. Simultaneously, southern and eastern industries fear that they will be crushed by northern industrial might.

4.1 The regional production implications of a deeper, wider Europe

The possibility of a haemorrhaging of industry played an important role in the membership referendums in the Nordic countries. The popular idea was that the combination of globalisation (as defined by increased ease of shifting production abroad) and discrimination arising from the Single Market programme might lead EFTA industry to head South in a massive way. EU membership, even more than EEA membership, would help circumscribe this loss of industry employment. In chapter 8, Jan Haaland and Victor Norman use a computable general equilibrium model to take a first look at the very broad implications of the combined effect of a deeper and wider Europe. The main focus is on the increased integration of European capital markets. In particular, they look at the impact of perfect capital mobility under a variety of assumptions concerning trade in goods. The analysis is organised around two questions. The first is: 'How will the regional pattern of industrial production in Europe be affected by product market integration and capital mobility?' The second is: 'Does product market integration tend to act as a substitute for capital movements?'

The model the authors use can be thought of as the son of their earlier, seminal model described in Haaland and Norman (1992). It therefore helps to briefly review the earlier study. In that paper, which examined the impact of the Single Market on EFTA, the authors conceived of the Single Market programme as producing two changes: lower trade cost and integrated markets. The market integration aspect is an attempt to capture the notion that the Single Market programme would force firms to look upon Europe as a unified market, instead of a set of small, fragmented markets. In terms of mechanics, Haaland and Norman calibrated their base case assuming that firms believe that the amount sold in one market does not affect prices in other markets. In the market integration case (as opposed to the fragmented market case), firms are forced to charge a single producer price throughout the Single Market. The impact of such market integration, which was first explored in a partial equilibrium model by Smith and Venables (1988), can be surprisingly large.

The base case in chapter 8 assumes that markets are fragmented and capital is immobile internationally. The authors assume that initially EFTA capital earns somewhat less than 'EU North' capital, which itself earns less than EU South capital. (EU North is the EU-12 *less* the EU South, which consists of Spain, Greece, Ireland and Portugal.) Specifically, if the rate of return in EU North is normalised to an index of 100, then Haaland and Norman assume that it is 95 in EFTA and 105 in the EU South.

The first simulation experiment is to consider the effects of allowing perfect capital mobility and lower trade costs throughout Europe (the old EU-12 plus the pre-1995 EFTA) by 2.5 per cent. Markets continue to be fragmented. The authors find that this leads to an important export of capital from EFTA to EU South. In fact, 17.6 per cent of EFTA capital is exported, with almost all of this going to EU South. This has the effect of reducing the output of capital-intensive industries in EFTA by about 6 per cent and increasing that in the EU South by about 7 per cent. The change in factor abundance boosts EFTA's output of skill-intense industries by about 5 per cent and shrinks that of EU South by about 3 per cent. The vast majority of this effect comes from perfect capital mobility, since the authors find that with capital mobility but without the trade-cost reduction, 18.4 per cent of EFTA capital leaves.

The second experiment adds market integration to perfect capital mobility and 2.5 per cent lower trade costs. Surprisingly, the authors find that market integration tends to increase the EFTA capital outflows slightly (from 17.6 per cent to 18.2 per cent). As in the previous experiment, EFTA tends to specialise more in skill-intensive industries while EU South specialises more in capital-intensive industries.

What do we learn from these simulations? First, there seems to be much less interaction between goods-market integration and capital-market integration than the popular debate suggests. To paraphrase the authors, those in EFTA who hope that EU membership will prevent capital outflows will find no support here. Second, even fairly small initial differences in the return to capital can create massive capital flows.

It is important, however, to keep in mind the exploratory nature of this study. This is – as Haaland and Norman point out themselves – only a first attempt. Perhaps the least satisfactory aspect of the model is perfect capital mobility. Until Europe has a single money as well as a single market, substantial differences in rates of return are likely to persist.

4.2 Migration in a deeper, wider Europe

Few economic issues can stir controversy and passion in the way migration can. Moreover, when it comes to migration, the question of deepening European integration cannot be separated from that of a wider Europe. The possibility of mass migration is an important issue both in members of the old EU-12 and in the new member countries. While no one in the EU-12 feared hordes of Nordic or Austrian migrants, migration is and will continue to be a deal-breaking issue in the prospective eastern EU enlargement. Recall that when Spain and Portugal acceded in 1986, they were excluded from the free movement of people for 5 years.

While the literature on migration is vast and quite sophisticated, many writers on the subject continue to perpetrate misunderstanding of the phenomenon. In chapter 6 Riccardo Faini provides a calm and factual discussion of migration and EU membership expansion. The factual points that are worth highlighting are:

1 The 1958–74 period saw an important migration from Southern Europe to Northern Europe
2 After 1974 the migration flow plummeted and many southern migrants returned home; in absolute and relative terms, the stock of Southern European migrants in Northern Europe fell

3 Southern European nations have themselves experienced sharp increases in the stock of migrants since 1980; most of these are non-EU
  nationals from developing countries.

In explaining the second fact above, Faini dispels a common myth about
intra-EU migration. Many writers presume that income differentials are
the key to migration. Faini, however, argues econometrically that the
reduced flows are due mainly to a reduced supply of Southern European
workers willing to migrate, and he associates this with rising Southern
income levels. This notion has important implications for the prospective
eastern enlargement. If Faini is correct, the migration flows that would
come with an eastern EU enlargement depend upon the level of income
in Eastern Europe as well as the income differentials.

A frequently-heard misapprehension about the third fact above has
caused much concern in Northern EU nations. According to the
common (incorrect) view, this rise in foreign residents stems from lax
migration policy in the South and tighter controls in the North.
Accordingly, one important phase of the deepening of Europe –
implementation of the Schengen Agreement in spring 1995 – could
produce a big movement of non-EU migrants from the South to the
North. Faini argues that while some of this might happen, the
magnitudes are likely to be small. His basic reasoning is that these new
migrants came to work in Southern Europe, not to gain access to
Northern Europe.

The rise in foreign residents in Southern Europe is largely accounted for
by three facts. First, due to rapid income growth in the South (except in
Greece) and sluggish growth in the North, the income gap between
Southern Europe and poor Mediterranean nations has widened since the
1970s. The gap between Northern Europe and poor Mediterranean
nations has not. Consequently, it is natural that the South should
attract migrants. Second, the informal sectors in Southern Europe are
much larger than those in the North, so non-EU workers (especially
illegal ones) are likely to continue to find it easier to work in the South.
Third, overall employment growth – which is often an important
determinant of migration – has been more sustained in the South than
the North. All three of these reasons suggest that few of the new
migrants in Southern Europe view it as a staging ground for migration
to Northern Europe.

Faini also addresses the issue of potential East–West migration after
the eastern enlargement occurs. Judging from historical (mainly South–
North) European migration patterns, the current East–West wage
differentials are sufficient to trigger fairly large migration flows. In fact,

it is somewhat surprising that so little East–West migration has occurred, although data is scarce. A partial explanation for this comes from the fact that Eastern workers may be expecting rapid growth in their own nations.

Faini closes his chapter with a call for further integration of European migration policies. He suggests that the wide variance of regulations in the EU-15 could provide potential migrants with an incentive to relocate simply to take advantage of better regulations. The harmonisation of both admission and labour market regulations is consequently a pressing matter.

4.3   Effectiveness of regional policies in Europe

As Europe becomes wider and more diverse, EU policy makers are devoting an increasing fraction of EU resources to policies aimed at narrowing income differentials. In 1980, the year before Greece became a member, 11 per cent of the EU budget was spent on Structural, Regional and Social policies (all of which are intended to help poor regions). In 1994 the EU spent over 20 billion ECU on these policies, i.e. about 30 per cent of the EU budget. Most of this money is spent on public infrastructures such as roads, airports, telephone lines, etc. in the old poor-4 member states (Spain, Portugal, Greece and Ireland). For these countries, the funds are quite important: Portugal, for instance, receives EU transfers that amount to about 3.5 per cent of its GNP.

Despite the magnitude of this so-called structural spending, very little academic interest has been focused on it. In fact, even the thinking of EU policy makers seems to be rather vague on how these billions are supposed to affect the location of economic activity. In chapter 7 Philippe Martin and Carol Ann Rogers develop a theoretical model in which public infrastructure can affect industrial location. This gives us a simple, benchmark model around which we can organise our thinking about structural spending. The first result Martin and Rogers find is that deeper trade integration can increase the disparity among regions by inducing industry to relocate from regions with poor infrastructure to regions with good infrastructure. In practice, this means a shift out of poor regions and into rich ones. While this result is very much in the spirit of Krugman's new location theory (see Krugman, 1991 for an introduction), Martin and Rogers constitutes the first model in which public infrastructure plays an explicit role.

Martin and Rogers also estimate their model on regional EU data. They find that good public infrastructure is highly correlated with the location of industry. They also go on to study which forms of public infrastructure are most closely correlated with industry location. They find that telecommunication and education infrastructure are most highly correlated with industry location. Energy and transport infrastructure are typically insignificant factors.

Since the share of structural spending on energy and transport infrastructure is 16 per cent, 18 per cent and 22 per cent in Spain, Greece and Ireland respectively, the empirical findings of Martin and Rogers should raise many eyebrows in Brussels. Their investigation suggests that the billions spent on energy and transport infrastructure are not useful in furthering the goals of EU structural policies.

4.4   Deeper goods market integration and the 'quality of life'

During EU accession negotiations, prospective Nordic members expressed a great deal of apprehension about the regional consequences of deeper integration. Of particular concern was the possibility that integration would worsen living conditions in the remote regions.

In both Finland and Norway, policy makers have struggled for decades to keep their remote regions populated. For Finland, especially, this desire takes on national security dimensions given the remoteness of their long border with Russia. Moreover, concern for equality is a hallmark of the Nordic model of development; these countries have become rich due to rapidly rising productivity in their export industries and services providers. Rather than allowing this to create income inequalities, Nordic policy makers instituted a wide range of policies that permitted nearly all members of society to share in the prosperity created by these fairly narrow economic activities. Such policies range from raising farmers' incomes via heavy protection of agriculture to direct social payments. Lavish infrastructure spending and industrial subsidies in remote regions are part of this.

In chapter 4 Pertti Haaparanta and Tiina Heikkinen present theoretical models in which deeper regional integration can have conflicting effects on welfare. In particular, they are interested in modelling the trade-off between lower prices and some notion of the 'quality of life'. There are two real-world concerns addressed here. The first is basically the idea that while opening markets may lower the price of consumer goods available at retail outlets, it may also narrow the range of goods carried by the retailers. The second is very similar to that addressed by Martin and Rogers in chapter 7, namely the tendency for international integration to foster greater concentration of economic activities in large urban areas.

The issues raised in this chapter are important, and have hitherto been little studied. The Haaparanta and Heikkinen models are hardly the final contribution to this area, but hopefully they will stimulate further theoretical and empirical research.

5   Economic consequences of membership for entrants

Finally, we turn to a classic trade policy question: 'What is the impact of EU membership on entrants?' In chapter 10, Kari Alho investigates this question, focusing mainly on the Finnish case.

The methods that are necessary to answer this question are not as simple as one might expect. The main difficulty is that the countries that acceded to the EU were already members of the EEA. As such, they had already agreed to a big increase in integration with the incumbents. Alho first outlines the main differences between EEA and EU membership. The most important of these may be summarised as the four Cs: the CAP, common external tariffs (entrants must adjust tariffs on third-country trade to match the EU's tariffs), cash (entrants will receive EU monies and contribute to the EU budget) and control (entrants will have a say in future EU legislation and the enforcement of existing EU laws). Additionally, membership will eventually remove border controls and imply participation in the monetary union.

Alho's overall estimate of the long-term welfare gain for Finland is 4 per cent of GDP. This is quite large compared to estimates for other countries. Much of this difference, however, is accounted for by the fact that Alho considers many economic channels ignored by others. For instance, instead of taking the farm sector to be static, he presumes that competition will force farms to merge into larger, more efficient units. Alho also calculates the economic gains from Finland's EMU participation. The mechanics of this involve the assumption that EMU would eliminate the Finnish Mark's interest rate premium over the German Mark.

6   Conclusions

This volume should be thought of as a beginning, not an end. The contributions were written before the EFTA countries made their choices regarding EU membership. Their relevance has not disappeared although Austria, Finland and Sweden have become EU members, and the issues will continue to be increasingly important in years to come. European integration will deepen, and the EU may get new members. Whether economists provide the detailed analysis or not, practical men will have to make hard choices concerning the eastern enlargement of Europe at IGC96.

NOTES

1   In this sense, Nordström's chapter 3 can be seen as a refinement to the 'Is regionalism bad?' literature begun by Krugman (1991). For a review of that literature, see Winters (1994).
2   An 'optimum tariff' drives a wedge between domestic and border prices. This creates government revenue and a distortion in domestic resource allocation. The domestic incidence of the tax is simply a transfer, but the incidence of the tax on foreigners is a net gain to the home country. Since the distortion effect is second order small while the taxation of foreigners is first order small, a sufficiently low tariff must be welfare improving. If the wedge is created by a non-tariff barrier, there is no implicit taxation of foreigners to offset the distortion loss.

REFERENCES

Baldwin, R.E., 1994. *Towards an Integrated Europe*, London: CEPR Press
Begg, D. *et al.*, 1991. *The Making of Monetary Union*, London: CEPR Press
Haaland, J. and V. Norman, 1992. 'Global production effects of European integration', in L.A. Winters (ed.), *Trade Flows and Trade Policy After '1992'*, Cambridge: Cambridge University Press
Krugman, P.R., 1991. 'Is bilateralism bad?', in E. Helpman and A. Razin (eds.), *International Trade and Trade Policy*, Cambridge, MA: MIT Press
Smith, A. and T. Venables, 1988. 'Completing the internal market in the European Community: some industry simulations', *European Economic Review*, 32, 1501–25
Tyers, R., 1993. 'Economic reform in Europe and the former Soviet Union: implication for international food markets', IFPRI, *Research Report*, 99, Washington, DC: IFPRI
Werner, P., 1970. *Report to the Council and the Commission on the Realisation by Stages of Economic and Monetary Union*, Brussels: Office of Publications of the European Communities
Winters, L.A., 1994. 'The EC and world protectionism: dimensions of the political economy', CEPR, *Discussion Paper*, 987, London: CEPR
Winters, L.A. (ed.), 1992. *Trade Flows and Trade Policy After '1992'*, Cambridge: Cambridge University Press
Winters, L.A. and A. Venables, 1991. *European Integration: Trade and Industry*, Cambridge: Cambridge University Press

Part One
Theoretical issues

2   A domino theory of regionalism

RICHARD E. BALDWIN

1   Introduction

In the past 10 years, regional trade liberalisation has swept the world
trading system like wildfire while the multilateral GATT talks proceeded
at a glacial pace. This conspicuous contrast raises the question: 'Why are
countries eager to open markets regionally, but reluctant to do so
multilaterally?' Perhaps the most-widely heard answer to this question
focuses on two assertions.[1] The first is that regional integration has
prospered as an alternative to multilateralism since multilateral trade
negotiations have become too cumbersome to deal with today's complex
trade issues. The second assertion is that the 'conversion' of the US from
a strong backer of multilateralism to an avid participant in regional
schemes has been a driving force.

This chapter discusses the shortcomings of these assertions, and
proposes an alternative answer. The chapter has four sections after the
Introduction. Section 2 presents a few facts about recent regionalism,
criticises the standard explanation for the recent rise in regionalism and
proposes an alternative answer. Section 3 presents the basic economic
and political economic model. Section 4 discusses how the domino effect
operates in the model, and Section 5 contains a summary and some
concluding remarks.

2   Facts, the standard explanation and an alternative

Before discussing the shortcomings of the standard assertions and
proposing an alternative answer, it is necessary to get a few facts straight.
First, it is important to be more precise about the nature of the recent
wave of regionalism. The initiatives that constitute the recent revival of
regionalism should be thought of as falling into two categories: deep
initiatives and shallow initiatives. Second, it is necessary to understand
the relative size (as measured by the amount of trade covered) of these

various initiatives. Lastly, one must get the facts straight on the timing and motives of the two major regional initiatives – those in Europe and in North America.

2.1   Deep and shallow regional integration arrangements

Deep regional integration schemes go far beyond the liberalisation of statutory border measures such as tariff and quantitative restrictions. These schemes involve the further opening of product and service markets to international competition by removing regulatory and fiscal barriers to competition from foreign firms. Typically, this involves modification of laws, regulation, practices and policies that many nations view as purely domestic matters. Most of these deeper integration schemes are in West Europe. Examples are the completion of the Single Market, the Treaty on European Union signed in Maastricht, the European Economic Area (EEA) agreement and the accession of Spain, Portugal, Austria, Finland and Sweden to the EU. These involved a substantial deepening of pre-existing arrangements, or promises thereof. For instance, the Single Market programme instituted free movement of capital in the EU, and alleviated many non-border barriers to trade in goods and services.[2] It harmonised VAT rates, required mutual recognition of product standards (with minimum harmonisation), strengthened rights of establishment and further opened public procurement. The EEA basically extended the Single Market to EFTA countries (except Switzerland), and prohibited all anti-dumping and countervailing duties on intra-EEA trade.

These initiatives did not expand regional integration. They merely deepened existing schemes. Before the Single Market programme (also known as EU'92'), West European regional integration was marked by two concentric circles. The outer circle, which encompassed all EU and EFTA members, was a 'virtual' free-trade area for industrial goods. That is, the confluence of the Treaty of Rome, the Stockholm Convention (EFTA's founding document) and the bilateral EU–EFTA free-trade agreements ensured duty-free treatment for industrial trade between each pair of these countries. The inner circle consisted of the EU's common market, which went beyond duty-free industrial trade. The EU'92' programme and the EEA deepened the extent of integration in both the inner and outer circles. The 1986 EU enlargement brought one new country (Spain) into the system and moved another (Portugal) from the outer to the inner circle. The 1995 EU enlargement merely switched three countries from the outer to the inner circle.

The Australia–New Zealand Closer Economic Relations Trade Agreement, ANZCERTA, is also a deep integration scheme. It applies to most food trade in addition to duty-free trade in industrial goods. Moreover, it goes far beyond border measures in that it includes explicit commitments to harmonise standards and other regulations that may impede trade, and to make business laws and regulatory practices compatible. Labour mobility in the area is also relatively free.

Most of the other recent regional schemes – such as the US–Canada free-trade area (FTA), the US–Israel FTA, NAFTA, MECOSUR – and the revivals of old regional schemes in Latin America and Africa have involved fairly shallow integration. These are principally limited to liberalisation of tariffs and quantitative restrictions over longer transition periods. For example, the NAFTA tariff and quota liberalisations will not be completed until the year 2009.

2.2   The size of regional integration arrangements

The second point of fact that needs to be mentioned is the size of the various regional schemes. In terms of the volume of trade affected, Western European schemes dominate all others. Table 2.1 shows that the EEA now covers about a third of world exports. This figure is more than $4\frac{1}{2}$ times larger than the amount of trade covered by the next largest regional scheme, NAFTA.[3] All of the other successful regional initiatives are tiny. de Melo and Panagariya (1993) considered all regional integration arrangements in the world (well over 100 in number) and defined as 'successful' only those for which intra-arrangement trade was at least 4 per cent of the members' total exports on a sustained basis. As they point out, this is a very permissive definition of 'successful'. As table 2.1 shows, none of the other arrangements covers even as much as 1 per cent of world trade. Several of them cover less than one hundredth of 1 per cent of world trade. The main point is that in terms of the volume of world trade covered, the European and North American regional integration schemes are really the only important ones.

2.3   The timing and motivation of regional arrangements

Given the dominance of Europe and North America in the recent revival in regionalism, it is therefore worth reviewing the timing and motives of regional integration on these two continents.

American regionalism

In the Western hemisphere, the recent wave of regionalism may be traced back to the US–Canada FTA. According to Schott (1988), the germ of this initiative was a March 1985 summit meeting between President

Table 2.1   West European regional arrangements

1990 data	Intra-regional exports ($ billion)	Intra-regional exports as share world exports (%)
West Europe free trade zone (EU + EFTA)	1128.5	33.9
of which:		
EU-12	821.8	24.7
NAFTA	237.9	7.1
ANZCERTA	3.8	0.1
ASEAN	26	0.8
Andean Pact	1.4	0.0
CACM	0.5	0.0
LAFTA	12.0	0.4
ECOWAS	1.2	0.0
PTA	0.6	0.0

Source: IMF, *Direction of Trade Yearbook 1992*, EFTA, *Trade 1991*, and de Melo and Panagariya (1993) for smaller arrangements.
Note: 0.0 per cent indicates less than one-hundredth of 1 per cent. ANZCERTA is the Australia–New Zealand arrangement, ASEAN is the South-east Asian arrangement, the Andean Pact is an FTA among South American nations, CACM is the Caribbean common market, LAFTA is the Latin America FTA, ECOWAS is the West African arrangement and PTA is the Eastern and Southern African preferential trading area. Many of the last six arrangements cover substantially less than all intra-group trade, so the figures in table 2.1 are overestimates of the trade actually influenced directly.

Reagan and Prime Minister Mulroney. Reagan formally announced his intention to negotiate this FTA in December 1985. It is important to note that this was almost a year *before* the Uruguay Round was launched. The US–Canada talks in fact proved difficult, and the agreement did not come into force until 1989.

The following year, the US and Mexico announced their intention to form an FTA. This bilateral FTA was initiated by President Salinas of Mexico as a means of fostering stability in Mexico by boosting growth and locking-in unilateral pro-market reforms. The motives for this initiative had little to do with the US's desire to liberalise trade. In 1990, US exports to Mexico accounted for only 7.2 per cent of its total exports, so it seems highly unlikely that the US viewed this politically exacting, yet commercially unimportant, initiative as substituting in any way for global trade liberalisation. Since the Mexican economy is smaller than that of the Los Angeles basin, Mexico is not likely to become an important trading partner of the US in the coming decades.

Canadian concerns that the US–Mexico FTA might erode their preference margins, especially in automotive parts, led to NAFTA. Canada requested that the bilateral US–Mexico talks be broadened into a trilateral negotiation. The US and Mexico agreed and the North American Free-Trade Agreement (NAFTA) was born.

Following the resurgence of regional integration in North America, many smaller regional initiatives were launched, re-launched or seriously discussed in Latin America. For instance, Chile, Brazil, Argentina, Uruguay and Paraguay, formally or informally, approached the US to begin bilateral FTA talks. Moreover, interest in President Bush's Enterprise for the Americas Initiative boomed in 1991, with 26 countries signing so-called Framework Agreements. These require the countries to make unilateral concessions on trade and investment to the US in exchange for the promise of closer US relations, leading eventually to an FTA.

Few of these came to fruition, and it seems likely that even fewer will be ever carried out. De la Torre and Kelly (1992) analyse the reasons why South–South preferential trade arrangements are typically plagued by a low rate of implementation. The recent discussion of regional integration in the Asia–Pacific area is certainly a development to watch. However, it seems quite likely that nothing substantial will come of this. Trade frictions among the major trading nations, China, Japan and the US have been rising rather than diminishing: for instance, one may rightly question the likelihood of the US Congress agreeing to abolish all tariffs on Japanese and Chinese imports.

European regionalism
Recent European regionalism was sparked by the Single Market programme. In 1985 Jacques Delors took office with the intention of rekindling European integration. His strategy was to embark on a massive liberalisation that would turn the common market into a single market. The first formal step towards the Single Market programme was Lord Cockfield's June 1985 *White Paper*. This listed 282 measures necessary to complete the single market. The treaty that implemented these measures (along with many other changes) was the Single European Act. This was signed in February 1986 by the EU heads of government. In the same year, Spain and Portugal acceded to the EU after 6 years of membership negotiations.

The Single Market programme harmed the competitiveness of EFTA-based firms by lowering the costs of their EU-based rivals, as Krugman (1988) points out. In the mid-1980s, EFTA governments had decided that they must react. The idea of countering the threat with a new plurilateral agreement was first suggested at a meeting of EFTA and EU ministers in Luxembourg in 1984, even before the *White Paper* was published. This produced the so-called 'Luxembourg Declaration'. However, the difficulties of such an initiative, and the EU's preoccupation with the Single European Act and the Maastricht Treaty, led to long delays. Indeed very little was done until January 1989 when Jacques Delors proposed the European Economic Area (EEA) agreement (initially called the European Economic Space agreement). Talks on the EEA began informally in 1989, continuing more formally in 1990 and 1991.

The first version of the EEA, signed in 1991, was rejected by the European Court of Justice as inconsistent with EU law. Negotiations were reconvened and the second version of the EEA was signed on 2 May 1992 in Oporto. This was acceptable to the European Court; however, Swiss voters rejected it in a December 1992 referendum. Since the EEA formally included all EFTAns, this required a technical rewriting of the agreement. More important, since the EEA obliged the EFTAns to make financial transfers to poor EU regions, the withdrawal of Switzerland also forced a renegotiation of the size of these transfers. The final version of the EEA was signed in 1993, with implementation starting in January 1994.

Since the Single Market involves such a deep degree of integration it proved difficult for the EU to extend the Single Market to non-members. In particular, EU'92' constrains many economic policies that are not traditionally viewed as trade policy. It requires supranational surveillance and enforcement of competition policy (known as anti-trust policy in the US), state aids to industry, national public procurement policies, and regulation of the behaviour of state-owned monopolies. The member states of the EU can accept this sort of supranational control by the European Commission since the Commission itself is controlled by national political leaders via the Council of Ministers. Since non-member governments cannot vote or attend the Council of Minister meetings, the EEA agreement involved 'regulation without representation' for the EFTA side.

This so-called 'influence deficit' made the EEA a relatively unpalatable means of offsetting potential discrimination from EU'92'. As it turned out, virtually none of the EFTA governments were willing to live with the EEA. Even before the final version was adopted, all the EFTAns (except Iceland and Liechtenstein, which have a combined population of 0.29 million) had applied for full EU membership. Obviously, the end of the East–West conflict in Europe was also critical to this membership drive in that it removed traditional resistance to the EU. Applications were received from Austria (July 1989), Sweden (July 1991), Finland

(March 1992), Switzerland (May 1992) and Norway (November 1992). For these countries, the EEA was viewed as a transitional arrangement, not a long-term solution (note that the EU froze the Swiss application in response to the negative outcome of their EEA referendum). Accession talks for the four EFTAns were concluded in 1994, with entry to occur in 1995 subject to national referendums. Austrian, Finnish and Swedish voters responded positively in 1994. Norwegian voters said no.

The collapse of Communism also opened the Central and Eastern European countries (CEECs). The EU and EFTA (separately) signed bilateral free-trade agreements with several of these countries in the early 1990s. Since nearly all industrial trade in West Europe is duty-free and West Europe is the dominant market for the exports of Central and Eastern European nations, these bilateral free-trade agreements were essential to levelling the playing field for CEEC exporters. Most CEECs have applied, or plan to apply, to become full EU members, and the EU heads of state have agreed that they will eventually be admitted.

2.4   Critique of the standard explanation of recent regionalism

There is certainly some truth in the first pillar of the standard account of resurgent regionalism. Many contemporary trade issues are much more complicated than those (e.g. tariff liberalisation) dealt with in earlier GATT rounds. However, this assertion does not directly answer the question of why 'regional' instead of 'global'. We will first consider how relevant this explanation is to elucidate the recent deep integration schemes in Europe.

The primary forces behind European economic integration in the post-Second World War period have always been strategic and geopolitical motives. It seems quite far-fetched to propose that European frustrations with the GATT are what triggered EU governments to endorse Jacques Delors' proposal for completing the internal market. Two historical facts reinforce this assertion. Even when the GATT multilateral process was widely perceived as functioning well (in the 1950s and 1960s), West Europe continued to proceed with regional integration. Also, the Single Market programme, which is the first cause of most of the deeper integration schemes, was proposed and adopted long before frustration with the GATT talks emerged.

Given that the first part of the standard explanation is irrelevant to understanding European regionalism, we will turn to the second part. According to Bhagwati (1993), the single most important reason why regionalism is making a comeback is the conversion of the US from devoted multilateralist to ardent regionalist. Recall, however, that the

US conversion dates back only to late 1985. The resurgence of regionalism in Europe and the US thus occurred at approximately the same time. This timing suggests that the second part of the standard explanation also has little explicatory power when it comes to deep integration initiatives in Europe.

This line of argument, if accepted, should be enough to reject the standard explanation. If the standard explanation does not account for recent regionalism in Europe, then it does not account for the bulk of regionalism. At the very best, it accounts for the relatively small regional arrangement in North America and the tiny arrangements in Africa, Latin American and Asia. Taken together, all the non-European schemes deemed successful by de Melo and Panagariya (1993) cover only 8.5 per cent of world trade. As we shall see, however, the standard explanation has many shortcomings when applied to even these small arrangements.

Again we start with the first pillar of the standard explanation. Is it reasonable to assert that the shallow regional arrangements in Africa, Asia and the Western hemisphere are prompted by a disappointment with the lack of progress in the Uruguay Round and the functioning of the multilateral trading system? Consider the Canada–US FTA (CUSTA). The political decision to start negotiations was taken in the year before the Uruguay Round was launched. One would have to tell a very complicated story about American and Canadian motives to assert that sluggish progress on the GATT talks prompted the Canada–US FTA. The US–Mexico FTA talks and NAFTA were started after the Uruguay Round talks became bogged down. However, the motives for the triggering event, the US–Mexico FTA, had virtually nothing to do with global trade. It was pursued on both sides as a means of locking-in pro-market reforms in Mexico. It thus seems that the 'frustration-with-GATT' part of the argument is not applicable to the other major regional initiatives in the world, namely those in North America.

Next consider the second pillar of the traditional argument. When it comes to North American initiatives, all of which involve the US, the second pillar is a tautology. Indisputably the US acceptance of regionalism was a key to explaining NAFTA, but this sort of logic has no explanatory power.

Where does this leave the traditional explanation of regionalism? If it does not account for European or North American regionalism, then it is irrelevant. According to the figures in Table 2.1, all the other schemes cover less than 2 per cent of world trade.

The traditional explanation is appealing at first glance, and it has won over many adherents. Unfortunately, it is not consistent with the facts. West European and North American regionalism arrangements are the only ones that cover a significant fraction of global trade. Resurgent regionalism in both regions started well before the GATT talks became sluggish and cumbersome. Moreover, European regionalism was revitalised for purely European reasons. The US attitude was irrelevant.

2.5   The domino theory of regionalism

This chapter proposes a very different explanation of the question: 'Why are countries eager to open markets regionally, but reluctant to do so multilaterally?' The stark contrast between the ease of regional liberalisation and the glacial GATT talks does not reflect a GATT failure: GATT Rounds have always been protracted, have always been slow, and have always been difficult. Indeed it does not even reflect a systemic phenomenon. I propose that the current wave of regionalism stems from two idiosyncratic events – one in the New World and one in the Old – that have been multiplied many times over by a 'domino effect'.

The idiosyncratic event in the Western hemisphere was the US–Mexico FTA, which was itself motivated by the unilateral reforms undertaken by Mexico in the 1980s. Announcement of the US–Mexico FTA destroyed the *status quo* of trade relations in the Americas. Other countries in the region, which are heavily dependent on the US market, were faced with a *fait accompli*. Mexico-based producers would gain preferential access to the US market, thereby increasing the competition facing third-country exporters and diverting foreign investment to Mexico. Despite continuing domestic opposition to its first regional liberalisation – the Canada–US FTA – Canada decided that it had to be at the negotiating table. Other countries in the hemisphere, such as Chile, Brazil, Argentina, Uruguay and Paraguay enquired about the possibility of a bilateral FTA with the US. Faced with a flood of requests for bilateral FTAs, the Office of the US Trade Representative encouraged South American countries to form regional groups among themselves before applying *en groupe* for an FTA with the US. Similar pressures explain the booming interest in President Bush's Enterprise for the Americas Initiative.

The idiosyncratic event in Europe was the completion of the Single Market. Again the timing and motives for this suggest that this regional initiative was in no way a substitute for multilateral liberalisation, nor did it have anything to do with the US attitude towards the GATT system. This event triggered a domino effect. Austria, which had been previously restrained from joining the EU by pressure from the Soviet bloc, applied for EU membership in 1989. The deepening of the EU and pending enlargement of the EU to include several large EFTA countries made the potential loss of competitiveness even more threatening to

EFTA nations that chose to remain outside the EU. That is, each EFTA nation individually faced the prospect of losing out in the EU-12 markets *and* in the markets of those EFTAns acceding to the EU. Since the combined EU and EFTA markets on average account for three-quarters of EFTA exports, the pressure on the holdouts mounted. Sweden put in its application in 1991 and Finland, Norway and Switzerland requested EU membership in 1992. The Icelandic government, which gave much thought to joining in the early 1990s, was deterred by the EU's common fishery policy. By the time Iceland changed its mind in 1994, it was told by the EU that it was too late to participate in the 1995 EU enlargement, so Iceland did not put in an application.

The first draft of this chapter was completed before the accession negotiations were finished. However, additional evidence of the importance of the domino effect can be found in the ordering of the four referendums. Leaders of Austria, Finland, Sweden and Norway agreed to sequence the national votes in order of descending EU popularity. The heavily populated eastern part of Austria was occupied by Soviet forces until 1955, so intrinsic resistance to joining the West via EU membership was quite weak in Austria. Also, Austria is the EFTA country most heavily dependent on the EU market for its manufactured exports. Owing to this, it was decided that Austria should go first. Finland held its vote next. Parts of Finland were lost to the USSR in the Second World War, and the country was 'Finlandised' during the Cold War so, as with Austria, EU membership promised significant non-economic gains. Sweden came after Finland and before Norway. It was hoped that the widely anticipated positive results in Austria and Finland would tilt the fine balance in Sweden towards the 'Yes' side. Norway was last. Norway's current exports are dominated by oil and so are not threatened by the Single Market programme. Norwegian exports of manufactured goods (SITC 5–8) to the EU account for only 19 per cent of its total exports, the figure rises to 27 per cent when manufactured exports to other EFTA nations (mainly Sweden and Finland) are included.

As figure 2.1 shows, there is strongly positive correlation between the fraction of the population voting for EU membership and the importance of manufactured exports to the EU + EFTA area as a share of total exports. The exception, of course, is Switzerland whose voters rejected even the EEA despite the fact that about 60 per cent of its exports face discrimination from EU92.

The political economy forces driving this domino effect are strengthened by a peculiar tendency of special interest groups; they usually fight harder to avoid losses than they do to secure gains. In this light, it is important that joining the regional integration in Europe and North

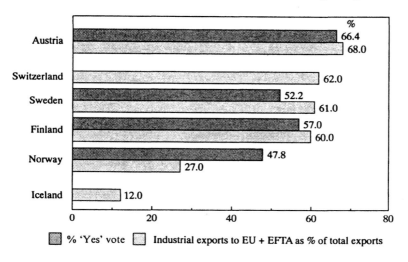

Figure 2.1 Importance of manufactures trade with EU and EFTA and referendum results

America would allow countries to avoid damage as well as to gain new commercial opportunities. While there may be many explanations for this asymmetric phenomenon, Baldwin (1993) proposes a simple economic interpretation based on sunk costs.

Entry into most industries and markets involves large unrecoverable investments in product development, training, brand name advertisement and production capacity. In such situations, established firms can earn positive profits without attracting new firms only in as far as these profits constitute a fair return on the entry investments. Another way to say this is that sunk costs create quasi-rents. In such industries, consider the incentive to lobby. If a country's exporters obtain additional access to foreign markets, their sales and profits will typically rise. The increase in pure profit, however, will attract new competition, so the size of the gains must be limited. In the extreme, entry continues until all pure profit disappears. Correspondingly, the incentive to lobby for new export opportunities will be limited, and in the extreme will disappear altogether. Next consider the reaction of an established firm to an unanticipated policy change (such as the '1992' programme, or the US–Mexico FTA) that would reduce its relative competitiveness and profitability. To be concrete, suppose that the change would wipe out half its quasi-rents. Since it would not actually be losing money, the firm would not shut down. More to the point, the firm should be willing to spend up to half its quasi-rents on lobbying for membership, if doing so would reverse the loss of relative competitiveness.

3   The basic model

Formalisation of the domino effect presented in the Introduction requires a model that first shows how closer regional integration affects the fortunes of industries based in non-member countries, and then connects these changing fortunes to the political decision making process. The economic framework adopted is closely related to the set-up used by Krugman (1991) in examining economic geography issues. The political economy model employed is related to Grossman and Helpman (1993).

3.1   The economic framework

Consider a world of g countries, h of which are members of the regional trade bloc. Without loss of generality, we refer to the trade bloc as the EC. Each country has two sectors: a differentiated-products sector (referred to as manufacturing) which is marked by increasing returns and imperfect competition, and a perfectly competitive, constant-returns sector (referred to as the A sector). Technology and preferences over goods are identical in all countries. There are two classes of workers, labourers and firm owners. The preferences of the firm owners are:

$$U^F = C_A^{1-\phi} C_M^{\phi}; \ \ C_M = [\Sigma_i \, c_i^{(\sigma-1/\sigma)}]^{\sigma/(\sigma-1)}, \qquad (1)$$
$$\sigma > 1, \ \ 0 \leq \phi \leq 1$$

where the summation is over goods that are actually available, σ is the elasticity of substitution between any two varieties and c_i is the consumption of food i. The income of firm owners derives solely from profits. The preferences of labourers are given by:

$$U^L = C_A^{1-\lambda} C_M^{\lambda}; \ \ C_M = [\Sigma_i \, c_i^{(\sigma-1)/\sigma}]^{\sigma/(\sigma-1)}, \qquad (2)$$

where σ is less than unity and λ is between zero and unity.

Utility maximisation by the representative consumers, subject to budget constraints, yields a typical country's demand function for a typical variety of manufactured good. This is:

$$c_j = (\frac{p_j}{P})^{-\sigma}E, \quad P = [\Sigma_i(p_i)^{-(\sigma-1)}]^{-1/\sigma} \qquad (3)$$

where E is the total expenditure of consumers on manufactured products. Labourers and firm owners spend a fraction $1-\lambda$ and $1-\phi$ on A respectively, so the demand for the A good is:

$$A = [(1 - \lambda)E^L + (1 - \phi)E^F]/p_A \qquad (4)$$

where p_A is the price of A, and E^L and E^F are the total expenditures of labourers and firm owners.

The labour input requirement for a typical manufactured variety is:

$$l_i = \alpha + \beta x_i, \quad \alpha, \beta > 0 \qquad (5)$$

where x_i is the output of variety i. α is a fixed cost. The cost of introducing a new variety is zero so, as usual, there will be only one firm producing each variety. Entry is ruled out, so the number of active firms is exogenous and equal to k per country. Each firm is owned entirely by the residents of the country in which it produces.

Two very strong assumptions on trade costs are made for tractability. Trade in the A good is costless while trade in manufactures is costly, with the costs being of the 'iceberg' type.[4] That is, shipping of manufactured goods between any two countries melts a fraction of the shipment. These trade costs are lower for intra-EC trade than for all other international trade. An EC-based firm that wants to sell a unit of manufactured goods in another EC country must ship $\mu > 1$ units. All other trade, that is all non-intra-EC trade, requires that $\tau > 1$ units be shipped for every unit sold. The essence of EC membership in this chapter is that $\mu < \tau$. There are no trade costs for domestic sales.

The production function of good A is linear homogeneous. Units of A are chosen such that A's unit labour input coefficient is unity. With perfect competition and costless trade prevailing, this choice of units implies that the price of A is equal to the wage rate. As long as all countries produce in both sectors, competition in the A good equalises the equilibrium wage in all countries. We take labour to be the numeraire.

Given the demand function, the typical manufacturer faces an isoelastic demand curve.[5] For producers based in a non-EC country, the first order conditions are:

$$p\left(1 - \frac{1}{\sigma}\right) = \beta, \quad p\left(1 - \frac{1}{\sigma}\right) = \beta\tau, \tag{6}$$

for home and foreign sales respectively. Here the ps are consumer prices, that is, c.i.f. prices. For a firm based in the EC, the first order conditions for sales to the home market and non-EC markets are the same as those for a non-EC firm; however they are:

$$p\left(1 - \frac{1}{\sigma}\right) = \beta\mu \tag{7}$$

for sales to other EC markets.

Manufactured goods are measured in units that are chosen so that the unit input coefficient β just equals $(1 - 1/\sigma)$. This implies that optimising firms charge the same f.o.b. price (namely unity) for all sales regardless of destination. The c.i.f. prices for home sales are unity in all countries, for intra-EC sales price equals μ and all other exports are prices at τ.

To simplify calculations of the general equilibrium demand patterns, we assume ϕ to be unity and λ to be strictly between unity and zero. By carefully choosing the units with which to measure national workforces, we can take E^L to be unity. Given that manufactured-goods prices are determined by profit maximisation, it is easy to calculate sales in the various markets using the demand curve. With a constant demand elasticity of σ, operating profits (i.e. profits gross of fixed costs) in manufacturing equal $(1/\sigma)$ times sales. In what follows, a crucial quantity will be the difference between equilibrium operating profit earned by the typical firm when it is based in a member nation and when it is not. This difference equals:

$$\Pi^{in} - \Pi^{out} = \lambda\frac{h(\mu^{1-\sigma} - \tau^{1-\sigma})}{\sigma}P_{ec}^{\sigma} + \frac{\lambda}{\sigma}(P_{ec}^{\sigma} - P_{non}^{\sigma}), \tag{8}$$

where

$$P_{ec} = (k[1 - \mu^{1-\sigma} + h(\mu^{1-\sigma} - \tau^{1-\sigma}) + g\tau^{1-\sigma}])^{-\frac{1}{\sigma}} \tag{9}$$

and

$$P_{non} = (k[1 + (g-1)\tau^{1-\sigma}])^{-\frac{1}{\sigma}}. \tag{10}$$

The first term in (8) is positive and represents the increase in profits the firm would experience in all incumbents' markets. The second term, which shows the change in profits earned on home market sales, is negative. The profit earned on sales to third nations is unaltered by EC membership and therefore cancels out.

3.2   General political economy modelling considerations

The median-voter model (see Mayer, 1984) is a popular and elegant framework much used in the political equilibrium literature. However, it does not seem to capture the principal aspects of the policy formation process affecting EC membership. Indeed, one of the most remarkable facts about the trend towards regionalism is the gap between the positions of governments and the positions of their electorates (as portrayed by public opinion polls). Both in Europe and North America, governments tend to espouse the views of pro-integrationist business leaders (and labour leaders as well in most of Europe), while the populace tends to be more wary. It would thus appear unreasonable to adopt a model of the political process in which the government was simply a mouthpiece for the people. In fact, direct democracy is not the usual way in which a country's government decides whether it wants to join a regional trade bloc.[6] Even if a referendum is held on the final negotiated accession treaty, the decision to engage in the negotiations is usually taken in the setting of representative democracy. The decision is thus influenced by pressure groups.

Both Hillman (1989) and Baldwin (1985) point out that under realistic assumptions elected officials may not be fully aware of the economic interests of their constituents. And their constituents may not be familiar with all the policies (and their economic consequences) championed by their elected representatives. Consequently, as Baldwin (1985) notes, groups of voters

> may have to engage in time-consuming and costly lobbying activities to bring its viewpoint to the attention of legislators. Similarly office-seekers need funds to inform the voters of how they have served them or will do so in the future.

The so-called pressure group model, or lobbying model, developed by Olson (1965) and others, focuses on the costs and benefits of lobbying and its impact on policy. Grossman and Helpman (1993) provide a modern, rigorous treatment of the lobbying model.

The basic political influence technology adopted in this chapter is similar to the Grossman and Helpman (1993) approach to the pressure group model. Two assumptions in the Grossman–Helpman approach are crucial to tractability: the policy maker's objective function is linear in campaign donations and social welfare, and interest groups can make donations contingent on the actions of the policy maker. Grossman and Helpman (1993) provide several justifications of the fixed-weight linear objective function. First, it can be taken as a reduced form for a political process where politicians' true objective is re-election and the odds of survival increase linearly in aggregate campaign donations and utilities of individual voters. Alternatively, they conjecture that it can be interpreted as a reduced form of a broad class of political process models in which

> politicians may value donations not only for the marginal effect that advertising and other campaign expenditures have on voter behaviour, but also because the funds can be used to retire campaign debts from previous elections (which many times are owed to the politician's personal estate), to deter competition from quality challengers, and to show the candidate's abilities as a fund raiser and thereby establish his or her credibility as a potential candidate for higher political or party office.

Regardless of the justification, this fixed-weight linear objective function allows us to think of campaign donations as direct payments to risk-neutral policy makers.

Grossman and Helpman (1993) also assume that organised special interest groups can specify donation contracts, or 'contribution schedules' that stipulate how large a donation will be made for each possible policy stance chosen. In the first of the two stages in the Grossman–Helpman model, contracts are announced by private groups and in the second, the government sets policy and collects donations. It is useful to think of these schedules as enforceable employment contracts where special interest groups 'employ' policy makers to do their bidding in exchange for performance-related compensation. Note that the donations are *ex post* in the sense that they are paid *after* the policy has been chosen by officials that have already been elected. Each group chooses the donation contract that maximises its own welfare, taking the contracts of other special interest groups as given.

Plainly one does not observe formal, enforceable contacts between policy makers and special interest groups (except when they are entered as evidence by the prosecution). It is, therefore, worth justifying the assumption in more depth. Even if not all real-world donations are made on this 'contractual' basis, one can think of the donation contracts as a simple way of capturing the potentially very complicated real-world compacts struck between special interest donors and policy makers. After all, regardless of the actual details of the informal agreements between policy makers and interest groups, the practical intent of these agreements is to reward the policy makers if and only if they choose policies that benefit the donating special interest group.

It would seem that the enforceability assumption could be dropped in a more complex model. For instance, using a repeated game set-up and the Folk theorem, I conjecture that *ex ante* donations would have the same effect as enforceable donation contracts. The equilibrium would involve politicians faithfully sticking to the bargain in order to avoid an off-equilibrium punishment consisting of the donators backing the politicians' opponents. It would be very interesting to model such a situation explicitly.

The fixed-weight linear objective function, together with performance-contingent donation contracts, makes it easy to frame the political process as a principal–agent problem where the government is the 'agent' and competing interest groups are the 'principals'. This, in turn, allows direct access to the well developed literature on principal–agent problems. Grossman and Helpman (1993) draw on the very general analysis of Bernheim and Whinston (1986a, 1986b), which enables them to consider an extremely broad class of 'contracts' between special interest groups and policy makers. This high level of generality makes it difficult to say very much about the nature of the resulting political equilibrium, apart from the fact that it exists. To characterise further the political equilibrium, Grossman and Helpman (1993) impose more structure on the problem in two steps. First they consider all donation contracts that are differentiable around the equilibrium. Second they focus on the Bernheim–Whinston notion of a 'truthful Nash Equilibrium', which restricts the contracts to a very specific form:[7] the donation of any special interest group equals the group's gross welfare minus a fixed amount that is chosen optimally. Bernheim and Whinston defend this concept by showing that such contracts would never be suboptimal and that equilibria supported by truthful contracts, and only these equilibria are stable to non-binding communications among the players.

3.3 Specific political influence technology

The government of the typical country chooses whether to join the EC or not. We capture this choice with the variable u, which equals unity if they decide to join, and zero otherwise. The choice is taken to maximise political support, which in turn depends positively upon the level of donations by industry, the level of social welfare net of donations, and on a third term R which reflects the support of groups that oppose EC membership on non-economic grounds. The government's problem is thus to choose u in order to maximise:

$$u[(1-a)D^{in} + aW^{in}] + (1-u)[(1-a)D^{out} + aW^{out} + R] \qquad (11)$$

where a is a parameter that lies between zero and one, the D and Ws are the levels of donations and social welfare when the country is 'in' or 'out' of the EC respectively, and R is the support from anti-EC groups that the government receives if it decides not to join the EC. R, which measures the country's general resistance to membership, varies across countries. The parameter a measures the extent of the political distortion. If a equals unity, the government acts as a social welfare maximiser. The further is a from unity, the greater is the political distortion. In this model, greater political distortion leads to the interest of exporters receiving greater weight in the policy making process. We take social welfare to be the sum of utilities, that is $W = U^L + U^F$, so:

$$W^{in} = (1-\lambda)^{1-\lambda}(\lambda)^\lambda P_{ec}^{\lambda\sigma/(1-\sigma)} + k\Pi^{in}$$
$$W^{out} = (1-\lambda)^{1-\lambda}(\lambda)^\lambda P_{non}^{\lambda\sigma/(1-\sigma)} + k\Pi^{out}. \qquad (12)$$

Following Grossman and Helpman (1993), the donation contracts in this chapter are restricted to be 'truthful' in the Bernheim–Whinston jargon and actual donations to be non-negative. All manufacturing firms in a country are organised into a lobbying group. The group's truthful donation contract is:

$$D^{in} = k\Pi^{in} + B, \quad D^{out} = k\Pi^{out} + B \qquad (13)$$

where B is a scalar and k is the number of manufacturing firms per country.

Given the donation contract, a typical government decides to join the EC if and only if:

$$R \le (1-a)k[\Pi^{in} - \Pi^{out}] + a[W^{in} - W^{out}]. \qquad (14)$$

Which can be rewritten as:

$$R \leq k[\Pi^{in} = \Pi^{out}] + a(1 - \lambda)^{1-\lambda}(\lambda)^{\lambda}[P_{ec}^{-\lambda\sigma/(\sigma-1)} = P_{non}^{-\lambda\sigma/(\sigma-1)}]. \quad (15)$$

3.4 The supply side of membership

The model so far describes only the demand for membership. We now turn to the 'supply' of memberships. As was mentioned in the Introduction, the truly remarkable fact is that the demand for membership in regional trading blocs has spread rapidly. The actual enlargement of the blocs has proved much slower.

To focus on why so many countries wish to join trading blocs, as opposed to focusing on how many actually get in, we assume that the supply of membership is perfectly elastic. That is to say, that the EU is an open club: any one who requests membership is admitted. Of course, this assumption does quite a bit of violence to the reality of EU politics. In future research, it would be quite interesting to specify a more realistic supply of membership schedule.

Having restricted special interests to 'truthful' donation contracts, the political choice of manufacturers is limited to the size of the constant term in the donation contract. Since there is only one organised donator, the level of B has no influence on the shape of policy, as long as the government is willing to accept the donation contracts. The way to tie down B in this simple principal–agent problem is to use the voluntary participation constraint.[8] That is if the agent (in this case, the government) is to accept the contract offered, the level of its equilibrium 'utility' must be at least as great as its reservation level. In our case, the government could refuse all contingent donation contracts. Thus if the lobbying groups are to have any influence over the government, they must choose a B such that the government is at least indifferent to refusing their donation contract.

Although all countries are symmetric economically, we assume that they differ in terms of the degree of non-economic resistance to EU membership. Arranging the countries in order of increasing resistance, we can plot the degree of resistance against the number of EU members. In figure 2.2, this is shown as RR. Clearly, we can think of there being a continuum of countries, so that h is a continuous variable, or we can view RR as the line that connects the points representing individual countries. In figure 2.2 we have assumed that there is negative resistance to membership in some countries. That is to say, the government loses political support for non-economic reasons if it does not choose membership.

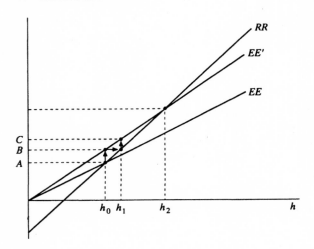

Figure 2.2   Non-economic resistance to EU membership

4   The '1992' programme and the domino effect

The political equilibrium, for a given τ and μ, can be found with the help of figure 2.2. The locus EE plots the right-hand side of (14). Since P_{ec} is decreasing in h, and $\Pi^{in} - \Pi^{out}$ is increasing in h, it is straightforward to show that right-hand side of (12) is upward-sloping, as shown in figure 2.2. The equilibrium number of members will be below the maximum of g, if there are countries in which there is sufficient resistance to EU membership to ensure that the locus RR will eventually rise above the EE schedule. The equilibrium number of members, h_0 in figure 2.2, is given by the intersection of the EE and RR schedules. For all countries to the right of h_0, the non-economic resistance to membership exceeds the net economic benefit from switching from non-member to member status. For all those to the left, the political support gained from being 'in' versus being 'out' outweighs the political resistance to membership. More precisely, respecting the integer constraint, we can say that equilibrium h is the highest integer that is less than h_0.

Given the economic and political economic components of the model, it is quite simple to see how a domino effect could occur. Consider the impact of a policy change, such as the Single European Act, that makes intra-EC trade cheaper. In our model this is reflected by a lowering of μ. The impact of a reduction in μ shows up in figure 2.2 as a shift of EE to

EE'. To show this, note that the derivative of the right-hand side of (14) with respect to μ is:

$$a(\lambda)^\lambda (1 - \lambda)^{1-\lambda} \left(\frac{-\lambda\sigma}{\sigma - 1} \right) P \frac{-\lambda\sigma}{\sigma-1}^{-1} (dP_{ec}/d\mu) + d(\Pi^{in} - \Pi^{out})/d\mu.$$

Since the EU price index falls with μ and the operating profit difference increases with μ, the derivative is clearly positive. Of course at $h = 0$, the price and operating profit differences are zero. The new equilibrium number of members is h_2. The difference between h_1 and h_2 is caused by the 'domino' effect: falling trade barriers in one set of countries triggers a fall in the barriers of other countries. Although there are no formal dynamics in this model (see the Discussion by Gylfason, p. 51 for a consideration of dynamics), it is useful to illustrate the domino effect by telling the story of the increase from h_0 to h_2 as if the increase in EU applications took place over time.

The initial shock of closer EU integration (lower μ) raises the political economic gains from membership enough to overcome the intrinsic resistance to membership in some countries. In particular in the first round of effects, the political economy support for member-ship rises from A to B in Figure 2.2. Thus, in the first round, all countries whose resistance is between A and B would join, thus boosting membership from h_0 to h_1. The rise in h, however, affects the choices of the remaining non-members. In particular, governments would judge that the political economy support for membership was equal to C in figure 2.2. This would prompt applications from all non-members whose resistance was between B and C. Of course, this further rise in membership would provoke a fresh batch of member-ship applications, and the process would continue until the new equilibrium was reached. Thus although the fundamental cause of enlargement is the exogenous deepening of EU integration, this initial shock is amplified by the way in which enlargement makes non-membership even more costly.

5   Summary and conclusions

This chapter presents a simple model of how an idiosyncratic shock, such as deeper integration of an existing regional bloc, can trigger membership requests from countries that were previously happy to be non-members. The basic logic is simple. The stance of a country's government concerning membership is the result of a political equilibrium that balances anti- and pro-membership forces. Among the pro-EU forces are firms that export to the regional bloc. Since closer integration within a bloc is detrimental to the profits of non-member firms, closer integration will stimulate the exporters to engage in greater pro-EU political activity. If the government was previously close to indifferent (politically) to membership, the extra activity may tilt the balance and cause the country to join the bloc. If the bloc enlarges, the cost to the non-members increases, since they now face a cost disadvantage in an even greater number of markets. This second-round effect will bring forth more pro-EU political activity in non-members, and thus may lead to further enlargement of the bloc. The new political equilibrium will involve an enlarged regional trading bloc. Meanwhile it would appear that regionalism is spreading like wildfire.

In future research, it should be possible to develop a set of hypotheses based on this simple model that could be tested against the experience of the EU. Stepping away from the strong symmetry in the model, it should be possible to show that those countries that partake in the enlargement depend rather heavily on exports to the EU (since their export profits would be greatly affected), and have a rather small home market (since the loss of profits on home sales due to the market opening would be small).

NOTES

1   See for instance, discussions by Bhagwati and Krugman in de Melo and Panagariya (1993).
2   The European Economic Community (EEC) was one of the four communities. The Treaty of European Union changed its name to the European Union (EU). This chapter uses EU throughout.
3   Under NAFTA, tariffs and other border measures are to be phased out between 1994 and 2009, so it is hard to know how much trade it will cover. The figure in table 2.1 shows the sum of exports between Canada, Mexico and the US in 1990.
4   As will become clear below, these two assumptions facilitate calculation of the equilibrium, since costless trade in the constant returns goods pins down the prices of labour in terms of A in all countries and iceberg costs allow consideration of trade costs without altering the homogeneity of the manufacturers' first order conditions.
5   Actually the elasticity is only approximately constant, with the approximation improving as the number of varieties increases.
6   In the one country where direct democracy is the political norm, Switzerland, the government's demand for membership was effectively overturned by a referendum on the EEA agreement.
7   The adjective 'truthful' comes from the fact that in the principal–agent set-up, these contracts imply that the principals pay the agent her full marginal

product minus some fixed amount. This, of course, means that the incentives of the agent to change her behaviour on the margin truthfully reflects the worth of such changes to the principals.

8   Grossman and Helpman (1993) show how to find the equilibrium Bs when the problem is too complicated to use the participation constraint.

REFERENCES

Anderson, K. and R. Blackhurst (eds.), 1993. *Regional Integration and the Global Trading System*, Brighton: Harvester-Wheatsheaf
Baldwin, R.E., 1985. *The Political Economy of US Import Policy*, Cambridge, MA: MIT Press
   1992. 'The economic logic of EFTA membership in the EEA and the EC', EFTA, *Occasional Paper*
   1993. 'Asymmetric lobbying: why governments pick losers', GIIS, mimeo
Bernheim, B. and M. Whinston, 1986a. 'Common agency', *Econometrica*, **54**, 923–42
   1986b. 'Menu auctions, resource allocation and economic influence', *Quarterly Journal of Economics*, **101**, 1–31
Bhagwati, J., 1993. 'Regionalism and multilateralism: an overview', in K. Anderson and R. Blackhurst (eds.), *Regional Integration and the Global Trading System*, Brighton: Harvester-Wheatsheaf
CEPR, 1992. 'Is bigger better? The economics of EC enlargement', *Monitoring European Integration*, **3**, London: CEPR
De la Torre, A. and M. Kelly, 1992. 'Regional trade arrangements', IMF, *Occasional Paper*, **93**, Washington, DC: IMF
de Melo, J. and A. Panagariya, 1993. 'Introduction', in J. de Melo and A. Panagariya (eds.), *New Dimensions in Regional Integration*, Cambridge: Cambridge University Press
de Melo, J. and A. Panagariya (eds.), 1993. *New Dimensions in Regional Integration*, Cambridge: Cambridge University Press
Dixit, A. and J. Stiglitz, 1977. 'Monopolistic competition and optimal product diversity', *American Economic Review*, **67**, 297–308
Grossman, G. and E. Helpman, 1993. 'Protection for sale', CEPR, *Discussion Paper*, **827**, London: CEPR
Hillman, A., 1989. *The Political Economy of Protection*, New York: Harwood Academic
Krugman, P. 1979. 'Increasing returns, monopolistic competition and international trade', *Journal of International Economics*, **9**, 469–80
   1988. 'EFTA and 1992', EFTA, *Occasional Paper*, **23**, Geneva: EFTA Secretariat
   1991. 'Increasing returns and economic geography', *Journal of Political Economy*, **99**(3), 483–99
   1993. 'Regionalism versus multilateralism: analytic notes', in K. Anderson and R. Blackhurst (eds.), *Regional Integration and the Global Trading System*, Brighton: Harvester-Wheatsheaf
Mayer, W., 1984. 'Endogenous tariff formation', *American Economic Review*, **74**, 970–85

Olson, Mancur, 1965. *The Logic of Collective Action*, Cambridge MA: Harvard
    University Press
Schott, J. 1988. 'United States–Canada free trade: an evaluation of the
    argument', *Policy Analyses in International Economics*, **24**, Washington, DC:
    Institute for International Economics

Discussion

THORVALDUR GYLFASON

As is his wont, Richard Baldwin has in Chapter 2 written a very
interesting study that combines sophisticated analysis of economic policy
with sound common sense. I share his view of European economic
integration for the most part, and I want to use this Discussion to
indicate how his story can be refined and extended.

Actually, my only serious reservation about the study concerns its title.
I do not think we have a 'domino theory' here. Unlike dominoes,
countries do not stoop or fall to EU membership, as I see it – they *rise* to
membership. Indeed, several of Baldwin's writings in recent years reflect
his view, shared by most other economists, that substantial economic
benefits can probably be derived from continued economic integration in
Europe. The process by which an increase in EU membership makes it
more attractive, from an economic point of view at least, for outsiders to
join the Union is not therefore well described by comparing prospective
entrants to falling dominoes.

1   Demand for EU membership

Chapter 2 tells an essentially dynamic story by static means. At the risk
of oversimplification, I think one can paraphrase Baldwin's model in
three simple equations:

$$h = \theta + \alpha e, \tag{1}$$

$$e = \lambda \Delta \pi, \tag{2}$$

$$\Delta \pi = \beta h - \gamma \Delta p, \tag{3}$$

where h is the number of EU members; e is a measure of pro-EU political effort; $\Delta\pi(=\pi^{in} - \pi^{out})$ is what Baldwin calls the profit differential, that is, the net economic benefit from joining the Union; and Δp is a measure of price differentials within the EU. The degree of economic integration is inversely related to the price differential Δp by assumption. The Greek parameters, α, β, γ, λ and θ are positive constants.

(1) tells us that the number of EU members is positively affected by pro-EU political activity. (2) expresses the positive relationship between the profit differential and pro-EU political effort: the greater the economic benefits of membership, the greater the political support for joining. (3) indicates how the profit differential increases with increasing membership: the idea here is that as the number of insiders h increases, so does the disadvantage of being an outsider; this increases the desire to join the Union. In other words, the larger the common market, the more costly it is to be excluded from it. (3) also shows the profit differential $\Delta\pi$ as a decreasing function of the price differential Δp within the EU and, by implication, as an increasing function of economic integration. In sum, then, (3) tells us that increased economic integration, through widening (higher h) or deepening (lower Δp), increases the economic advantages of EU membership.

(1), (2) and (3) can be combined so as to give

$$h = \frac{\theta - \alpha\lambda\gamma\Delta p}{1 - \alpha\beta\lambda},$$
(4)

so that

$$\frac{\partial h}{\partial\Delta p} < 0.$$
(5)

Here we have the number of EU members as a decreasing function of the price differential within the Union. In other words, by reducing the price differential, economic integration increases the demand for membership. In jargon, deepening calls for widening. This is the main point of Baldwin's study. The downward-sloping demand curve for membership is shown in figure D2.1.

2   Supply of membership

But demand curves, as we know, usually tell only half a story. We need to consider supply to choose Baldwin's model. There is reason to suspect

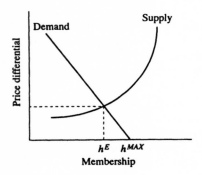

Figure D2.1   Demand and supply of EU membership

that further economic integration in Europe may actually increase the temptation among existing EU members to keep potential entrants out, so as not to spread the gains from membership too widely. If so, the number of members h can be modelled as an increasing function of the price differential Δp, as shown by the upward-sloping supply curve in figure D2.1.

Moreover, as the number of outsiders decreases, the potential benefits of being the sole outsider, or one of a few, may seem more attractive to some. Take Norway, for example. Rather than join the crowd, the Norwegians might conceivably find it worthwhile to attempt to outperform the EU from the outside by undertaking on their own a radical liberalisation of their economy (including, perhaps, agriculture, to increase macroeconomic efficiency, and labour markets, to reduce unemployment, as in New Zealand); by revamping the public sector; by floating the krone; and so forth: by seeking, in short, to establish an economic 'Hong Kong' of sorts on the fringes of Europe. That could be a shrewd move, provided that the government of the country is capable of unilateral liberalisation.

The main point of figure D2.1, however, is that EU membership (h) and the extent of economic integration (which is inversely related to Δp) are both determined endogenously. The equilibrium number of members, h^E, may well wind up somewhere below the maximum, h^{MAX}, i.e. the number of potential members. Put differently, the interaction of demand and supply in the market for EU membership need not necessarily result in a 'full house' ($h^E = h^{MAX}$) and complete integration ($\Delta p = 0$), when all possible influences and interactions have been taken into account. I find it more plausible to suppose that the equilibrium outcome will be one where $h^E < h^{MAX}$ and $\Delta p > 0$. In any case, figure D2.1 shows that there is no simple relationship between the two main dimensions of economic integration, widening and deepening, when the supply side is included in the model. The process of economic integration can widen or narrow and deepen or become more shallow at the same time, depending on the forces that affect demand and supply.

3   Dynamics

To see this clearly, it may help to consider the dynamic nature of the problem posed by Baldwin. To this end, I propose two simple changes in his model as I have paraphrased it in equations (1), (2) and (3). Specifically, let me replace equation (1) by

$$h = \theta + \alpha e - \mu h^2 \tag{1'}$$

where $\mu > 0$ and $h = dh/dt$ is the *flow* of new members into the EU rather than the existing *stock* of members h, the left-hand side variable in (1). This formulation seems more reasonable: pro-EU political activity is intended to induce new members to join old ones. The last term on the right-hand side of (1') has been added to ensure that membership stops expanding after reaching a critical level, $h^C = \alpha\beta\lambda/2\mu$, as shown below.

Let me also replace (2) by

$$e = \lambda\Delta\pi + \sigma\Delta p \tag{2'}$$

where the first term reflects the economic argument for EU membership as before, and where a second term has been added to represent the political argument for ($\sigma < 0$) or against ($\sigma > 0$) membership. The idea here is that a smaller price differential Δp means a closer economic *and political* union, and hence also a more extensive sharing of national sovereignty, and that this can be used as an argument either for or against membership in political debate.

Now, combining (1'), (2'), and (3), we get

$$h = \theta + \alpha\beta\lambda h + \alpha(\sigma - \lambda\gamma)\Delta p - \mu h^2 \tag{6}$$

so that

$$\frac{\partial h}{\partial h} = \alpha\beta\lambda - 2\mu h \tag{7}$$

and

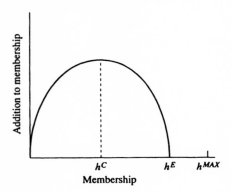

Figure D2.2   Dynamics of EU membership

$$\frac{\partial h}{\partial \Delta p} = \alpha(\sigma - \lambda\gamma). \tag{8}$$

(7) tells us that there is perceived to be safety in numbers, as the saying goes, but only up to a point: the bigger the Union, the more attractive it is for outsiders to join until the critical size, $h^C = \alpha\beta\lambda/2\mu$, is reached. Thereafter, the inflow of new members declines and then stops when an equilibrium is reached at $h = h^E$ such that $h = 0$ in (1′). As before, this equilibrium does not have to imply a 'full house' (see figure D2.2). Without the restraining influence, however (i.e. with $\mu = 0$), h converges on h^{MAX}, as in Baldwin's story.

(8) confirms that there is no general presumption that deepening calls for widening – or vice versa, for that matter. Suppose, for example, that a closer political union is construed as an argument against membership (i.e. $\sigma > 0$) and that this political argument outweighs the economic argument for membership in a popular referendum. Then we have $\sigma > \lambda\gamma$ and hence $\partial h/\partial \Delta p > 0$. This means that increased integration *reduces* the inflow of new members into the Union. In this case, there may be a conflict between deepening and widening in the integration process. There is a similar ambiguity concerning the effect of the price differential Δp on the equilibrium number of EU members, h^E, as can be shown by solving (1′) for h by setting $h = 0$.

4   Bargaining

I have argued here that one needs to consider both demand and supply, and also dynamics, in the market for EU membership to deal with the interaction and ultimate destination of the ongoing widening and deepening of the economic integration process in Europe. But even that may not be enough. The market for EU membership is by no means atomistic. On the contrary, it consists of a few players, some of whom are quite strong. One probably also has therefore to introduce bargaining and games to be able to tell a complete story about the ebbs and flows in economic integration. Richard Baldwin has done us a great service by showing the way.

NOTE

I am grateful to Harry Flam for his comments.

3 Customs unions, regional trading blocs and welfare

HÅKAN NORDSTRÖM

1 Introduction

There are some indications today that the multilateral trading system is yielding to, or is complemented by, a system of regional trading arrangements.[1] The Uruguay Round of multilateral trade negotiations was long overdue, and the big players with the power to resolve the deadlock, the EU and the US, seemed more interested in their own regional integration initiatives than in furthering the process of multilateral trade liberalisation. The foot-dragging at the negotiation table was surely strategic to some extent – a manoeuvre to get additional concessions from the more eager parties – but it may also have reflected a more negative attitude or disillusionment with the GATT-centred multilateral trading system. Indeed, while GATT has been effective in reducing tariffs since the Second World War, it has encountered increasing difficulties in stemming the proliferation of non-tariff trade barriers and in extending the coverage to new areas, such as services, agricultural products and protection of intellectual property rights.

In the view of many observers, the EU has become increasingly inward-looking as it has grown larger, and there are widespread concerns that the more protectionist-inclined members will dominate the policy process and turn the EU into a 'European Fortress', an increasingly closed market to the rest of the world. The direction of US trade policy is also unclear. Advocates of (aggressive) bilateralism seem to have won ground, fuelled by the perception that the Japanese market is 'closed' and that other nations do not play by the GATT rules. The fear of curtailed market access is probably an, or perhaps *the*, important force behind the drive to seek alliances with powerful neighbours or establish new trading blocs among like-minded nations. The loss of momentum in the multilateral process and the movements towards regional and bilateral arrangements has sparked a renewed debate over the relative merits of the two approaches to trade liberalisation.

The debate over regionalism can, following Bhagwati (1993), be divided into two parts: the 'static impact question' and the 'dynamic time-path question'. The former focuses on the short-run effect of regional trading blocs and their interaction, and the latter on whether regionalism may constitute an alternative route to global free trade. This chapter addresses both questions. The analysis is based on a multicountry regional version of Krugman's (1980) workhorse model of intra-industry trade. The main issues and results are briefly discussed in this introductory section.

The analysis of regional trading blocs is still in its infancy. It draws mainly on the traditional customs union analysis of Jacob Viner (1950), generally without any explicit treatment of regions. The main point in Viner's analysis of customs unions, whether regional or not, is that they may cause welfare losses if trade is diverted from low-cost external sources to high-cost internal ones, rather than being created by increased specialisation within the unions. However, trade diversion need not be a problem, it can be eliminated, or at least alleviated, by an appropriate downward adjustment of the external tariff. A customs union is, therefore, always *potentially* welfare improving, a point made formally by Kemp and Wan (1976).

However, it is unlikely that a customs union will volunteer a tariff reduction at the time it is formed. On the contrary, the incentive goes the other way: the optimal tariff is higher for the customs union than for the constituent countries, because their common market power is larger. The best we can hope for is, perhaps, that customs unions play by the GATT rules, as regulated in Article 24. This states, in short, that the common duties and other regulations shall not on the whole be higher or more restrictive than those previously applicable in the constituent countries.[2] According to Schott (1989), no trading arrangement has so far been declared GATT-incompatible. This suggests that the incentive to defect is not overwhelmingly large (or that GATT panels screening the arrangements are reluctant to rule against powerful interests). The temptation is probably tempered by the risk of provoking a 'trade war' with the rest of the world. Indeed, as will be shown, if other countries retaliate, which is permissible after going through the GATT dispute settlement process, the prospective gain may turn into a loss. Let me outline the argument.

Assume that tariffs are semi-cooperative, perhaps negotiated under the auspices of GATT. The regime is sustained by the threat of retaliation; an immediate return to optimal tariffs towards the offending part, while the rest of the world continues with their tariff cooperation. The latter qualification is important. If a defection provoked a general 'trade war,' instead of a selective punishment of the offending part, the deterrence would be much weaker. As will be shown, this scheme is sufficient to keep the customs union in line unless the union is very large or the cooperative tariffs are close to the non-cooperative rates. In the latter cases, the punishment does not 'bite'. The analysis suggests that a customs union, out of fear of retaliation, may play by the GATT rules until it has reached a certain critical size, and thereafter withdraw to exercise its market power in the world. Consequently, small trading blocs constitute no threat to the GATT-centred multilateral trading system, but large ones do.

Even if a customs union abides by Article 24, outsiders are generally harmed by the arrangement (although to a much less extent than if exploited by optimal tariffs). Demand for their products falls as members of the customs union substitute internal tariff-free goods for external goods. This leads to a terms of trade deterioration for outsiders that reduces their welfare. The impact is rather minor as long as the customs union is small. The trade that is diverted can easily be compensated by increased trade among outsiders. However, the repercussions become worse at each stage of enlargement. Countries that were previously happy to be non-members, for some (non-economic) reason, may therefore want to reconsider membership later on. It may then, however, be too late. It is not in the interest of the customs union to include all countries in the world (except under the hypothetical case that unions are forced to set tariffs à la Kemp and Wan). The customs union is simply better off trading with outsiders at favourable terms. The above points are elaborated in section 3 of the chapter.

Are the effects of *regional* trading blocs much different from those of trading blocs in general? According to Krugman (1991),

> if trading arrangements follow the lines of natural trading regions, they will have a much better chance of improving welfare than trading arrangements between 'unnatural' partners.

The argument is, perhaps, best understood in the terms of Viner's (1950) seminal concepts 'trade diversion' and 'trade creation.' Recall that a trade-creating customs union is welfare improving while a trade-diverting union is, at least for outsiders, harmful. Think of a 'natural trading region' as a group of countries with low 'natural' trading costs (do not confuse these with tariffs and other man-made barriers). They may be located near each other, understand each other's language and (business) culture, and have similar legal systems. These factors tend to make trade more intense within regions than between regions, even in the absence of formal trading arrangements. Thus, if such arrangements are signed, there is a good chance that they will improve welfare since there is little scope for trade diversion.

There is one caveat to Krugman's argument. All countries in a 'natural trading region' may not be included in the deal. It depends on the size of the region and the cost of inter-regional trade. Intuitively, if the region is small and inter-regional trading costs low, most trade is with other regions in the world. All countries in the region may then be encouraged to join the local trading bloc to get the best possible 'leverage' on the external terms of trade. However, if the region is large or if the trade with other regions is minor because of high inter-regional trading costs, the local bloc is better off leaving some countries outside. The prospect for regional outsiders is not good at all. They are, in a sense, 'locked-in' by inter-regional trading costs, leaving little choice other than to trade with the local bloc, even at unfavourable terms. Thus, while a regional trading arrangement may have a small impact on the rest of the world, the consequences for regional outsiders may be quite severe.

The final issue addressed in the chapter is whether regional integration may be a step towards global free trade. The starting point is the observation that a large trading bloc may lose out from a multilateral free trade agreement. The consumption distortion would decrease, but not enough to compensate for the terms of trade deterioration. The bloc may therefore try to thwart the process of multilateral trade liberalisation. The incentive changes if unorganised countries join forces in a counter-balancing trading bloc. Free trade then becomes a mutually beneficial solution as long as the trading blocs are of about equal size. Consequently, the formation of (regional) trading blocs may be a first, and possibly necessary, step towards global free trade. This is shown at the end of section 4.

2 The model

Consider a world with n symmetric countries that trade in differentiated goods produced with a single factor of production, labour. The labour endowment per country is fixed and normalised to one. Consumers have identical preferences represented by a CES utility function

$$U_h = \left[\sum_g c_{h,g}^{\frac{\sigma-1}{\sigma}} \right]^{\frac{\sigma}{\sigma-1}} \tag{1}$$

where $c_{h,g}$ is consumption (*per capita*) of good g in country h, and σ is the elasticity of substitution between different goods. All goods in the world are produced with the same technology, which requires a fixed input of labour per good and a constant input of labour per unit of output,

$$l_g = \alpha + \beta x_g, \qquad (2)$$

where l_g denotes labour employed in production of the gth good and x_g denotes output of that good. In other words, there is a fixed cost and a constant marginal cost which suggests that average production cost declines with output. In addition, there are transportation costs between markets. These take Samuelson's 'iceberg' form: of a unit of a good shipped from market h to f, only a fraction $1 - \gamma_{f,h}$ arrives (see chapter 2 in this volume). The structure of transportation costs will be specified later on. We will now turn to the optimisation problem of firms.

Consider a representative firm in country h producing a single good that is exported to all markets. The firm sets prices in different markets to maximise profit,

$$\pi_h = p_{h,h} x_{h,h} + \sum_{f \neq h}^{n} \frac{p_{f,h}(1 - \gamma_{f,h}) x_{f,h}}{1 + t_{f,h}} - w_h l_h, \qquad (3)$$

where $p_{h,h}$ is the price charged to domestic consumers, $p_{f,h}$ is the price charged to foreign consumers (including transportation and tariffs), $t_{f,h}$ is the *ad valorem* tariff in market f on goods imported from country h and w_h is the domestic wage rate. Given that the firm's market share is negligible in all countries, it faces a uniform demand elasticity across markets that is approximately equal to the elasticity of substitution between competing varieties. The optimal prices in the home market and in export market f are then given by the usual mark-up rules:

$$p_{h,h} = \left(\frac{\sigma}{\sigma - 1}\right) \beta w_h, \quad p_{f,h} = \frac{1 + t_{f,h}}{1 - \gamma_{f,h}} p_{h,h}. \qquad (4)$$

Note that firms receive the same revenue on all units (equal to the domestic price). Consumer prices may, of course, differ across markets to the extent that import tariffs and transportation costs vary. Substituting the above pricing rules into (3) and assuming free entry and exit, and thus zero profit in equilibrium, we can solve for the (long-run) output per good

$$x_h = (\sigma - 1)\alpha/\beta \tag{5}$$

and, imposing full employment, the number of varieties produced in country h,

$$v_h = (\alpha\sigma)^{-1}. \tag{6}$$

These are the same in all countries since technologies, preferences and endowments are identical by assumption. Hence, we may drop the country index on x and v.

Let us now turn to the utility maximising problem of the representative consumer in country h. She derives income from two sources: wages and tariff revenue (taken as given by individual consumers). The optimal consumption is derived by equating the marginal rate of substitution to the relative price of different goods. For instance, the relative consumption of a representative domestic good h and a representative foreign good f is

$$\frac{c_{h,h}}{c_{h,f}} = \left(\frac{p_{h,h}}{p_{h,f}}\right)^{\sigma} \Rightarrow c_{h,f} = (1 + t_{h,f})^{-\sigma}(1 - \gamma_{h,f})^{\sigma} q_{h,f}^{\sigma} c_{h,h}; \quad q_{h,f} \equiv p_{h,h}/p_{f,f}, \tag{7}$$

where $q_{h,f} = q_{f,h}^{-1}$ is the relative world market price of the goods; that is, the terms of trade between country h and f.[3] Imposing balanced trade,

$$\sum_{f \neq h}^{n}\left(\frac{p_{h,h}}{1 - \gamma_{f,h}}\right)c_{f,h} = \sum_{f \neq h}^{n}\left(\frac{p_{f,f}}{1 - \gamma_{h,f}}\right)c_{h,f} \Rightarrow x = c_{h,h} + \sum_{f \neq h}^{n}\left(\frac{q_{h,f}^{-1}}{1 - \gamma_{h,f}}\right)c_{h,f}, \tag{8}$$

and substituting (7) for $c_{h,f}$, we can solve for consumption of domestic and foreign goods, respectively:

$$c_{h,h} = \frac{1}{1 + \sum_{f \neq h}(1 + t_{h,f})^{-\sigma}(1 - \gamma_{h,f})^{\sigma-1}q_{h,f}^{\sigma-1}}x, \tag{9}$$

$$c_{h,f} = \frac{(1 + t_{h,f})^{-\sigma}(1 - \gamma_{h,f})^{\sigma}q_{h,f}^{\sigma}}{1 + \sum_{f \neq h}(1 + t_{h,f})^{-\sigma}(1 - \gamma_{h,f})^{\sigma-1}q_{h,f}^{\sigma-1}}x, \tag{10}$$

and, substituting $c_{h,h}$ and $c_{h,f}$ into (1), the corresponding utility level,

$$U_h = \frac{\left[1 + \sum_{f \neq h}(1 + t_{h,f})^{1-\sigma}(1 - \gamma_{h,f})^{\sigma-1} q_{h,f}^{\sigma-1}\right]^{\frac{\sigma}{\sigma-1}}}{1 + \sum_{f \neq h}(1 + t_{h,f})^{-\sigma}(1 - \gamma_{h,f})^{\sigma-1} q_{h,f}^{\sigma-1}} \, v^{\frac{\sigma}{\sigma-1}} x. \tag{11}$$

Finally, the $n - 1$ relative prices (terms of trades) are determined from the balanced trade conditions (for all but one country). This is the entire model.

3   Customs union in a world without regions

As a point of departure, let us consider a simple case with only one trading bloc in the world and symmetric transportation costs between markets, γ. What makes this case simple is that there are only two groups of countries – members and outsiders – and hence only one relative price to determine. (Intra-group relative prices are all one since countries are symmetric within each group.) We will derive some basic insights in this framework and then go on to the more complex analysis of regional trading blocs.

Assume that the trading bloc is a customs union (CU) with zero internal tariffs and a common external tariff (CET) towards the rest of the world. We shall analyse the economic consequences of the customs union under three tariff policies:[4]

1   the CU imposes optimal tariffs towards outsiders
2   the CU maintains the (average) pre-union tariff level of its members (to comply with Article 24)
3   the CU sets the external tariff under the restriction that outsiders shall not be worse off than before the formation of the customs union.

The external tariff that keeps outsiders unharmed (3) is denoted a 'Pareto Efficient Tariff' (PET) or a Kemp–Wan (1976) tariff. It is Pareto efficient, or more accurately Pareto improving, in the sense that members are better off while outsiders are held unharmed. In practice, it means that the customs union must reduce its external tariff when formed and at each stage of enlargement. With the appropriate rate there will be *no* trade diversion; only welfare improving trade creation among countries that join the customs union. This is our reference case for evaluating other tariff policies.

Before we go on to the analysis, we have to derive the optimal tariff and the Pareto efficient tariff. Let m countries, index $i = \{1, \ldots, m\}$, form a customs union with a common external tariff, t_i, towards outsiders, index

$j = \{1, \ldots, n - m\}$. Let i' and j' index countries other than the representative one in each group. We allow non-members to set different tariff rates towards the customs union, $t_{j,i}$, and towards each other, $t_{j,j'}$. They can then retaliate against a tariff provocation from the customs union without compromising their own tariff cooperation. The consumption of different types of goods for members and outsiders, respectively, is given by (9) and (10):

$$c_{i,i} = \frac{1}{1 + (1 - \gamma)^{\sigma-1}[(m - 1) + (n - m)(1 + t_i)^{-\sigma} q_{i,j}^{\sigma-1}]} x, \quad (12a)$$

$$c_{i,i'} = (1 - \gamma)^{\sigma} c_{i,i}, \quad (12b)$$

$$c_{i,j} = (1 - \gamma)^{\sigma}(1 + t_i)^{-\sigma} q_{i,j}^{\sigma} \, c_{i,i}, \quad (12c)$$

$$c_{j,j} = \frac{1}{1 + (1 - \gamma)^{\sigma-1}[(n - m - 1)(1 + t_{j,j'})^{-\sigma} + m(1 + t_{j,i})^{-\sigma} q_{i,j}^{1-\sigma}]} x, \quad (13a)$$

$$c_{j,j'} = (1 - \gamma)^{\sigma}(1 + t_{j,j'})^{-\sigma} c_{j,j}, \quad (13b)$$

$$c_{j,i} = (1 - \gamma)^{\sigma}(1 + t_{j,i})^{-\sigma} q_{i,j}^{-\sigma} c_{j,j}. \quad (13c)$$

By substitution of (12) and (13) into the balanced trade condition,

$$(m - 1)c_{i',i} + (n - m)c_{j,i} = (m - 1)c_{i,i'} + (n - m)q_{i,j}^{-1} c_{i,j},$$

where $c_{i',i} = c_{i,i'}$, we get an implicit expression for the terms of trade between members and outsiders, $q_{i,j} = p_{i,i}/p_{j,j}$:

$$[(m - 1) + (1 - \gamma)^{\sigma-1}](1 - t_i)^{\sigma} q_{i,j}^{1-\sigma} + (n - m) - m q_{i,j}$$
$$- [(n - m - 1)(1 + t_{j,j'})^{-\sigma} + (1 - \gamma)^{1-\sigma}](1 + t_{j,i})^{\sigma} q_{i,j}^{\sigma} = 0. \quad (14)$$

The optimal tariff for the customs union is derived by maximising the utility of a representative member,

$$U_i = \frac{\left[1 + (1 - \gamma)^{\sigma-1}[(m - 1) + (n - m)(1 + t_i)^{1-\sigma} q_{i,j}^{\sigma-1}]\right]^{\frac{\sigma}{\sigma-1}}}{1 + (1 - \gamma)^{\sigma-1}[(m - 1) + (n - m)(1 + t_i)^{-\sigma} q_{i,j}^{\sigma-1}]} v^{\frac{\sigma}{\sigma-1}} x, \quad (15)$$

with respect to t_i, where $dq_{i,j}/dt_i$ is calculated from (14). The first order condition can, after a fair amount of algebra, be simplified to the standard expression for optimal tariffs

$$\hat{t}_i = \frac{1}{\varepsilon_i - 1}; \quad \varepsilon_i = \sigma - (\sigma - 1)s_{j,i}, \tag{16}$$

where ε_i is the elasticity of demand for the customs union exports to the rest of the world and $s_{j,i}$ is the rest of the world's (a representative country) expenditure share on customs union goods at world market prices:

$$s_{j,i} = \frac{m(1 - \gamma)^{\sigma-1}(1 + t_{j,i})^{-\sigma}q_{i,j}^{1-\sigma}}{1 + (1 - \gamma)^{\sigma-1}[(n - m - 1)(1 + t_{j,j'})^{-\sigma} + m(1 + t_{j,i})^{-\sigma}q_{i,j}^{1-\sigma}]}. \tag{17}$$

The larger the expenditure share, the higher the tariff charged by the customs union. The share is, of course, endogenous, depending on tariffs and transportation costs as well as on the size of the customs union.

What is the optimal tariff for outsiders? The answer is indicated in (16) and (17). A customs union with a negligible share of the world market has an optimal tariff that is approximately $1/(\sigma - 1)$; the standard expression for small countries exporting differentiated goods. This is the (approximate) optimal tariff for non-members, provided that n is large.

Let us now derive the Kemp–Wan or Pareto efficient tariff. It is derived from the condition that outsiders' post-union welfare shall be identical to the pre-union welfare. Outsiders are assumed to be passive; they neither raise nor lower their tariffs as a response to the customs union's benevolent tariff policy. Specifically, they do not discriminate between imports from different sources; $t_{j,j'} = t_{j,i} = t_j$. Consider the welfare index of a representative outsider.

$$U_j = \frac{\left[1 + (1 - \gamma)^{\sigma-1}(1 + t_j)^{1-\sigma}[(n - m - 1) + mq_{i,j}^{1-\sigma}]\right]^{\frac{\sigma}{\sigma-1}}}{1 + (1 - \gamma)^{\sigma-1}(1 + t_j)^{-\sigma}[(n - m - 1) + mq_{i,j}^{1-\sigma}]} v^{\frac{\sigma}{\sigma-1}} x. \tag{18}$$

A sufficient condition for U_j to be constant is that the term within the inner brackets, $(n - m - 1) + mq_{i,j}^{1-\sigma}$, is constant. The pre-union value of this term is $n - 1$ since m is one and $q_{i,j}$ is one (the initial 'customs union' has one member and its terms of trade against the rest of the world is one). Thus, setting $(n - m - 1) + mq_{i,j}^{1-\sigma} = n - 1$ and solving for $q_{i,j}$, we find that the external tariff of the customs union must be set so that the terms of trade against the rest of the world do not change ($q_{i,j} = 1$). From (14) we find that the following restriction is imposed on the external tariff:

$$\tilde{t}_i = \left[\frac{m - 1 + (1 - \gamma)^{1-\sigma}(1 + t_j)^{\sigma}}{m - 1 + (1 - \gamma)^{1-\sigma}}\right]^{\frac{1}{\sigma}} - 1. \tag{19}$$

The customs union must set a lower tariff than other countries ($t_i < t_j$ if $m > 1$). Moreover, it must reduce its tariff at each stage of enlargement ($dt_i/dm < 0$). If the external tariff is set according to (19), there will be no repercussions on outsiders; they will continue to consume the same basket of goods and end up with the same utility level. In other words, there will be no detrimental 'trade diversion'; only welfare improving 'trade creation' within the customs union. The external tariff is in that sense Pareto efficient or, more accurately, Pareto improving. Moreover, as pointed out by Kemp and Wan (1976), such a restriction may facilitate global free trade because members are better off the more countries that join the customs union. The simple logic is: the more countries that join, the more trade creation and the higher the welfare. (Recall that by construction there is no trade diversion.)

This is about as much as one can say analytically. To get further, we have to simulate the model numerically. The first scenario is the following: assume that the initial tariffs are semi-cooperative, say 10 per cent (the optimal, or non-cooperative, tariff is 20 per cent for a small country, given the assumption that $\sigma = 6$). A customs union is formed and it can choose between the three tariff policies discussed above. What are the consequences for members and non-members, given that non-members keep their tariffs constant? The result is presented in figure 3.1. The solid lines refer to the optimal tariff case, the long-dashed to the constant (Article 24) case, and the short-dashed to the PET case. On the x axes we have the share of countries belonging to the customs union, m/n, and on the y axes the external tariff of the customs union, the terms of trade between the customs union and the rest of the world, and the welfare of members and outsiders, respectively, expressed as a fraction of welfare in the pre-union stage. Note that $x = (\sigma - 1)\alpha/\beta$ and $v = (\alpha\sigma)^{-1}$ disappears by this normalisation, so there are only three parameters that need an assumption: n, σ, and γ, set to 100, 6 and 0.1, respectively.

What do we learn from this exercise? The first point is that Article 24 provides at best a partial safeguard for outsiders. Demand falls for their products as members of the customs union substitute internal tariff-free

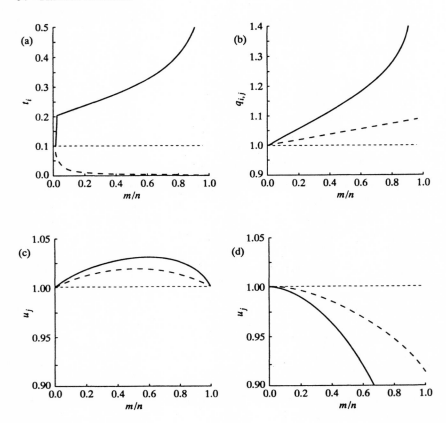

Figure 3.1   Customs union and three tariff policies
a   **External tariff, customs union**
b   **Terms of trade, customs union/Rest of World**
c   **Welfare, customs union**
d   **Welfare, Rest of World**

products for external products. This leads to a terms of trade deterioration for outsiders that reduces their welfare. The impact is rather minor as long as the customs union is small; the trade that is diverted can easily be compensated by increased trade among outsiders. However, as more countries join the customs union, the remaining outsiders have little choice but to trade with the customs union, even at increasingly unfavourable terms.

A complete safeguard would require that the customs union reduces its external tariff when formed, and at each stage of enlargement.

However, it is unlikely that a customs union will volunteer a tariff reduction since it is better off with constant tariffs or indeed higher tariffs *if*, as assumed in this example, outsiders do not retaliate. (In the next example we shall allow outsiders to retaliate if the customs union violates Article 24.) In fact, the customs union does not gain much at all if it has to reduce its external tariff to keep outsiders unharmed. (The modest gain does not show in the plot because of the chosen scale.) The welfare gain comes in that case *only* through reduced consumption distortion – note that there are no output effects in this model – which is modest in comparison to the gain that comes through the terms of trade improvement. Thus, the welfare gain of members comes primarily at the expense of outsiders.

Given the above conclusion, it follows that the customs union has no interest in including all countries in the world (except if forced to set Pareto efficient tariffs). A gradual expansion leads at first to improved welfare for members as more goods become available at non-distorted prices and the terms of trade against outsiders improve. Although the terms of trade continue to improve as the customs union grows, the gain becomes less and less valuable since there will be fewer and fewer outsiders to trade with at the favourable terms. Eventually a point is reached where the marginal contribution to welfare of an additional member is zero; by definition the optimal size of the customs union. The optimal size depends, among other things,[5] on the tariff policy of the customs union; it is larger if the customs union exploits its size by optimal tariffs than if it keeps the external tariff constant. A marginal member is in the former case more valuable by pushing the optimal tariff upwards, giving a better 'leverage' on the terms of trade.

Finally, the incentive to join the customs union increases with the size of the union for two reasons: first, the larger the customs union, the larger the welfare gap between members and outsiders, and hence the gain of becoming a member. The second reason is somewhat speculative. Countries that are considering applying for a membership know that there is a cut-off point beyond which it is not in the interest of the customs union to grow. The larger the customs union, the larger the risk of being turned down. Hence, as the customs union grows, countries may rush to become members before other countries take their chances and it is too late (or before the entrance terms become unfavourable).[6]

In the previous case there was no (economic) reason for the customs union to abide by Article 24. It could do better by exploiting its market power in the world through optimal tariffs. However, the example presupposed that the rest of the world remained passive. What if they retaliate? (This is permissible after going through the GATT dispute

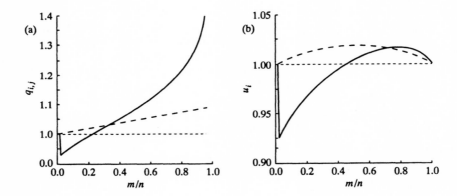

Figure 3.2   The retaliation case
a   Terms of trade, customs union/Rest of World
b   Welfare, customs union

settlement process.) Is the threat of retaliation a sufficient deterrence to keep the customs union in line? This is the question we shall address next.

Assume that a violation of Article 24 is met with an immediate return to optimal tariffs towards the offending part, while the rest of the world continues with their tariff cooperation. The latter qualification is important. If a defection provoked a general 'trade war', instead of a selective punishment of the offending part, the deterrence would be much weaker. The semi-cooperative tariffs are, as before, 10 per cent and the optimal tariffs are 20 per cent for individual countries (under the assumption that $\sigma = 6$). The retaliation case is illustrated in figure 3.2.

Note that, under the threat of retaliation, it does not pay for the customs union to impose 'optimal' tariffs, unless the union is extremely large ($m/n > 0.75$). A small to medium-sized customs union does much better to abide by Article 24 or even to 'volunteer' a tariff reduction to the Pareto efficient level.

The size at which it pays to defect, the critical size, depends on the degree of tariff cooperation in the world. Why? Intuitively, a low initial tariff makes it more costly to defect. For instance, if the initial tariffs are 5 per cent it hurts a great deal more to have them raised to the punishment level 20 per cent than if the initial tariffs are 19 per cent. The customs union must be very large to gain from a defection in the former case, but not necessarily in the latter. It suggests that it is easier to keep a customs union in line the lower are the cooperative tariffs. However, this is not entirely true. If tariffs are negotiated below 5 per cent, it becomes harder again to deter defection, in the sense that slightly smaller customs

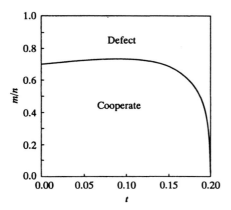

Figure 3.3 Critical size of customs union

unions may defect. I do not have any good intuition why this is the case. From a practical point of view, it may not matter much. A trading bloc must still cover above 70 per cent of the world to gain from a defection. The 'critical' size at which defection pays is plotted in figure 3.3 against the cooperative tariff rate. On the x axis we have the cooperative tariff rate, t, ranging from zero (free trade) to 0.2 (the optimal rate for an individual country), and on the y axis the 'critical size' of the customs union, m/n.

Note the hump-shaped relationship, suggesting that the GATT is most stable in the presence of customs unions at intermediate tariff levels. The general conclusion is that a customs union, out of fear of retaliation, may play by the GATT rules until it has reached a certain critical size, and thereafter withdraw to exercise its market power in the world. Consequently, small trading blocs constitute no threat to the GATT-centred multilateral trading system, but large ones do.

4 Regional trading blocs

The previous discussion abstracted from the fact that customs unions, free-trade areas (FTAs) and other forms of preferential trade arrangements tend to be regional.[7] Regions are in a sense 'natural' trading areas: transportation costs are relatively low, language and cultural barriers may be relatively easy to overcome, and the political and legal framework may be fairly similar. The above factors tend to keep regional transaction costs down and make trade relatively more intense between neighbouring countries than between countries in different parts of the world.[8] Regional trading blocs may, therefore, have somewhat different consequences than those suggested in section 3 of the chapter. For instance, Krugman (1991) argues that

> if trading arrangements follow the lines of natural trading regions, they will have a much better chance of improving welfare than trading arrangements between 'unnatural' partners.

The argument is, perhaps best understood in the terms of Viner's (1950) seminal concepts 'trade diversion' and 'trade creation.' Recall that a trade–creating customs union is welfare improving while a trade-diverting union is, at least for outsiders, harmful. A trading arrangement between natural trading partners may cause very little trade diversion, and hence be welfare improving, simply because these countries did not trade much with other 'unnatural' trading partners to start with.

There is one caveat to Krugman's argument. All countries in a 'natural trading region' may not be included in the deal. It depends on the size of the region and the cost of inter-regional trade. Intuitively, if the region is small and inter-regional trading costs low, most trade is with other regions in the world. All countries in the region may then be encouraged to join the local trading bloc to get the best possible 'leverage' on the external terms of trade. However, if the region is large or if the trade with other regions is modest because of high inter-regional trading costs, the local bloc is better off leaving some countries outside. The consequences for regional outsiders do not look good at all. They are, in a sense, 'locked-in' by inter-regional trading costs, leaving little choice other than to trade with the local bloc, even at unfavourable terms. Thus, while a regional trading arrangement may have a small impact on the rest of the world, the consequences for regional outsiders may be quite severe. This is shown in the first part of this section.

Imagine a world composed of two 'natural' trading regions, A and B, of equal size: $n_A = n_B = 50$. One may, for instance, think of region A as the Western hemisphere and region B as the Eastern hemisphere. The transaction cost of regional trade is, by assumption, lower than the cost of inter-regional trade; the former is, for simplicity, set to zero while the benchmark for the latter is $\gamma = 0.1$. At the outset there is only one trading bloc in the world; a customs union in region A. (We shall introduce a trading bloc in region B later on.) Members are index $A = \{1, \ldots, m_A\}$, outsiders in the region $a = \{1, \ldots, n_A - m_A\}$, and countries in the other region $b = \{1, \ldots, n_B\}$.

To reduce the number of tariff cases, I assume that the cooperative tariff regime (GATT) is sustainable by threats of retaliation. This was shown

Table 3.1   Trading bloc in one region

(1)	$m_A=1$ (2) Con.	$m_A/n_A=10/50$ (3) Con.	(4) PET	$m_A n_A=25/50$ (5) Con.	(6) PET	$m_A/n_A=40/50$ (7) Con.	(8) PET
$t_{A,a}$	0.1	0.1	0.012	0.1	0.005	0.1	0.003
$t_{A,b}$	0.1	0.1	0.012	0.1	0.005	0.1	0.003
$q_{A,a}$	1	1.013	1	1.032	1	1.049	1
$q_{A,b}$	1	1.013	1	1.029	1	1.042	1
$q_{a,b}$	1	1.000	1	0.997	1	0.994	1
$\Delta c_{A,A}$	1	-12.6	-39.2	-25.4	-41.8	-33.0	-42.5
$\Delta c_{A,A'}$	0.565	54.9	7.7	32.2	3.1	18.7	1.9
$\Delta c_{A,a}$	0.565	-5.5	0	-10.0	0	-10.8	0
$\Delta c_{A,b}$	0.300	-5.7	0	-11.4	0	-14.2	0
$\Delta c_{a,a}$	1	0.9	0	5.2	0	13.3	0
$\Delta c_{a,a'}$	0.565	0.9	0	5.2	0	13.3	0
$\Delta c_{a,A}$	0.565	-6.7	0	-12.7	0	-14.9	0
$\Delta c_{a,b}$	0.300	0.6	0	3.6	0	9.0	0
$\Delta c_{b,b}$	1	0.4	0	2.3	0	5.5	0
$\Delta c_{b,b'}$	0.565	0.4	0	2.3	0	5.5	0
$\Delta c_{b,A}$	0.300	-6.9	0	-13.9	0	-17.6	0
$\Delta c_{b,a}$	0.300	0.7	0	3.9	0	9.7	0
U_A	1	1.008	1.00043	1.015	1.00046	1.016	1.00047
U_a	1	0.998	1	0.990	1	0.975	1
U_b	1	0.999	1	0.995	1	0.989	1

to be effective in the last section. Only extremely large trading blocs could gain from withdrawing from the tariff cooperation to exercise their market power in the world.[9] The semi-cooperative tariff rate is, as before, assumed to be 10 per cent. As a reference, we shall also simulate the PET case. The Pareto efficient tariffs are solved numerically from the restrictions that outsiders shall be unharmed. Note that there are two restrictions since there are two groups of outsiders: regional and external. Thus, the customs union may have to set different tariffs for the two groups: $t_{A,a}$ and $t_{A,b}$. The simulations for three sizes of the regional customs union, $m_A/n_A = \{0.2, 0.5, 0.8\}$, are reported in table 3.1.

A few comments before we go on to the results. The consumption patterns of each group, A, a and b, are derived from (9) and (10). They are not reported to save space. Relative prices, $q_{A,a}$, $q_{A,b}$ and $q_{a,b} = q_{A,a}$, are determined from the balance trade conditions. Column (2) of table 3.1 ($m_A = 1$) is the pre-union semi-cooperative equilibrium with 10 per cent tariffs. The associated welfare is normalised to one, and α and β are chosen so that domestic consumption is one. $\Delta c_{i,j}$ is the percentage change in consumption in country i of goods from country j, induced by the formation of the customs union.

What do we learn from this exercise? Let us take the changes in trade pattern as a point of departure. The countries that join the customs union will trade a great deal more with each other than before ($\Delta c_{A,a}, > 0$), partly at the expense of trade with outsiders ($\Delta c_{A,a}, \Delta c_{A,b} < 0$). This increases their welfare for two reasons: first, it reduces the consumption distortion (they consumed 'too many' domestic goods in the pre-union state). Second, it leads to a terms of trade gain; particularly against regional outsiders that are 'locked in' by inter-regional trade costs ($q_{A,a} > q_{A,b}$). The welfare gain is considerably lower if the customs union is restricted to set Pareto efficient tariffs. The welfare gain in the latter case comes *only* through reduced consumption distortion, which is modest in comparison to the gain that comes through the terms of trade improvement with constant tariffs. It suggests that the welfare gain to members comes primarily at the expense of outsiders, in particular regional ones.

Let us take a closer look at the latter. They suffer a terms of trade loss not just against the customs union but, although to a much less extent, against region B. The reason is the following: the trade diverted from the customs union ($\Delta c_{A,a} < 0$) can only partially be compensated by increased trade with other outsiders in the region ($\Delta c_{a,a\prime} > 0$), especially if most countries in the region are members. Trading partners must thus be looked for in other regions ($\Delta c_{a,b}, \Delta c_{b,a} > 0$), although it means higher trade costs. Life is easier for countries in region B. They have greater scope for regional substitution for two reasons: first, the number of countries in region B exceeds the number of outsiders in region A. Second, due to the inter-regional trade cost they didn't trade much with region A to begin with (in the pre-union state). Hence, the volume of trade to substitute is much less. This is the reason for the terms of trade loss for outsiders in region A against countries in region B.

To conclude, the welfare gain to members of the customs union comes primarily at the expense of outsiders; in particular, regional outsiders that are locked-in by inter-regional trade costs, forcing them to trade with the local bloc even at unfavourable terms. The other region is relatively unharmed because the trade between the regions was modest at the outset due to high inter-regional trade costs. The negative repercussion on outsiders can be nullified, or at least reduced, if the customs union is restricted to set a lower external tariff than the average pre-union level of its members.

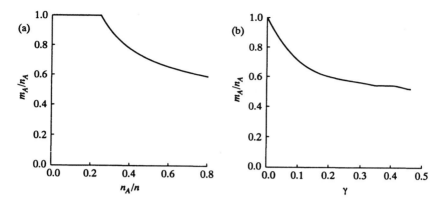

Figure 3.4   Optimal size of customs union
a   Optimal size of customs union and region size
b   Optimal size of customs union and inter-regional trade costs

What determines the optimal size of a regional customs union? There are two obvious candidates in this framework: the size of the region and the degree of inherent regionalism (as measured by the inter-regional trade cost). Intuitively, if the region is small, the majority of the goods are imported from other regions and, therefore, it is the terms of trade against the rest of the world that is of primary interest to the customs union, not the terms of trade against a few regional outsiders. All countries in the region may, therefore, be encouraged to join the customs union to get the best possible 'leverage' on the external terms of trade. However, even in a small region, a customs union may choose to leave some countries outside if inter-regional trade is unimportant because of high inter-regional trade costs. The case is illustrated in figure 3.4, where the optimal size of the customs union is plotted against the relative size of the region, $m_A/n_A = f(n_A/n)$, for given trade costs, $\gamma = 0.1$, and against trade costs, $m_A/n_A = f(\gamma)$, for a given size of the region, $n_A/n = 0.5$. The smaller is the region and the lower is the inter-regional trade cost, the larger is the optimal size of the customs union.

Assume now that a customs union is formed in region B. Members of the customs union are index $B = \{1, \ldots, m_B\}$, and regional outsiders $b = \{1, \ldots, n_B - m_B\}$. Let us make the following experiment. Assume that the customs union in region A is already in existence. The size of the customs union is optimal given the initial situation with no customs union in region B; $m_A/n_A = 35/50$. Let us trace out changes in the trade

Table 3.2   Trading blocs in both regions

(1)	m_B = 1 (2)	m_B/n_B = 10/50 (3)	m_B/n_B = 25/50 (4)	m_B/n_B = 40/50 (5)	(6)	m_B = 1 (7)	m_B/n_B = 10/50 (8)	m_B/n_B = 25/50 (9)	m_B/n_B = 40/50 (10)
$q_{A,a}$	1.043	1.043	1.044	1.045	$q_{B,a}$	1.005	1.018	1.035	1.049
$q_{A,b}$	1.038	1.039	1.042	1.047	$q_{B,b}$	1	1.014	1.033	1.051
$q_{A,B}$	1.038	1.025	1.008	0.996	$q_{B,A}$	0.963	0.976	0.992	1.004
$\Delta c_{A,A}$	0.692	0.3	1.8	4.3	$\Delta c_{B,B}$	1.043	−13.0	−26.0	−33.6
$\Delta c_{A,A'}$	0.692	0.3	1.8	4.3	$\Delta c_{B,B'}$	0.589	54.1	31.1	17.6
$\Delta c_{A,a}$	0.503	0.4	2.3	5.6	$\Delta c_{B,b}$	0.589	−5.6	−10.1	−10.6
$\Delta c_{A,b}$	0.260	0.7	3.9	9.8	$\Delta c_{B,a}$	0.322	−5.9	−11.5	−14.0
$\Delta c_{A,B}$	0.260	−7.2	−14.5	−18.5	$\Delta c_{B,A}$	0.250	−6.0	−12.0	−15.1
$\Delta c_{a,a}$	1.102	0.5	2.7	6.7	$\Delta c_{b,b}$	1.043	0.9	5.7	14.6
$\Delta c_{a,a'}$	0.606	0.5	2.7	6.7	$\Delta c_{b,b}$	0.589	0.9	5.7	14.6
$\Delta c_{a,A}$	0.482	0.4	2.2	5.4	$\Delta c_{b,B}$	0.589	−6.9	−13.0	−14.9
$\Delta c_{a,b}$	0.321	0.7	3.9	10.9	$\Delta c_{b,a}$	0.322	0.7	4.1	10.2
$\Delta c_{a,B}$	0.321	−7.1	−14.5	−17.6	$\Delta c_{b,A}$	0.250	0.6	3.5	8.9
U_A	1.017	1.016	1.012	1.005	U_B	0.992	1.000	1.007	1.007
U_a	0.981	0.980	0.975	0.968	U_b	0.992	0.990	0.980	0.965

pattern, terms of trade and welfare when a customs union is formed in region B. The simulations for three sizes of the customs union, $m_B/n_B = \{0.2, 0.5, 0.8\}$, are reported in table 3.2, under the assumption that tariffs are maintained at the semi-cooperative 10 per cent level.

The action is now mainly in region B. Countries that join the customs union will trade more with each other and less with others. As a consequence, relative prices in the world market changes to their advantage; in particular towards outsiders in both regions. Their welfare increases at the expense of other countries, but mostly at the expense of regional outsiders that 'lose' a part of their natural trading partners and are 'forced' to trade more (it is optimal under the circumstances) with other regions at higher transaction costs.

4.1   Interaction between trading blocs

In the above exercise we held the size of the customs union in region A constant. The question is: if it is optimal to change the size when new customs unions emerge on the world market, or rather, before they emerge, to influence their size optimally? This model is not really

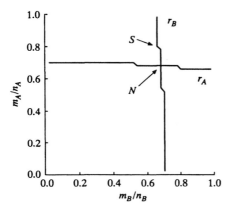

Figure 3.5   Reaction curves

designed for such game theoretic issues, but we can at least get a first shot at the issue. In figure 3.5 is simulated the optimal size for the A union given different sizes of the B union, and vice versa, under the assumption that both trading blocs abide by Article 24. The best response function (reaction curve) for each union, $m_A/n_A = r_A(m_B/n_B)$ and $m_B/n_B = r_B(m_A/n_A)$, is plotted in figure 3.5.

The Nash equilibrium, marked by N in figure 3.5, is given by the crossing of the two reaction curves. The Nash equilibrium encompasses in this symmetric case 68 per cent (34/50) of the countries in each region. If the two regions were of unequal size, the smaller region would encompass a larger fraction (possibly all countries) and the larger region a smaller fraction.

Note that the reaction curves are downward-sloping. It suggests that a first mover can influence the size of latecomers to its own advantage by committing to a larger size than otherwise. There should be no problems with credibility in this case. One can always set stringent rules for under which circumstances a member can and cannot be excluded. The Stackelberg equilibrium, marked by S in figure 3.5, with the A union as leader and the B union as follower (the A union chooses the number of members optimally given the reaction curve of the B union) encompasses 80 per cent (40/50) of the countries in region A and 66 per cent (33/50) of the countries in region B. Compared to the symmetric Nash equilibrium, welfare is marginally higher for the A union and lower for the B union. Hence, a customs union may choose to expand above the static optimum (34/50) to influence the size of an emerging trading bloc. It may pay off in a smaller rival than otherwise, and in the end higher welfare.

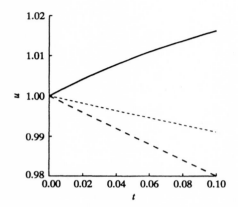

Figure 3.6   Welfare, customs union and outsiders, at different tariffs

4.2   The scope for free-trade agreements

The final issue I would like to address is whether regional integration may be a step towards global free trade. The starting point is the observation that a single dominating trading bloc may lose out from a multilateral free trade agreement. This is shown in figure 3.6. The example builds on the following assumptions: There exists only one trading bloc in the world, in region A. The size of the customs union is optimal, $m_A/n_A = 35/50$, given the initial semi-cooperative tariff level: 10 per cent. On the x axis we have the tariff rate and on the y axis the welfare level of the customs union (solid line), outsiders in region A (long-dashed), and countries in region B (short-dashed). Note that welfare decreases for the customs union as the tariff rate is negotiated down to the free-trade level (zero). The consumption distortion decreases, but not enough to compensate for the terms of trade deterioration. It may, therefore, try to block the process of multilateral trade liberalisation.

The incentive changes if unorganised countries join forces in a counter-balancing trading bloc. To simplify, let us assume that all countries are members of the local trading bloc; $m_A = n_A$ and $m_B = n_B$.[10] The blocs negotiate over tariffs, t_A and t_B, under the threat of imposing optimal tariffs against each other (trade war). The negotiation range, bounded by the indifference curves through the threat points (optimal tariffs), are plotted in figure 3.7 for two relative sizes of the regions (trading blocs): $n_A/n_B = 25/75 = 1/3$ and $n_A/n_B = 50/50 = 1$.

Note that trading blocs *may* reach a mutual beneficial free-trade

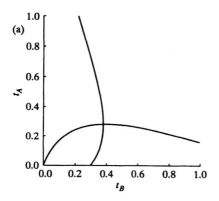
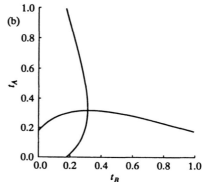

Figure 3.7   Negotiation ranges
a   Negotiation range, $n_A/n_B = 1/3$
b   Negotiation range, $n_A/n_B = 1$

agreement *if* they are not too different in size. The free-trade solution is within the negotiation range unless one bloc is more than three times larger than the other bloc (given the parameters of the model).[11] In the limiting case it is only the small bloc that gains from a free-trade agreement. The large bloc is indifferent between free trade and trade war. The most likely outcome in this situation is perhaps not a complete elimination of tariffs; rather an asymmetric reduction that 'balances' the gains. It may, therefore, be hard to reach a free-trade agreement unless the blocs are of about equal size.

The analysis suggests that countries may join forces in a trading bloc to improve their chances of a negotiated free-trade agreement with other blocs in the world. What a single country cannot achieve on its own may be possible for a group of countries acting together. Thus, the formation of (regional) trading blocs may be a first, and possibly necessary, step towards global free trade. Necessary because the current blocs may not find it to their advantage to enter into a multilateral free-trade agreement unless their dominating position in the world market is counter-balanced by other blocs of similar economic strength.

5   Conclusions

The process of regional integration has its hopes and its fears. On the one hand, it may provide a track for expediting trade reforms in different parts of the world. On the other hand, trading blocs may turn into exclusionary, trade-diverting entities that may bring harm to world welfare, in particular to regional outsiders. Indeed, there are widespread concerns that trading blocs are becoming inward-looking, curtailing the market access for non-participants. Countries that were previously happy to be non-members are, therefore, taking steps to seek a closer alliance with their major trading partners (see chapter 2 in this volume). The cost of standing outside has simply become too high, or is becoming so as other trading partners enter. Whether the local trading bloc will accommodate all prospective candidates is an open question. It depends above all on the size of the region. If the region is small, it probably will; in particular, since it may improve the chances of negotiating free trade agreements with other blocs in the world. Indeed, joining forces in a trading bloc may be a necessary step towards global free trade. Necessary because the current blocs may not find it to their advantage to enter into a multilateral free trade agreement unless their dominating position in the world market is counter-balanced by other blocs of similar economic strength.

NOTES

I would like to thank Harry Flam, Peter Ludvik and participants at the conference for useful comments and Molly Åkerlund for proofreading the manuscript. Financial support from the Tore Browaldhs Foundation for Scientific Research and Education is gratefully acknowledged.
1 In Europe it is manifest in the '1992' programme and the EC–EFTA accord; in North America in the free trade agreement between Mexico, Canada and the US (NAFTA); and in Asia in renewed efforts among ASEAN members to establish a free-trade area. See de Melo and Panagariya (1993) for an excellent discussion of 'the new regionalism in trade policy'.
2 See Finger (1993) for a comprehensive discussion of GATT's influence on regional arrangements.
3 Note that relative wages are equal to the terms of trade: $w_h/w_f = p_{h,h}/p_{f,f} = q_{h,f}$.
4 The only trade policy instrument in this model is tariffs. What I have in mind, however, is the tariff equivalent of the overall barriers to trade.
5 The optimal size of a regional trading bloc is discussed at some length in section 4.
6 A similar result is derived by Baldwin (1995) in a more sophisticated political economy framework (chapter 2 in this volume). Baldwin shows that a deeper integration of an existing trade bloc, such as the EC '1992' programme, may trigger membership requests from countries that were previously happy to be non-members. The campaign for membership is driven by firms that fear they will lose out in the internal market due to cost disadvantages. The cost of standing outside increases as other countries enter and eventually the political equilibrium is tilted in favour of a membership in more and more countries. Baldwin's 'domino effect' is strengthened further, as suggested in this chapter, if governments fear that they may not be given a second chance.

7 There are a few exceptions such as the free-trade agreement between the US and Israel and the preferential treatment by the EU of some former colonies.
8 The main exception is Africa, where (the official) trade between neighbouring countries is relatively modest. Part of the reason is that they export the same type of primary goods, as opposed to the industrialised world, that exports mainly differentiated (manufactured) goods.
9 Whether this result holds in a regional setting is left for future research. It may be weakened by inter-regional trading costs that make punishment from external sources less effective.
10 The optimal size of a trading bloc may indeed be the entire region if (i) there are more than two regions in the world, (ii) the excluded countries are expected to form a competing trading bloc, or (iii) this strengthens the bloc's bargaining power towards other trading blocs.
11 A similar result is derived by Gros (1987), studying trade wars between individual countries.

REFERENCES

Baldwin, R.E., 1995. 'A domino theory of regionalism', chapter 2 in this volume
Bhagwati, J., 1993. 'Regionalism and multilateralism: an overview', in J. de Melo and A. Panagariya (eds.), *New Dimensions in Regional Integration*, Cambridge: Cambridge University Press
de Melo, J. and A. Panagariya, 1993. 'The new regionalism in trade policy'. Washington, DC: The World Bank
Finger, M., 1993. 'GATT's influence on regional arrangements', in J. de Melo and A. Panagariya (eds.), *New Dimensions in Regional Integration*, Cambridge: Cambridge University Press
Gros, D., 1987. 'A note on the optimal tariff, retaliation and the welfare loss from tariff wars with intra-industry trade, *Journal of International Economics*, 23, 357–67
Kemp, M. and Wan, H., 1976. 'Elementary proposition concerning the formation of custom unions', *Journal of International Economics*, 6, 95–7
Krugman, P.R., 1980. 'Scale economies, product differentiation, and the pattern of trade', *American Economic Review*, 70, 950–9
1991. 'Is bilateralism bad?', in E. Helpman and A. Razin (eds.), *International Trade and Trade Policy*, Cambridge, MA: MIT Press
Schott, J., 1989. 'Free trade areas and US trade policy', Washington, DC: Institute for International Economics
Viner, J., 1950. *The Customs Union Issue*, New York: Carnegie Endowment for International Peace

Discussion

ILKKA KAJASTE

Nordström's chapter 3 is highly stimulating. It is important that the effects of different trade policy developments are examined. The impacts of integration are in most cases sensitive to assumptions concerning the policy stance adopted. It is obvious that exact, unequivocal estimates of the most likely consequences of integration cannot be given. However, certain conclusions may be drawn.

In studying these questions, the global approach which Nordström adopts is essential, and increases the usefulness of the model. Also the European integration process should be considered predominantly in a global context, as part of a global liberalisation process. Nordström's chapter therefore contains the assumption that the final target of the regional integration processes is 'natural', not 'strategic' integration.

The analysis of regional outsiders is interesting. One of the central questions relating to the effects of integration in the new entrant countries has been the cost of joining the common trade policy, that is, the loss of independent room of manoeuvre *vis-à-vis* third countries. Nordström's model seems to clarify this problem effectively. However, as pointed out elsewhere,[1] there might exist also useful strategic options as to how to exploit the position of a regional outsider (e.g. Hong Kong).

Here, the natural trading area seems to be a key concept. It is obvious that it covers the original Community area and also those former EFTA countries which became members at the beginning of 1995. No major adjustment of industrial structures is expected due to the deepening and widening of integration, at this stage. These countries share largely similar structures, technologies, preferences, etc. In addition, it could be expected that the integration will further emphasise these common features, so that the growth of intra-regional trade will lead also to increasing intra-industry specialisation. It is obvious that the internal market programme and EMU will further diminish transaction costs within the EU region.

The starting point of the potential new entrants from Central and Eastern Europe is, however, different. Finland has currently experienced two major changes in her foreign trade relations; the western integration and the eastern disintegration. Finland was not integrated with the CMEA. However, because of the geographical proximity and the clearing trade system between Finland and the former Soviet Union the collapse of the East European economies also affected the Finnish economy. The collapse of the Finnish exports to the East revealed how distorted the trade relations based on central planning (Soviet Union), imperfect competition (Finland) and bilateralism (clearing trade) basically were (see Kajaste, 1993). One could therefore wonder to what extent the industrial capacities of the Central and Eastern European countries (CEECs) really reflect their comparative advantages. If this is not the case, a too rapid integration in a regional, European context might lead to very painful adjustment. Against the background of the results of chapter 3, it would be interesting to examine also other possible options open to these countries. There is an obvious risk that bilateralism in economic relations *vis-à-vis* European Union could marginalise these countries further.

NOTE

1   See chapter 9 in this volume.

REFERENCE

Kajaste, I., 1993. 'Finland's trade with the Soviet Union: its impact on the Finnish economy', *Economic Bulletin for Europe*, **44**, New York: United Nations

4   Consumer services and economic integration

PERTTI HAAPARANTA and
TIINA HEIKKINEN

1   Introduction

One common criticism of economic integration is that while integration can increase welfare in price terms it may lead to a deterioration in the non-price terms of consumption. Geroski (1989), for example, has argued that integration may reduce the variety of goods available to consumers if economies of scale in production are strong. At the policy level, Finnish and Swedish governments during the EU membership negotiations demanded the right to continue their present regional policies to ensure the availability of services everywhere (Ministry of Foreign Affairs, 1993).[1] Indeed one of the hardest issues in the negotiations during spring 1994 was which areas in Finland and Sweden were entitled to receive special funding from the EU regional programme. In this chapter we study these issues by looking at how the quality of consumer services is affected by economic integration. Another issue on which we hope to shed some light is whether one can expect the relative prices of basic consumer goods to fall when the restrictions on the imports of these goods are lifted. In the light of the fact that the relative prices of food products, for example, are highest in the OECD area among Nordic countries, one major argument in favour of EU membership has been an expected decline in related consumer prices.

This point of view is relevant also to the integration theory in general, since almost all the goods traded internationally reach consumers via a distribution system and the distribution sector (comprising only a part of consumer services) is a sizable sector in itself. In Finland, the share of the labour force in retailing, transportation and financial services is around 33 per cent, and some of the most important effects of integration will remain unappreciated unless the distribution sector is taken into account. Rousslang and To (1993) found that the domestic distribution system seems to impose significantly higher transport costs

80

on imported goods than on identical domestic goods, thus biasing trade against foreign goods.

As such, the main theories of international trade and integration shed little light on consumer services. These theories give strong support to claims that consumers will benefit from free trade even when it is recognised that free trade does not deliver the first best outcome (see, for example, Krugman, 1993), yet they do not take into account the distinctive features of service production and consumption. Here we focus on two of the most important.[2] First, service production is characterised by the fact that the act of production cannot be separated from the act of consumption; most services are both intangible and non-storable. Secondly, focusing on consumer services like retailing and retail banking, we assume that services must be provided where consumers are located and, hence, pricing decisions are also made locally.[3] Since service production is almost everywhere the most regulated industry and regulations particularly hit the operations of foreign firms, the most significant effect of integration in service industry may be the entry of foreign firms. The policies in use seem to have a major effect by imposing high barriers of entry.[4]

We model the production of consumer services by modifying the monopolistic competition–product differentiation model now familiar in trade theory to include a non-trivial choice of product variety. The product variety offered by a firm corresponds in our model to the 'quality' of services. The specific modelling attempts to take into account some of the issues relevant for the 'real' economies (see n. 4 above). In section 2 we present and consider a model suitable for an analysis of integrated wholesale–retail firms or retail banking with a given number of firms. The model is especially valuable for the analysis of how the reduction of barriers to trade on visible goods affects the service sector.[5] Section 3 explains what happens with the entry of foreign firms. Finally, in section 4 we use the traditional urban economics models surveyed in Fujita (1989) to account explicitly for the regional impacts of integration.

Before going into the detailed analysis, we should mention that, in contrast to consumer services, producer services have received increasing attention in trade and integration theory (Ethier and Horn, 1991; Francois, 1990a, 1990b; Hoekman, 1992a, 1992b; Jones and Ruane, 1990; Markusen, 1989; Melvin, 1989). These studies[6] emphasise the role of service in improving the Smithian international division of labour and thus increasing the efficiency of goods production. They are based on the models by Ethier (1982) and Edwards and Starr (1987). In these settings the expansion of markets due to integration permits an increasing division of labour; this effect appears even when producer services are not traded internationally, since the expansion of goods trade indirectly expands the markets for producer services also. Here we focus on the production of services to (internationally) immobile consumers, so the issues emphasised in the literature on producer services are not directly relevant. Instead, integration will work here through changes in the quality of services and service prices. The quality of services has a role similar to the division of labour in producer services: the 'efficiency' of final consumption is affected by the change in the number of varieties consumed.

2   Model I: do we still get bananas in Lapland?

The basis of the modelling is that consumers' welfare is affected by both the quantity and the quality of the goods they consume. Here we identify 'quality' with product variety. In modelling variety, we assume that consumers like variety as such. In this section, we want to stay at a general level, but one of our preferred interpretations is that product variety refers to geographic variety in points of supply, i.e. each variety corresponds to the supply of a good in a different place. With this interpretation the love-for-variety approach means that the representative consumer is mobile within the home country but is always restricted to consuming in the place where she happens to be and thus prefers, *ceteris paribus*, that there exist many points of supply.[7] Consider, then, the representative consumer with the following S–D–S-preferences with c as the differentiated (i.e. the service) good and d as the homogeneous good:

$$u = \left\{ \left[\int_0^m c(i)^\alpha di \right]^{1/\alpha} \right\}^\delta d^{1-\delta} \tag{1}$$

Here $0 < \alpha < 1$, indicating that the consumer loves variety, $c(i)$ is the amount of the ith variety consumed, m is the total number of varieties consumed (points of supply) and δ is the weight of the utility derived from the consumption of the differentiated good in the overall utility of the consumer. Since the utility (1) is separable in the consumption of the differentiated goods the consumer choice can be presented in two stages. If E is the expenditure allocated to the differentiated goods, the demand for the ith variety is

$$c(i) = p(i)^{1/(\alpha-1)} E / \left[\int_0^m p(j)^{\alpha/(\alpha-1)} dj \right]. \tag{2}$$

If D denotes the expenditure on the d-good and r is its price, the consumer welfare, (using (1) and (2)), is:

$$u = \left[E^\delta / P(m)^{(\alpha-1)/\alpha} \right] (D/r)^{1-\delta}$$

$$P(m) = \int_0^m p(j)^{\alpha/(\alpha-1)} dj \tag{3}$$

where $P(m) =$ the price index for the aggregate consumption of differentiated goods. Hence, if Y is the aggregate income then $E = \delta Y$ and $D = (1 - \delta) Y$.

We assume that service production needs two types of inputs. First, intermediate inputs consisting of goods either imported or produced in the home country are needed, one good for each variety produced (e.g. retailing firms demand goods to bring to consumers). Secondly, the service firms use labour in transportation and other tasks related to selling the goods. The labour requirements reflect the underlying technology of service production. For the firms to be willing to supply a variety of goods, the production technology must imply that there are economies of scope to be utilised. We also require that the technology shows *marginal dis*economies of scope, i.e. that increasing variety can be produced only with increasing cost. In the sphere of retailing, our model firms can be best interpreted as integrated wholesale–retail chains and the assumption of marginal diseconomies of scope materialised if, for example, an increase in variety of products supplied increases the demand for special storage, etc. which increases costs disproportionately to the variety. The assumption is also needed for analytic purposes: we want the firms to provide only a finite number of varieties.[8] A convenient form for the use of labour by a service firm satisfying these requirements is

$$\left[\int_0^z c(i)^\beta di \right]^{1/\beta} + \phi, 0 < \beta < 1, \tag{4}$$

where $z =$ the number of varieties produced by the firm and ϕ is the fixed cost of production. This form was first used by Ethier and Horn (1991) to characterise input requirements of a competitive supplier of producer services. The presence of fixed costs implies that no variety will be produced by more than one firm. We assume that there are n firms indexed by k. Hence the number of varieties produced is $m = \Sigma z(k)$. The firms aim at maximising their profits, which for firm 1 (similar expressions hold for other firms) are:

$$\pi = \int_0^{z(1)} p(i)x(i)di - \int_0^{z(1)} q(i)x(i)di - w\left\{\left[\int_0^{z(1)} x(i)^\beta di\right]^{1/\beta} + \phi\right\} \quad (5)$$

where w = the wage rate, $q(i)$ = the price of the ith intermediate input and $x(i)$ is the amount of variety i produced. The firm now chooses $z(1)$ and $p(i)$ for all i in $[0,z(1)]$ with $x(i)$ equal to (2) to maximise (4). Our model of the service firm can be seen as a special case of the model of retailing firms developed by Betancourt and Gautsch (1988, 1989), especially in its emphasis on the simultaneity of the quality choice with the pricing decision.

Without loss of generality we assume that all intermediate goods are priced equally, $q(i) = q$ for all i. We assume further that all firms take the aggregate price level of consumption $P(m)^\delta r^{1-\delta}$ as given. Hence firms regard the demand for variety i as independent of the prices of other varieties. With these assumptions we can focus on symmetric equilibria where all firms produce the equal number of varieties, $z(k) = z$ for all k, and all varieties are priced equally, $p(I) = p$ for all i. Hence, the first order conditions for profit maximisation:

$p(i)$:

$$\int_0^z \left(\frac{1}{\alpha-1}+1\right)p(i)^{1/(\alpha-1)}\frac{E}{P(m)}di - \int_0^z\left(\frac{1}{\alpha-1}\right)q(i)p(i)^{(1/(\alpha-1))-1}\frac{E}{P(m)}di -$$

$$w\left\{\frac{1}{\beta}\left[\int_0^z\left(p(i)^{1/(\alpha-1)}\frac{E}{P(m)}\right)^\beta di\right]^{(1/\beta)-1}\int_0^z \beta\left(p(i)^{1/(\alpha-1)}\frac{E}{P(m)}\right)^{\beta-1}\right.$$

$$\left.\left(\frac{1}{\alpha-1}\right)p(i)^{(1/(\alpha-1))-1}\frac{E}{P(m)}di\right\} = 0 \quad (6)$$

z :

$$[p(z) - q(z)]c(z) - \frac{w}{\beta}\left[\int_0^z c(i)^\beta di\right]^{(1/\beta)-1}c(z)^\beta = 0 \quad (7)$$

where $c(z)$ is given by (2), reduce to

$$p - \frac{q^*(1+\tau)}{\alpha} - \frac{w(p,z,\tau,n)z^{(1-\beta)/\beta}}{\alpha} = 0 \tag{8}$$

$$p - q^*(1+\tau) - \frac{w(p,z,\tau,n)z^{(1-\beta)/\beta}}{\beta} = 0 \tag{9}$$

where we have used the facts that $m = nz$ and $P(m) = nzp^{\alpha/(\alpha-1)}$ and (2). It is obvious that for there to exist a solution to (8) and (9) the condition $\beta < \alpha$ must hold. To get the general equilibrium solution, we have to specify the production in the rest of the economy to determine the wage rate.

The rest of the economy produces two goods: the intermediate input with price q and the homogeneous consumption good with price r. The intermediate good is used only by the consumer service sector as modelled above. We assume that the intermediate good sector is the sector protected by trade policies and is also a sector whose products are imported in net terms. In Nordic countries, food products are an important example of goods belonging to this group. The other non-service sector is, thus, the non-protected exportable good sector. Production in both sectors takes place under conditions of perfect competition. Hence, if L^c is the amount of labour these sectors use, their production decisions can be presented by a revenue function (Dixit and Norman, 1980; Woodland, 1983):

$$G = G(q, r, L^c). \tag{10}$$

The properties of the revenue function are well known (see, for example, Dixit and Norman, 1980): G_q and G_r give the supplies of the intermediate input and the homogeneous consumption good. In equilibrium $L^c = L - L^s$, where L is the total labour force and $L^s =$ the labour used in the consumer service sector and, hence, the wage rate is

$$w = G_L(q, r, L - L^s). \tag{11}$$

The domestic price q is given by $q = q^*(1+\tau)$, where $\tau =$ the tariff equivalent of the protection of the intermediate input sector and q^* is the world market price of these goods. r is also determined completely in the world market, $r = r^* = 1$ if it is chosen as the numeraire. Finally we assume that all tariff revenues are returned to the consumers as lump-sum transfers. The national income Y is then

$$Y = n\pi + wL^s + G + q^*\tau(mc - G_q). \tag{12}$$

Since $c(i) = c = p^{1/(\alpha-1)}\delta Y/nzp^{\alpha/(\alpha-1)} = \delta Y/nzp$ and profits π are given by (5), the national income can be solved from the equation

$$Y = n\left(zp\frac{\delta Y}{nzp} - zq\frac{\delta Y}{nzp}\right) + G\left(q^*(1+\tau), r, L - n\left[z^{1/\beta}\frac{\delta Y}{nzp} + \phi\right]\right)$$
$$+ q^*\tau\left(nz\frac{\delta Y}{nzp} - G_q\right). \tag{13}$$

This gives $Y = Y(p, z, \tau, n)$. The derivation of the properties of the solution is straightforward. First $Y\tau < 0$ for the reasons known from the basic trade theory: an increase in the rate of protection worsens the misallocation of resources in the competitive sector of the economy. Otherwise the effects depend on the degree of protection and on how labour-intensive the sector producing x goods is, though most likely $Y_p > 0$ but $Y_p p/Y < 1$. An increase in the number of services provided reduces the labour resources available in the other sectors but, if the production of x goods is labour-intensive, reduces the x good production and, hence, increases tariff revenue. If protection is not very severe then the first effect dominates, and $Y_z < 0$ and with high levels of protection $Y_z > 0$. With similar reasoning $Y_n < 0$ with mild protection, $Y_n > 0$ with severe protection. Hence, we get

$$Y = Y(p, z, n, \tau), Y_p > 0, \quad Y_z < (>) 0, Y_n < (>) 0, Y_\tau < 0 \tag{14}$$

where the signs in parentheses refer to the case of severe protection and labour-intensive production of the x goods. The wage rate can be solved from (11) by using (14). If $G_{LL} = 0$ which is the case if the competitive sector is a mini-Heckscher–Ohlin-type sector in the economy, then it is clear that the wage rate depends only on the trade policy-changes in p, z, and n do not have any effect on it. Hence, we assume that $G_{LL} < 0$. With this, the wage rate is

$$w = w(p, zn, \tau) \tag{15}$$

with $w_p < 0, w_z < 0$ for mild protection, $w_z > 0$ for severe protection, $w_n > 0$ and $w_\tau = ?$ the ambiguity in the effect of trade policy on the wage rate is due to two opposing effects. First if the x good protection is labour-intensive then an increase in the rate of protection tends to increase the

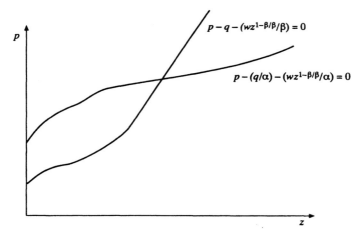

$$p - q - (wz^{1-\beta/\beta}/\beta) = 0$$

$$p - (q/\alpha) - (wz^{1-\beta/\beta}/\alpha) = 0$$

Figure 4.1   Economic integration, pricing and product choice decisions

wage rate. At the same time, the reduction in the demand for differentiated goods due to the decline in income increases the supply of labour to the competitive sector, and thus tends to push the wage rate down.

With (15) we can go on to study how economic integration affects the pricing and product choice decisions of firms. The solution to (8) and (9) is described in figure 4.1, the exact properties of the solution are easy to characterise. Here we simply explain the findings.

First, a reduction in trade barriers will through its direct effect on the costs of imported inputs tend to push price down. Since there are marginal diseconomies of scope in production, this creates a pressure to reduce the product variety, i.e. z tends to become smaller. Hence, both prices and product variety will be reduced: consumers obtain better price terms of trade but worse non-price terms of trade. With product variety meaning also variety in the locations of supply we will thus tend to see a reduction in the number of supply locations.[9]

This need not, however, be the only outcome. If the wage rate declines when trade is liberalised then it can be the case that $(q^* + w_\tau z^{(1-\beta)/\beta})/\alpha < q^* + w_\tau z^{(1-\beta)/\beta}/\beta$. Then the curve describing (9) shifts down by more than the curve describing the optimal pricing decision (8) when trade is liberalised. The outcome is uncertain: only the possibility that price will go up and product variety will go down can be excluded. In particular, it is possible that with trade liberalisation price declines and product variety increases. The intuition is that while the decline in the price of the imported intermediate input creates pressure to reduce the price proportionately more, the simultaneous stronger downward pressure on the wage rate makes the reduced price compatible with the increase in marginal cost due to the increase in product variety.

The results of this section can be summarised by considering the welfare implications of trade liberalisation. Using (3), the welfare of the representative consumer can be written as

$$u = \delta^\delta (1 - \delta)^{1-\delta} Y \left(\frac{(nz)^{(1-\alpha)/\alpha}}{p} \right)^\delta$$

where Y is given by (13) and p by (14) and (15) (we have set $r = 1$). We take the case $p_\tau, z_\tau > 0$ to be the benchmark case. Hence, the welfare effects of trade liberalisation are threefold. First, aggregate income, and consequently welfare, increase because the allocation of resources in the competitive sector of the economy improves. Secondly, since p decreases the real income Y/p increases.[10] This will show up as an increase in welfare if the share of the service sector products in consumption, δ, is high enough. Finally, the product variety decreases when trade is liberalised and welfare is adversely affected. Thus, in general the welfare effects of liberalising trade in visible goods appear to be ambiguous. And in total contrast to the new trade theory, the ambiguity arises because of the possibility that the product variety available to consumers may decrease. The difference in results is most easily explained by referring to the basic Krugman (1979) model. First, in our world products have to be distributed to the consumers through service firms, while in the Krugman model the consumers can costlessly utilise the product available in the whole world economy. Secondly, in the Krugman model the product variety is determined by the entry of firms to the industry, and here we have thus far considered only the case where the number of firms is given.[11]

It is clear that allowing entry of new firms may change the results in our model since the product variety nz can increase if enough new firms are born even when the product variety of each individual firm narrows. For a preliminary view on the effects of entry, consider how a change in the number of *home* firms affects price and product variety. (8) and (9) imply that the only channel through which entry/exit of firms has an effect is through wage costs. If the number of firms increases, the wage rate goes up. In terms of figure 4.1 both of the curves shift up with the curve associated with (9) shifting (rotating) by more. The number of product varieties produced by individual firms thus falls, though naturally the total number of varieties may increase. The impact on price is unclear. In particular, we can have the 'worst' case, both higher prices and reduced product variety after entry.

Finally, note that in this section we have considered only non-preferential liberalisation. With preferential liberalisation, as in the case of Finland joining the EU, there are trade-diversion effects to be taken into account. In the above framework, however, instead of Vinerian diversion we may observe something like trade modification (Ethier and Horn, 1984), i.e. substitution between varieties imported from member and non-member countries.

3 Service production and entry by foreign firms

Barriers to entry, against both domestic and foreign potential entrants, seem to be especially high in service production. As argued in n. 5 above in the case of Finland entry barriers are significant, at least in retail banking and in retail trade.

When trade barriers on imports of visibles are changed, the profits of a service sector firm change by

$$\partial\pi/\partial\tau = zp^{\alpha/(\alpha-1)}(1-\alpha)\partial(\partial Y/nzp)/\partial\tau - zp^{1/(\alpha-1)}q^*(\delta Y/npz) - w_\tau$$
$$\left[z^{1/\beta}p^{1/(\alpha-1)}(\delta Y/npz) + \phi\right]. \tag{16}$$

In the benchmark case where $p_\tau, z_\tau, w_\tau > 0$, it is clear that profits increase when trade is liberalised.[12] Hence, one would expect the integration at the level of goods trade to have a positive effect on entry. As we noticed above, there is nothing to guarantee that reduction of trade barriers leads to a reduction in prices and wages and in product variety. Hence, in general, one cannot be sure that profits increase, though the direct impact working through the cost of imported input is certainly positive. We assume, however, that the effect is positive to make sure that there are incentives to entry.

To concentrate on the liberalisation of trade in services, which here is equivalent to the establishment of local production by foreign producers, we consider entry by foreign firms only. The assumption can, however, be defended also on the grounds of realism. If we consider retail banking or retail chains, the building of distribution networks will probably be so expensive that entry will be feasible only for foreign firms having already established their position abroad.

To make the analysis of the mode of entry simple, we assume that if the foreign firm enters domestic markets then share μ of its labour costs arises from the use of domestic labour and share $(1 - \mu)$ from the use of foreign labour of their residence countries. We take μ to be parametric to the firm and we also treat it as a policy variable. If $\mu = 0$ the service production does not require the establishment of production facilities in the home country, while if $\mu = 1$ then production is not possible at all without foreign direct investment (FDI).

The unit labour costs of foreign firms supplying the home market[13] are thus $\mu w + (1 - \mu)w^*$, where $w^* =$ the foreign wage rate. Since we allow the wage rates to differ we also allow for the possibility that domestic and foreign producers' pricing and product choice decisions differ. Hence, since we are going to consider the case where all producers within a group behave symmetrically, in equilibrium all domestic firms charge price p and produce z different goods, while all foreign producers charge price p^* and produce z^* varieties. In our interpretation of product variety as variety in the location of distribution outlets, this means that we assume that the same good may be sold at different prices at different places. But this is exactly what we observe in reality.[14]

We consider here entry only as an increase in the exogenously given number of foreign firms in the home markets. This is sufficient to raise the main issues associated with entry by foreign competitors.[15]

In equilibrium there will be $m + m^*$ varieties produced, with $m = nz$ and $m^* = n^* z^*$, $n^* =$ number of foreign firms. The demand curves facing the producers of a variety are (using (1) with $m + m^*$ to substitute for m):

$$c(i) = p(i)^{1/(\alpha-1)} \frac{E}{\left[\int_0^m p(j)^{\alpha/(\alpha-1)}dj + \int_m^{m+m^*} p^*(j)^{\alpha/(\alpha-1)}dj\right]},$$

$$i \in [0, m] \tag{17a}$$

$$c^*(i) = p^*(i)^{1/(\alpha-1)} \frac{E}{\left[\int_0^m (j)^{\alpha/(\alpha-1)}dj + \int_m^{m+m^*} p^*(j)^{\alpha/(\alpha-1)}dj\right]},$$

$$i \in [m, m + m^*]. \tag{17b}$$

Assuming again that the firms take the aggregate price index as given, the pricing and product variety decisions in equilibrium are determined by the following equations:

domestic firms:

$$p - \frac{q}{\alpha} - \frac{w(p, p^*, z, z^*, n, n^*, \mu)z^{(1-\beta)/\beta}}{\alpha} = 0 \tag{18a}$$

$$p - q - \frac{w(p, p^*, z, z^*, n, n^*, \mu)z^{(1-\beta)/\beta}}{\beta} = 0 \tag{18b}$$

foreign firms:

$$p^* - \frac{q}{\alpha} - \frac{[\mu w(p, p^*, z, z^*, n, n^*, \mu) + (1 - \mu)w^*]z^{*(1-\beta)/\beta}}{\alpha} = 0 \quad (19a)$$

$$p^* - q - \frac{[\mu w(p, p^*, z, z^*, n, n^*, \mu) + (1 - \mu)w^*]z^{*(1-\beta)/\beta}}{\beta} = 0. \quad (19b)$$

To solve the model completely we need to know how the wage rate behaves. To get to that, we need to know how the demand for the differentiated goods is determined and, hence, how the income of the domestic private sector is determined. We assume that visible trade is liberalised, i.e. $q = q^*$. (17a) and (17b) imply (with $E = \delta Y$) that

$$c = p^{1/(\alpha-1)} \frac{\delta Y}{mp^{\alpha/(\alpha-1)} + m^* p^{*\alpha/(\alpha-1)}},$$

$$c^* = p^{*1/(\alpha-1)} \frac{\delta Y}{mp^{\alpha/(\alpha-1)} + m^* p^{*\alpha/(\alpha-1)}} \quad (20)$$

with $m = nz$, $m^* = n^* z^*$. Equilibrium income is then determined from

$$Y = nz(p - q^*)c + n^* \mu w(z^{*1/\beta}c^* + \phi)$$
$$+ G[q^*, r, L - n(z^{1/\beta}c + \phi) - n^* \mu(z^{*1/\beta}c^* + \phi)] \quad (21)$$

where c and c^* are given by (21) and $w = G_L$. We assume that the solution is as follows:

$$Y = Y(p, p^*, z, z^*, n^*, \mu),$$
$$Y_p > 0, \ Y_{p*} > 0, \ Y_z > 0, \ Y_{z*} < 0, \ Y_{n*} < 0, \ Y_\mu > 0. \quad (22)$$

$Y_p > 0$ partly for the same reasons as in (14). Here income tends to rise also because the increase in p increases demand for products supplied by foreign firms and, thus, the income of the domestic workers at foreign firms increases (if $\mu > 0$). $Y_{p*} > 0$ because an increase in price charged by foreign producers increases income by increasing the profits of domestic producers. Simultaneously the wage income of those working for the foreign firms (assuming that the effect of a price change of a good on its own demand is larger than on demand for substitutes) declines. We have assumed the first effect to dominate. $Y_z > 0$ because if domestic firms increase their product niche their revenues increase at any given level of demand for individual goods, but the level of demand goes down since the aggregate price level increases, reducing real income. It can be shown that the elasticity of demand for domestic goods with respect to z is less than one. Hence, the first effect dominates. Simultaneously the wage rate increases, increasing the domestic income obtained from foreign firms. These two effects are due to the presence of foreign firms within (14). The effect producing (14) also occurs here: the income from the competitive sector declines when labour is shifted away from it. To bring out clearly the implications of the presence of foreign firms we have assumed that the first two effects dominate. $Y_{z*} < 0$ because an increase in z^* reduces demand for goods supplied by domestic firms, and we assume this effect dominates. Y is thus assumed to decline when z^* increases, even though the expansion of production by foreign firms pushes up the wage incomes earned by domestic labour at these firms. $Y_{n*} < 0$ because an increase in the number of foreign firms reduces, *ceteris paribus*, the demand for all goods because the given income must be shared with a larger number of goods. It can be shown that the aggregate demand for labour by foreign firms increases despite the fall in demand for individual goods, but we assume the first effect working through the income created by domestic firms to dominate; entry by foreign firms thus crowds out markets for domestic producers. $Y_{\mu} > 0$ because an increase in μ increases unambiguously the demand for labour and, hence, increases the wage rate and wage income obtained from the foreign firms.

It is now straightforward to use (23) to solve for the wage rate:

$$w = w(p, p^*, z, z^*, n^*, \mu),$$
$$w_p < 0, w_{p*} > 0, w_z > 0, w_{z*} < 0, w_{n*} = ?, w_{\mu} > 0. \tag{23}$$

The properties of the solution are clear on the basis of the discussion relating to (22). The ambiguity of the effect of the number of foreign firms on the wage rate arises because the demand for all individual goods falls when n^* increases, while the aggregate demand for labour by foreign firms increases. If μ is small then the first effect dominates, while with a large μ the second effect may be larger.

Using (24) the price of the goods produced by domestic firms and the size of their product niche can be solved from (18), just as in section 2, now in terms of the price and product niche of foreign producers, the number of foreign producers and the degree of supply through FDI. An increase in the price of goods made by foreign firms reduces the product variety supplied by domestic firms, but may increase or decrease the price of goods produced by domestic firms. For the sake of completeness, we assume that the price increases; this is the case if $\alpha - \beta$ is not too large and corresponds to the benchmark case studied above. Similarly, an increase in the share of local production by foreign firms leads to a reduction in the number of products by domestic firms, while the price effect is unclear; we assume that price increases. The widening of the product niche of individual foreign firms makes the domestic firms also widen their niches; the price charged by domestic producers is assumed to decline. Thus we have

$$p = p(p^*, z^*, n^*, \mu), p_{p*} > 0, p_{z*} < 0, p_{n*} = ?, p_\mu > 0$$
$$z = z(p^*, z^*, n^*, \mu), z_{p*} < 0, z_{z*} > 0, z_{n*} = ?, z_\mu < 0. \tag{24}$$

(24) and (23), when substituted in (19), allow one to calculate the price p^* and product niche z^* of the foreign firms.

There clearly are a plethora of possible cases to consider; to be able to concentrate on the most crucial issues in service trade liberalisation we have decided to concentrate on just a few. We assume that $w > w^*$ since the EFTA countries are generally regarded as high-wage countries compared with the average of EU countries.

Take first the case where μ is policy-determined and set at a level higher than would be the case without restrictions. Hence, deregulation of service trade implies a decline in μ for any given n^*. When μ declines, the unit wage cost of a foreign firm changes by $w^* - w - \mu w_\mu$, which is always negative. We assume this to hold even when the adjustment of p and z to changes in μ are allowed for. With declining labour costs the foreign firms will reduce prices; they will increase the number of varieties they supply, while the impact on the price they charge is unclear. If p^* declines then we can see that domestic firms follow: p will decline and z will increase. Hence, allowing foreign producers to utilise cheap inputs can reduce retail prices overall without any sacrifice in the quality of service. On the other hand, if p^* increases then the reactions of domestic firms are ambiguous (see (24)).

The welfare implications, even in the case where retail prices decline and product variety increases, are, however, ambiguous. While the gains emphasised in the new trade theory are present welfare may decline, since the switch of the supply base abroad can reduce domestic income (see (22)): if foreign firms base their operations in the home country then home country income is higher, *ceteris paribus*, since the home country receives a larger income transfer from these firms in the form of higher wage income. The mode of entry to domestic markets may thus raise serious issues in the political economy of service trade: direct consumer interests (in terms of prices and product variety) may be in conflict with overall economic interests.

Similar issues arise if we consider the impacts of an increase in the number of foreign firms. If most of the production of foreign firms is satisfied from their production facilities abroad then the wage rate declines when n^* increases, making them expand their product niche and lower prices. Simultaneously the domestic firms also reduce prices and increase the range of products they supply. On the other hand, if the foreign firms supply domestic markets through FDI (μ is large) then the wage rate can increase. If this happens, then the entry by foreign firms leads to a reduction in the number of varieties supplied by all individual firms, and higher prices for all goods. Whether the total number of varieties decreases depends on how elastic the product variety choice of foreign companies is with respect to n^*. But even when we take the best of cases, i.e. product prices decline and the total number of varieties increases, (23) tells us that the aggregate income may decline. The crowding out of domestic producers by the increasing number of foreign producers and the ensuing decline in income may be so strong that the increased welfare from reduced prices and larger product varieties withers away.

It is thus clear that the effects of the liberalisation of trade in services depend on the entry mode of the foreign entrants. In our model, the difference between the entry modes arises from their different impacts on factor markets. With FDI the entrants push up the wages of the factors the service sector shares with the other sectors. With entry from their home bases the foreign firms have an effect only by increasing, *ceteris paribus*, the number of goods supplied to consumers, and thus putting a downward pressure on prices of individual goods and then on the returns on factors the service sector uses. The FDI channel of course also has this latter effect. The FDI mode then seems in any case to provide a smaller number of varieties and higher prices than the entry from own home base. Hence, there is, *ceteris paribus*, a case for claiming that entry through FDI may not be as beneficial to the home country as other modes.[16]

4   Regional impacts of integration

In earlier sections the conclusions with regard to the effect of integration on the number of supply points were based on the interpretation of product variety as variety of locations. This section extends the single-area economy model in section 2 to a multi-area urban economics model, in order to see whether the conclusions continue to hold under explicit modelling of the multiplicity of locations.

As the local availability of services is an important determinant of the welfare of the residents in a region, the recent work in economic geography (Krugman, 1989) is directly relevant for the issues now at hand. There are several approaches to modelling the location of economic activities in space, over and above Krugman (1989). In view of an older (and mainstream) tradition in regional and urban economics, the basic force behind the localisation of activities is the need for people to reside in some place. The birth of business areas is then explained by the existence of commuting costs for residents in the area. Fujita (1989), extending this tradition, shows how, in a given economy, external or internal increasing returns to scale affect the size and number of central business districts.[17] Both of these are determinants of the regional availability of services, i.e. channels through which integration may have an impact on the provision of services. Here we rely on these types of models, surveyed in Fujita (1989).

Consider now an economy built on homogeneous land (in Fujita's terminology) which has L inhabitants and which has A identical business areas each having a population of L/A. Each business area is characterised by the same structure of production as the economy in section 2. The production of goods does not require land as an input, land is used for residential purposes only.

All the economic activity takes place at the centre of the business area, called the central business district (CBD), and thus residents have to commute, which creates costs of transportation. Costs of commuting to work and for shopping rise with distance from the CBD. The other inputs move with their owners and, hence, are also equally divided between the areas. The c goods, following the notation in section 2, are always produced for local consumption only, i.e. there is no trade in them between the various business areas.

The demand for labour in the competitive sector is determined by

$$G_L(q, r, L^c, A) = w, \text{i.e.}$$
$$L^c = L^c(w, A, q, r), \tag{25}$$
with
$$L^c_w < 0, L^c_A < 0, L^c_q = ?$$

in each region. Here we have assumed labour and other inputs to be complements in production, and so $G_{LA} < 0$.

Similarly, demand for labour by the service sector in a given region is given by

$$L^s = n \left[\int_0^z c(i)^\beta di \right]^{1/\beta} + \phi. \qquad (26)$$

In (26) $c(i)$ is the regional equilibrium consumption, i.e. it also depends on w in the manner studied below.[18] With (25) and (26) the labour markets are in equilibrium when

$$(L^s + L^c) = L/A. \qquad (27)$$

In equilibrium, when citizens choose where to live they make sure that they get at least the same level of welfare in the chosen area as elsewhere. We assume that the citizens have the option of migrating abroad. The welfare level (net of costs of migration) they can achieve abroad is exogenously given to the country, i.e. we assume the home country to be small in world labour markets. If the reservation utility is u then, as Fujita has shown, the demand for income by a citizen planning to live in an area having a population L/A is[19]

$$Y^d = Y(u, L/A), \ Y_u > 0, \ Y_{L/A} > 0. \qquad (28)$$

(See appendix, p. 100, for the derivation of (28)).

In equilibrium, this demand has to equal the supply of *per capita* income in the area, which is

$$Y^s = (A/L) \left[n \int_0^z p(i)c(i)di + G(q, r, L^c(w, A, q, r)) + T \right] \qquad (29)$$

where T are the lump-sum transfers from the government.[20] We study the properties of an equilibrium where aggregate supply of labour, L, to the whole economy is given. Hence, while we think of the reservation utility as referring the possibility of migration, we assume that the migration within the country proceeds faster than the migration over national borders. Accordingly, we consider only A adjusting when there are changes in the economic environment. In general, both L and A would adjust.

For a given u the total number of trading areas can be studied as a function of the exogenous variables of interest. We are naturally interested in whether the integration of the national economy with the rest of the world through reduction in trade barriers integrates the national economy, i.e. reduces the number of business areas, making varieties geographically less available.

We focus only on the equilibrium where all firms are identical. The aggregate income in any area is then determined by (12), with $G(q, r, L^c(w, A, q))$ substituted. Similarly, p and z are determined for any w from (8) and (9). The solutions for p and z are

$$p = p(w, \tau), \partial p/\partial w > 0, \partial p/\partial \tau > 0$$
$$z = z(w, \tau)\partial z/\partial w < 0, \partial z/\partial \tau > 0. \tag{30}$$

With (30), the aggregate income in the area is given by

$$Y = Y(w, A, \tau), \partial Y/\partial w = ?, \partial Y/\partial A < 0, \partial Y/\partial \tau < 0. \tag{31}$$

The reaction of the aggregate income to change in wage rate is ambiguous, the sign of the effect depending on the height of trade barriers.[21] An increase in the number of business areas has also an ambiguous effect on the regional income, but we assume that the direct effect through the availability of resources per region dominates. Finally, stricter trade policy implies larger loss of income from the competitive sector, which leads to a decline in the aggregate income.

Equation (27) can now be used to solve for the equilibrium wage rates after (30) and (31) have been substituted in (2) to get the demand for labour in the service sector. To ensure stability in the labour market we assume that aggregate demand for labour declines when the wage rate increases. With this assumption, it is obvious that the wage rate behaves as

$$w = w(A, \tau), \partial w/\partial A = ?, \partial w/\partial \tau < 0. \tag{32}$$

The ambiguity with respect to the number of areas is due to the fact that with a larger A the supply of labour in each area is reduced. Hence, since the demand for labour in an area decreases when the area becomes smaller, the net impact on excess demand for labour at any given wage rate is unclear.

Finally, substituting (31) and (32) in (29) gives the supply of *per capita* income in any region as a function of the number of areas and the trade policy. It is clear that the supply of *per capita* income may increase or decrease when the number of areas increases. With smaller regions a

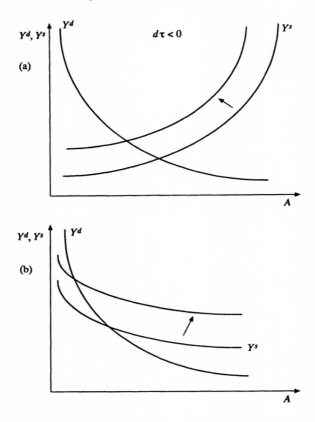

Figure 4.2 Supply of *per capita* income in a region as a function of number of areas and trade policy
a   Increasing *per capita* income
b   Decreasing *per capita* income

given income is shared by fewer people, but the income is also smaller. There are thus two possible cases to consider, given in figure 4.2. In figure 4.2a the case of *per capita* income increasing with A is shown, in figure 4.2b the other case.

Since the regional income increases when the trade barriers are reduced, it is obvious in figure 4.2a that the number of business areas is reduced. Hence trade liberalisation leads to the concentration of economic activity in fewer areas. With figure 4.2b, the situation looks ambiguous. It can, however, be argued that only the case where the income demand is steeper is stable: it is natural to think that the equilibrium is achieved so that people move to an area if the income there is higher than the income required to achieve the reservation welfare. Given this, trade liberalisation will concentrate economic activities, as in figure 4.2a.[22]

It seems to be a safe conclusion that there exist strong economic forces promoting a larger concentration of economic activities when economic integration proceeds. Hence, the criticism of integration that it may create regional problems, when taking into account migration and other transition period costs, by reducing services in far-away areas, may have some validity. In the current model integration increases average commuting distances, etc.[23] These issues must, however, be separated from the welfare issues: e.g. if integration leads to an increase in the reservation utility u by increasing welfare on the average in the integrating area, then integration may even reduce the concentration of economic activity and lead to smaller business areas. In figure 4.2a an increase in the reservation utility shifts the demand for income curve up and hence tends to increase A.

5   Conclusions

In this chapter we have studied whether the popular fear, highly relevant in policy making, that economic integration can reduce the 'quality of life' while simultaneously improving the price terms of consumption, has any validity. We have found the answer to be affirmative by using a model of production of consumer services including the quality dimension as a decision variable for firms. We have shown that a reduction of trade barriers in both the visible goods and service trade may reduce the variety in supply while simultaneously reducing the prices of the varieties supplied. Consequently, the welfare effects of trade liberalisation remain ambiguous, even when we allow entry by new firms.

One of the most interesting areas of study would be to combine the analysis of consumer and producer services. One would then be able to consider the efficiency-creating aspects of integration simultaneously with the quality of consumer services: an interesting question is whether the improvement in the division of labour allows consumers to consume larger variety with reduced prices.

Another timely extension would be to analyse entry in greater detail, using some well defined concept of entry. This problem is related to the problem of modelling the production of consumer services. As we noted in the Introduction, our model is best conceived as a model of integrated wholesale–retail firms. But as integration will probably lead to a prohibition of exclusive distribution rights the vertical structure now widely observed may be destroyed and retailers start to utilise supplies from various wholesalers. One must then differentiate between entry to wholesaling and entry to retailing.

Finally, we have assumed that trade policies are given exogenously to private agents. In practice, however, trade policies tend to be formulated on the basis of actions of various pressure groups, and this may be especially true for trade in services. Future work must take this into account.

Appendix: derivation of (28)

The demand for income by residents of an area is derived as in Fujita (1989, ch. 5). Assume that the welfare of a representative resident is given by the following utility function:

$$\psi U = U(u, s) = u^{\gamma} s^{1-\gamma}, \tag{4A.1}$$

where u is given by (1) in the text and $s =$ consumption of housing services in terms of area occupied. Since $u = E/P$, by inverting (4A.1) we get

$$\frac{E}{P} = \frac{U^{\gamma}}{s^{\gamma/(1-\gamma)}} \tag{4A.2}$$

which can be used to derive 'demand price of housing' $\psi(I, U)$ at the given level of income and welfare

$$\psi(I, U) = \max_{s} \frac{I - \frac{U^{\gamma}}{s^{\gamma/(1-\gamma)}}}{s}. \tag{4A.3}$$

In equilibrium income, $I = Y - T(r)$, where $Y(r) =$ commuting costs at distance of r km from the central business district in which the resident works. The solution to problem (4A.3) is given by the function $s(Y - T(r), U)$

$$s(Y - T(r), U) = U^{1-\gamma} [(1 - \gamma)(Y - T(r))]^{-\frac{1-\gamma}{\gamma}} \tag{4A.4}$$

With (4A.4) it is easy to see that $\partial \psi / \partial (Y - T) > 0, \partial \psi / \partial U < 0$. The last piece of land occupied by a resident of the given CBD, r_f if determined by equating the demand price of housing services with the supply price which is assumed to be exogenously given: land is assumed to have an alternative use, and the return from this use is independent of the supply of land. If r_a is the return from the alternative use then

$$\psi(Y^d - T(r_f), U) = r_a \tag{4A.5}$$

giving

$$r_f = r_f(Y^d, U), \partial r_f/\partial Y^d > 0, \partial r_f/\partial U < 0, \tag{4A.6}$$

where we have denoted by Y^d the income needed to support welfare U, i.e. the 'demand for income'. If the population living at distance r from the CBD is $M(r)$ the total area of land used at the distance r from the CBD, N is given by

$$N(Y^d, U) = \int_0^{r_f(Y^d, U)} \frac{M(r)}{s(Y^d - T(r), U)} dr \tag{4A.7}$$

with $\partial N/\partial Y^d > 0, \partial N/\partial U < 0$. Given $N = N(Y^d, U)$, Y^d can be solved as $Y^d = Y^d(N, U)$. With $N = L/A$ we get (28).

NOTES

We thank Anne Brunila and Risto Vaittinen, and especially Bernard Hoekman, for comments.

1 This view of integration causing a decline in the regional availability or in quality may be partly based on experiences gained from deregulation of financial markets: the improvement in the price terms of services was accompanied by the reduction in the number of branch offices.

2 See (Hoekman, 1992a, 1992b; Jones and Ruane, 1990; Ruane, 1990, Sapir, 1990, 1991). Also, importantly but not dealt with here, the specific nature of service production gives rise to issues of political economy different from those arising in the context of goods trade. One such issue relates to the mode of entry to markets: different groups may be affected depending on the entry mode as emphasised by Hoekman (1992a, 1992b) and Leidy and Hoekman (1993) (see also Jones and Ruane, 1990).

3 Most services still seem to require physical proximity (Sapir, 1990) though increasingly financial services to any location, for example, can be provided from almost everywhere. For these services one must raise the question of the mode of delivery: they can be provided either from a local base or from a base elsewhere. Examples of consumer services where the consumer is mobile are tourism and education.

4 In Finland, retailing is almost completely concentrated in four integrated wholesale–retail chains, among which the degree of competition is very low (Brunila, 1992; Haaparanta and Puhakka, 1992; Hyvönen, 1990). Brunila

(1990, 1992) identifies exclusive distribution rights as the main entry barrier. These rights will disappear when Finland joins the EU. In retail banking, five banking groups share the market. In banking, the existing firms share a joint payments transfer system to which they can deny access by new (foreign) firms (Lindberg, 1992). Lindberg argues also that since in banking product packaging involving cross-subsidisation is not prohibited by the Finnish law of competition, the existing banking groups can prevent effectively entry by increasing consumer switching costs. Finally the degree of competition in the retailing of specialised goods (e.g. pharmaceutical, photographic equipment, etc.) is very low (Brunila, 1992; Vaittinen, 1993).

5 Currently the Finnish food processing industry is divided in two groups. Those relying on imported inputs are pushing towards a speedy dismantling of trade barriers towards the EU. These firms claim that the consumer prices could drop substantially if trade barriers were abolished. The rest of the industry, enjoying a position of little competition, fears the entry of foreign products and, thus, has requested a long transition period during which they continue to enjoy protection.

6 Except Jones and Ruane (1990), which studies the effects of mode of entry in the framework of the classical trade theory.

7 The love-for-variety approach is one of the two basic ways to model consumers' demand for variety (see Helpman and Krugman, 1985). The other, ideal-variety, approach assumes that each individual consumes only one variety, the variety closest to her ideal variety. Using this assumption we would assume that consumers are relatively immobile even within the home country and, thus, would like to have a point of supply close to where they reside permanently. We have chosen the love-for-variety approach to allow also for other meaningful interpretations. For example, among financial services means of hedging are among the most important services and the basic means to hedge is to diversify, i.e. hedging is equivalent to love-for-variety.

8 We shall assume that the firms decide on the prices and product variety simultaneously. Were we to assume that the choice of product variety was made before the pricing decisions, we could allow for marginal economies of scope. Analytic simplicity, and we think also realism, has dictated our choice.

9 In her study on Finnish retail markets for specialised goods (sports, home electronics and hardware) Brunila (1992) found that an increase in the scale of activity led to a deterioration in non-price terms of service.

10 Because $pY_p/Y < 1$.

11 In the Krugman model each firm produces only one variety and no variety is produced by more than one firm, yet the number of firms in each country is the same both with and without international trade.

12 This holds since $Y_p\, p/Y < 1$ as noted above.

13 We assume that the operations of foreign firms in domestic markets are separable from their activities in other markets. We allow their possible efficiency advantages, etc. to show in w^*, the foreign unit labour cost.

14 Vaittinen (1993) and Union of Finnish Labour (1992) give evidence on the persistence of price differences in consumer goods even within the same town.

15 In general we would have to apply some concept of entry to determine the equilibrium number of (foreign) entrants. Mercenier and Schmitt (1992) have noticed that if there are costs of entry which are sunk (which we have argued

above to be relevant, at least for some services) the implications of economic integration crucially depend on whether the incumbent firms use the gain they have because of these costs, or not. If the gain is used, the gains from integration calculated by Smith and Venables (1988) and Norman (1989), for example, may practically vanish.

16 Hence, in retail banking, for example, it is crucial whether domestic banks allow foreign entrants to use the ATM system they run jointly. If not, then foreign banks must build their own networks.

17 In Fujita (1989) external economies are due to division of labour in a manner suggested by Ethier (1982). Another related study is Rivera-Batiz (1988).

18 (26) is readily modified to the case where some firms supplying the goods are foreign firms.

19 In the appendix, p. 100, we show that the same idea is applicable in our model.

20 We follow here the tradition of urban economics by assuming that all land is owned by absentee landowners.

21 If the barriers are low, then an increase in wage rate reduces the income generated in the competitive sector. This is spread to the service sector as a decline in demand. Hence the aggregate income is also reduced. On the other hand, with high trade barriers an increase in the wage rate can alleviate the inefficiences due to the trade policy if production in the protected sector is labour-intensive, i.e. if $G_{qL} > 0$.

22 The second problem in figure 4.2b is that the equilibrium need not be unique. Then, even if we exclude unstable equilibria there may still exist a number of stable equilibria. Without a richer model it is impossible to say how the economy reacts to changes in exogenous parameters. One way could be to employ the distinction made by Krugman (1991) between historically determined and expectationally determined equilibria.

23 Also, in view of (30) and (32), and as in section 2 above, the reduction in trade barriers can reduce the variety of products supplied in each region. Hence, integration can reduce both the 'geographic' and the product variety.

REFERENCES

Betancourt, R. and J. Gautsch, 1988. 'The economics of retail firms', *Managerial and Decision Economics*, 9, 133–44

1989. 'Two essential characteristics of retail markets and their economic consequences', *Discussion Paper*, 89/25, Department of Economics, University of Maryland

Brunila, A., 1990. 'Erikoiskaupan markkinat ja tehokkuus 1988' (Retail markets for special goods and efficiency in Finland 1988), *Tutkimuksia* (Research Report), 38, Työväen taloudellinen tutkimuslaitos (Labour Institute for Economic Research)

1992. 'Kilpailu ja hinnoittelu välittävillä markkinoilla' (Competition and pricing in intermediating markets), *Tutkimuksia*, 31, Työväen taloudellinen tutkimuslaitos

Dixit, A. and V. Norman, 1980. *Theory of International Trade*, Cambridge: Cambridge University Press

Edwards, X. and R. Starr, 1987. 'A note on indivisibilities, specialization and economies of scale', *American Economic Review*, 77(1), 192–4

Ethier, W., 1982. 'National and international returns to scale in the modern theory of international trade', *American Economic Review*, 72(2), 389–405

Ethier, W. and H. Horn, 1984. 'A new look at economic integration', in Kierzkowski (ed.), *Monopolistic Competition and International Trade*, Oxford: Oxford University Press

    1991. 'Services in international trade', in E. Helpman and A. Razin (eds.), *International Trade and Trade Policy*, Cambridge, MA: MIT Press

Francois, J., 1990a, 'Trade in producer services and returns due to specialization under monopolistic competition', *Canadian Journal of Economics*, 23(1), 109–24

    1990b. 'Producer services, scale and the division of labor', *Oxford Economic Papers*, 42, 715–29

Fujita, M., 1989. *Urban Economic Theory*, Cambridge: Cambridge University Press

Geroski, P., 1989. 'The choice between diversity and scale', in *1992: Myths and Realities*, Centre for Business Studies, London Business School

Haaparanta, P. and M. Puhakka, 1992. 'Erikoisia tarjouksia' (Strange offers), *Kansantaloudellinen Aikakauskirja* (Finnish Economic Journal), 2:1992

Helpman, P. and P. Krugman, 1985. *Market Structure and International Trade*, Cambridge, MA: MIT Press

Hoekman, B., 1992a. 'Market access through multilateral agreements', *The World Economy*, 15

    1992b. 'Regional versus multilateral liberalisation of trade in services', CEPR, *Discussion Paper*, 749, London: CEPR

Hyvönen, S., 1990. 'Integration in vertical marketing systems: a study of power and contractual relationships between wholesalers and retailers', Helsinki School of Economics, Series A, 72

Jones, R. and F. Ruane, 1990. 'Appraising the options for international trade in services', *Oxford Economic Papers*, 42, 672–87

Krugman, P., 1979. 'Increasing returns, monopolistic competition and international trade', *Journal of International Economics*, 9, 469–80

    1989. *Geography and Trade*, Cambridge, MA: MIT Press

    1991. 'History versus expectations', *Quarterly Journal of Economics*, 106, 651–67

    1993. 'The narrow and broad arguments for free trade', *American Economic Review*, 83(2), 362–6

Leidy, M. and B. Hoekman, 1993. 'What to expect from regional and multilateral trade negotiations: a public choice perspective', CEPR, *Discussion Paper*, 747, London: CEPR

Lindberg, R., 1992. 'Ulkomaisten pankkien kilpailusta ja alalle tulon esteistä Suomessa' (On competition with foreign banks and barriers to entry in Finland), Kilpailuvirasto (Office of Competition), Selvityksiä (Report), 11/1992

Markusen, J., 1989. 'Trade in producer services and in other specialized intermediate inputs', *American Economic Review*, 79(1), 85–95

Melvin, J., 1989. 'Trade in producer services: a Heckscher–Ohlin approach, *Journal of Political Economy*, 97, 1180–96

Mercenier, J. and N. Schmitt, 1992. 'Free-entry equilibrium, sunk costs and trade liberalization in applied general equilibrium: implications for "Europe

1992"', paper presented at the European Economic Association Annual Conference (Dublin)

Ministry of Foreign Affairs, 1993. 'Jäsenyysneuvottelujen avajaiset, 1.2.1993' (Opening of the Finnish and Swedish EC membership negotiations, 1.2.93)

Norman, V., 1989. 'EFTA and the internal European market', *Economic Policy*, **9**

Rivera-Batiz, L., 1988. 'Increasing returns, monopolistic competition, and agglomeration economies in consumption and production', *Regional Science and Urban Economics*, **18**

Rousslang, D. and T. To, 1993. 'Domestic trade and transportation costs as barriers to trade', *Canadian Journal of Economics*, **26(1)**, 209–21

Ruane, F., 1990. 'Internationalization of services: conceptual and empirical issues', report prepared for the Commission of the European Communities, Department of Economics, Trinity College, Dublin, mimeo

Sapir, A., 1990. 'The structure of services in Europe', report prepared for the Commission of the European Communities, Université Libre de Bruxelles, mimeo

1991. 'From fragmentation to restructuring of service markets in the European Community', Université Libre de Bruxelles, mimeo

Smith, A. and A. Venables, 1988. 'Completing the internal market in the European Community: some industry simulations', *European Economic Review*, **32**, 1501–25

Union of Finnish Labour, 1992. Databank on local retail prices of consumer goods in Finland

Vaittinen, R., 1993. 'Erikoiskaupan kilpailullisuus' (The competitiveness of markets for special goods), Kuluttajatutkimuskeskus, *Julkaisuja* (National Consumer Research Centre, Publication), **12**

Woodland, A., 1983. *International Trade and Allocation of Resources*, Amsterdam: North-Holland

Discussion

BERNARD HOEKMAN

Chapter 4 nicely complements the recent literature on trade in services, which has emphasised the role of producer services in economic growth and specialisation. It is similar to that literature in terms of using a framework of monopolistic competition and product differentiation, but differs in that the focus is on consumer rather than on intermediate producer services. It also complements the literature – and some of the other chapters in this volume – by allowing for foreign direct investment and trade liberalisation. For example, Haaland and Norman in chapter 8 assume that non-manufacturing activities are non-tradable/non-contestable. By allowing explicitly for trade in services and FDI, as well as liberalisation of trade in tangible goods, a flavour is given of what might happen in the Haaland–Norman context if that model were made more general.

It is well known that services differ from goods in a number of ways. Differences that are often emphasised include: (1) intangibility, which leads to a need for regulation to offset market failure (e.g. quality uncertainty); (2) non-storability, implying that the joint presence of consumer and producer is required, with technology often such that this implies a physical proximity constraint; and (3) the fact that services production tends to be 'factor-intensive' in that the relative importance of intermediate tangible inputs is much less than in the case of the production of goods.[1]

Haaparanta and Heikkinen in chapter 4 focus on the second of these dimensions and investigate a specific case. Immobile consumers demand services that satisfy final demand, and may in principle source from domestic suppliers, foreign suppliers located abroad (cross-border trade), or foreign suppliers that have established a local physical presence. Of course, the extent to which the second option is technically feasible will vary, depending on the characteristics of the service involved. The focus of much of the chapter is on comparing the welfare implications of the mode through which foreign service suppliers contest the market. The modelling approach chosen implies that liberalisation of trade in tangibles leads to greater specialisation and thus changes in prices and the variety of services offered to consumers. Welfare impacts depend importantly on whether changes in prices are offset by changes in variety (which include the number of geographic locations where services are available). This in turn makes the possibility of entry by foreign firms an important determinant of the ultimate effect of liberalisation of goods *and* services.

Although the explicit focus on the non-storability characteristic of services is both very interesting and useful, it is important not to lose sight of the other distinguishing characteristics of services noted earlier. While any model must abstract from many aspects of the 'real world', care must be taken that in interpreting and applying the theoretical structure that is developed to specific service examples it is kept in mind that the other dimensions may have implications that need to be taken into account. For example, liberalisation *per se* may be pretty much irrelevant in increasing the contestability of those service markets that are subject to heavy regulation. Take the case of medical services. Even if foreign doctors or nurses are in principle allowed to provide services, it is likely that they will have to demonstrate that they satisfy local quality standards. Only if a regime of mutual recognition has been established will entry be relatively easy (abstracting from other barriers such as language, etc.).

The policy that is modelled in section 2 of chapter 4 is the impact of liberalisation of trade in goods. These are assumed to be intermediate inputs that enter into the production of the differentiated services. Two points can be raised with respect to this section. First, the liberalisation is assumed to be non-preferential. However, the focus of this volume is on preferential liberalisation, i.e. on the effects of joining the EU. It would have been appropriate to compare the analysis of the unilateral, non-discriminatory liberalisation approach with the preferential option. This allows trade and investment diversion effects to be taken into account. Presumably this is an important policy issue, as in principle a country contemplating accession to the EU should be interested not only in how this will compare with the status quo, but also how it compares with unilateral liberalisation *vis-à-vis* the rest of the world. This applies not only to liberalisation of goods, but also to liberalisation of services. Indeed, the distinction between non-discriminatory and preferential liberalisation may be particularly important for the results of the chapter, as much depends on the value of μ, which in turn is largely a function of the wage difference between home and host country for foreign entrants.[2] As EU firms can be expected to have much higher wages on average than non-EU providers, the wage difference between EFTA and foreign (EU) firms in their home markets will be much smaller in the preferential liberalisation scenario.

The assumption made that there are tariffs on imported goods and the classic assumption that all tariff revenues are returned in lump-sum fashion is not very realistic. To the extent that trade barriers between EFTA and the EU exist, these will be NTBs, with associated rents going to specific groups in society. In principle, there should not be any restrictions on trade in industrial products between EFTA and the EU. This is something that presumably affects trade with the rest of the world, and thus comes back to the issue noted earlier regarding the distinction between preferential EU-based liberalisation, and a non-discriminatory liberalisation strategy.

Care must also be taken to justify the production structure of the service sector. While it is certainly true that for retail distribution inputs of goods are crucial, this will be much less so for other services (e.g. banking or insurance). Indeed, for such services it may not be necessary to maintain the assumption that intermediate tangible goods are used in the production process. This would not imply, of course, that liberal-

isation of trade in goods becomes irrelevant, as this will still have indirect
effects.

Section 3 of the chapter adds liberalisation of services to the story,
'which here is equivalent to the establishment of local production by
foreign producers'. Entry costs for foreign suppliers depend on μ, the
share of labour costs incurred in the host country, as unit labour costs of
supplying in the host country are $\mu w + (1 - \mu)w^*$. If $\mu = 0$ we have pure
cross-border trade in services, while if $\mu > 0$ we have FDI. In principle,
therefore, the set-up can deal with foreign competition that is of a pure
cross-border variety, although this possibility is ignored. This is realistic
in the sense that in most cases $0 < \mu < 1$. Foreign firms must have some
kind of physical presence to provide the majority of consumer services.
For the types of services that the chapter focuses on – retail distribution
of goods, retail banking – the value of μ is likely to be close to one.

An important determinant of entry costs in service sectors will often be
the regulatory regime that applies. This may dominate labour costs for
many services (think of legal or medical services). The authors have tried
to capture this by making μ a policy variable as well. That is, policy can
raise μ, increasing the relative importance of local wage costs in the total
costs of a foreign firm.[3] This implies an increase in the variable costs of
supplying the host market. But frequently regulations will act on fixed
costs as well, and this should be taken into account. Indeed, regulatory
barriers are often prohibitive and preclude entry by domestic as well as
by foreign firms. If liberalisation occurs, entrants from both sources may
materialise, largely driven by the decline in the fixed (sunk) cost
associated with entry. The authors, however, assume that liberalisation
will lead only to entry by foreign firms. However, as they themselves note
in n. 4, in Finland retail distribution is highly concentrated, with
exclusive distribution one of the important barriers to entry. One of the
effects of EU membership will be the application of EU competition law,
which might be invoked in particular sectors to allow greater domestic as
well as foreign competition.

Greater precision regarding the policies that are involved in restricting
entry would have enriched the chapter, and made it easier for the reader
(and policy makers) to relate the model to the 'real world'. More on the
normative side would also have been useful. What should governments
be doing in principle? Is there any rationale for taxing/subsidising FDI?
What can be said about the opportunity costs of pursuing preferential
liberalisation as opposed to liberalisation on an MFN basis? Are there
aspects unique to consumer services that could make preferential liberalisation more attractive? More on the political economy forces that are set
in motion in the context of the model would also be interesting. For

example, what can be said in the context of consumer services liberal-isation regarding the stance of different interest groups with respect to both preferential and non-discriminatory liberalisation? Or as regards the policy stance on the 'mode of supply' that is preferred? Perusal of the liberalisation commitments that have been made by countries in the context of the Uruguay Round negotiations on services reveals that most countries are more liberal with respect to establishment than cross-border trade. Hopefully future research by the authors will focus on such questions.

Finally, I would strongly support the possible extension to combine producer and consumer services noted by the authors in their concluding comments (section 5). To the extent that the welfare implications of liberalisation of consumer services are ambiguous, this ambiguity may be offset if account is also taken of the fact that many traded services are producer services. A fall in the cost and increase in the variety of such services will generally be beneficial.

NOTES

1 Alternatively put, the 'roundaboutness' of production is substantially less.
2 For example, the size of μ determines the size of w_n. Also, the larger is μ, the more important will w^* (or rather $w^* - w$) be.
3 Greater generality might have been attained by defining μ in local content terms. Governments tend to focus on value added or local content, not on the share of labour costs incurred. As the two are of course closely related, this would not have significant implications for the analysis.

Part Two
Policy issues

5 Voting power and control in the EU: the impact of the EFTA entrants

MIKA WIDGRÉN

1 Introduction

National aspects and the balance of national voting power in the EU play an important role as long as the governments have direct influence in the decision making process. The decisive body of the Union is the Council of Ministers where Germany, Italy, France and the UK have 10 votes each; Spain 8 votes; the Netherlands, Greece, Portugal and Belgium 5 votes each; Denmark and Ireland 3 votes each and Luxembourg 2 votes. Decisions are made mainly by the qualified majority for which 54 votes out of 76 were required before the EFTA countries' entry. Among the new entrant countries, Austria and Sweden have 4 votes and Finland has 3 votes. The qualified majority in an expanded EU is made up of 62 votes out of 87.[1]

The Council of Ministers offers a nice example for cooperative game theory, since it is a weighted majority game with an asymmetric decision making rule. Since 1986, when the Single European Act came into force, the role of qualified majority voting has become more important. Recently there have been pressures towards simple majority or so-called double majority voting in the Council, due to the fear of Union's weakening abilities to operate after the enlargement.

The purpose of this chapter is to analyse national influence in the EU. The concept of 'influence' is divided into direct effect on outcomes of votings and to control (see section 2). Particular attention is paid to the impact of the new entrants. The analysis can be divided into three parts. First, we analyse the national influence on the current members' point of view. We thus intend to investigate the loss of current members' power both in absolute and relative terms. Second, we analyse the control of the new entrants over decisions and their opportunity to change the direction of policies pursued. Third, our purpose is to give measures concerning the rules of the decision making game. We thus investigate the effects of changes in voting rule.[2]

The analysis in this chapter is based on power and satisfaction indices of cooperative games (see section 2). Power indices have been mostly applied to institutions where voting takes place. Voting power in the EU Council of Ministers has been analysed earlier in Brams and Affuso (1985a, 1985b); Brams, Doherty and Weidner (1991); Widgrén (1993a, 1993b, 1993c, 1994a, 1994b, 1994c, 1995); Nurmi (1992); and Hosli (1993).

The rest of the chapter is organised as follows. In section 2 we present the measures of voting power and control. The results obtained for the current Community and for an expanded EU with three new EFTA countries as members are summarised in sections 3, 4 and 5; conclusions are presented in section 6.

2   Measuring the national influence in the EU

While the basic notion of influence is understood by everyone, it turns out to be quite tricky to define formally. For instance, in the EU Council of Ministers, while most would agree that Germany has more influence than does Luxembourg it is not obvious how one would quantify such a statement. We know that Germany has more votes than Luxembourg and it is intuitively acceptable that it should have more – or at least as much – influence as Luxembourg. However, as the following example illustrates, voting weights alone are poor proxies for influence, and hence what we need is a more appropriate measure of influence.

As it turns out, three separate measures have been explored in the literature. The first measure of influence, which we call *power*, answers the question 'How likely is it that a particular country's weighted vote will be essential to the passage of a proposal?'. A second natural measure, which we call *negative control*, answers a related but different question: 'How likely is it that a proposal will be rejected when a particular country votes "no"?' Finally a third measure, *positive control*, answers the question, 'How likely is a proposal to be adopted when a country votes "yes"?'

Having defined measures of influence, we are still a long way from quantifying them for current and potential EU members. The outcome of a weighted vote on a specific issue depends upon three things: the majority rule adopted (e.g. simple majority or qualified majority), the weights assigned to the various countries and the voting behaviour of the countries. Of these three, modelling the voting behaviour poses the greatest conceptual problems.[3] For instance, on a certain issue before the

Council of Ministers a very small country like Luxembourg might be absolutely crucial to obtaining a qualified majority. In such a situation, one could say Luxembourg had a lot of power. However, on many other issues, Luxembourg's votes might be quite irrelevant, so one might say that Luxembourg had no influence. This issue-by-issue approach, while appealing at first sight, is impractical. To make a general statement about how much influence Luxembourg has under certain voting rules would require us to predict each country's position on every conceivable issue. This sort of judgement would be far too subjective.

The approach adopted in the literature (and in this chapter) is to describe countries' voting behaviour in a more abstract way. We say that country i will vote 'yes' on a randomly selected issue by probability of p_i. The voting behaviour of n countries can thus be described by the so-called *acceptability vector*, which is an n-dimensional vector of the p_is. These p_is help us to quantify specific measures of power. To see how, we consider a simple example. Using this simple example, we illustrate and define power and control indices in order to fix ideas and introduce terminology.

Suppose that there are three countries – A, B, C – whose voting weights are 49 per cent, 49 per cent and 2 per cent, respectively. Moreover suppose that we were absolutely certain, for some reason, that each country was equally likely to vote for or against a randomly chosen issue, implying that the correct acceptability vector is $(1/2, 1/2, 1/2)$. Finally suppose that the voting is conducted according to the simple majority rule. Obviously there are 8 possible outcomes in the voting (that is $8 = 2^3$): YYY, YYN, YNY, YNN, NYY, NYN, NNY, NNN, using the notation that the first, second and third letters reflect the votes of A, B, and C, respectively and that Y indicates a 'yes' vote and N a 'no' vote. Given the acceptability vector, each outcome occurs with an equal probability of 1/8.

Careful inspection of the outcomes (keeping the weights in mind) shows that C's 'yes' vote is crucial to passage of a proposal whenever A and B disagree. This occurs in 4 of the 8 possible outcomes: YNY, YNN, NYY and NNY. The total probability that C's vote is crucial is the sum of the probability of YNY, YNN, NYY and NNY. Given the acceptability vector assumed, each of these occur with 1/8 probability, so the total probability is 0.5. Clearly 0.5 could be taken as a formal measure of country C's power. Country C's negative control is measured by the probability that the outcome of voting agrees with his/her no vote. This occurs in 3 out of 4 outcomes,[4] so C's negative control could be measured as 0.75. Likewise, its positive control is 3/4. One would measure power and control for A and B in similar fashion. It turns out that they have exactly the same power and control figures as C. Thus distribution of votes can indeed be a poor measure for influence.

Furthermore, maintaining the assumed acceptability vector, we could see how the power and control measures of the three countries change when we altered the majority rule to say a two-thirds majority rule, or changed the weights of the three countries, or added a fourth country. For each of these changes the voting system would give different power and control indices for each of the three countries.

The trouble with the primitive power and control indices introduced in this example is that they are sensitive to the exact acceptability vector we assumed.[5] To get around this problem, we would want indices that describe power and control for a wide range of acceptability vectors. The literature addresses this problem by calculating the indices, assuming a joint probability for the p_is.[6] In particular, the literature has focused on two standard joint probability distributions (pds) for the p_is. The first assumption is called *independence*. This assumes that the p_is are independently and uniformly distributed on the closed interval between zero and one. The second is called *homogeneity*. It assumes that all of the p_is in a given acceptability vector equal a fraction, which we call t, but that the value of t is uniformly distributed over $[0, 1]$.

To define the power and control indices that will be used to investigate the impact that EU enlargement has on various countries' influence in the Council of Ministers, it is useful to adopt a more structured approach than was taken in the simple example. First, following the terminology of cooperative game theory, we consider the outcomes in the simple example above as equal to coalitions. The list of outcomes in the simple example above can be written in a list of 'yes' vote (or 'no' -vote)[7] coalitions as follows: $\{A, B, C\}; \{A, B\}; \{A, C\}; \{A\}; \{B, C\}; \{B\}; \{C\}; \emptyset$. It can be easily seen that there are different coalitions. For our analysis, three different types of coalitions are essential. First, a country is crucial for the outcome and has power when it belongs to a minimum majority with respect to itself (i.e. it can swing the majority 'yes' vote coalition to a minority by voting 'no'). In our example, C is crucial in coalitions $\{A, C\}$ and $\{B, C\}$ (or outcomes YNY and NYY). Second, a country has negative control when it does not belong to a 'yes' vote coalition and only a minority 'yes' vote coalition is formed. In our example, coalitions $\emptyset$, $\{A\}$ and $\{B\}$ (or outcomes NNN, YNN and NYN) are such. Finally, a country has positive control when it belongs to a majority yes vote coalition.

Let N be the set of n ministers in the Council of Ministers. Supposing that they vote 'yes' or 'no' independently of each other, we can write for any coalition $S \subset N$ (or any particular array of 'yes' and 'no' votes), the probability that it will be formed as follows:

$$P\{\text{`coalition } S \text{ is formed'}\} = \prod_{i \in S} p_i \prod_{i \notin S}(1 - p_i) \tag{1}$$

which is no more than a binomial probability with varying p probabilities. In our example above, they were constant, and that is why the number of 'yes' votes in outcomes were binomially distributed, as we can see by having a closer look at the outcomes and their probabilities of occurrence in the example. The sum of the probabilities in (1) over all possible 2^n coalitions (or outcomes) is always 1.[8] Thus (1) defines formally a probability distribution over all possible outcomes. If we take the sum of these probabilities over the chosen classes[9] of coalitions (minimum majorities with respect to each voter, majorities where a particular voter is a member and blocking coalitions where a particular voter is a member), we will have the probabilities that we need for our measures of influence.

The assumptions that we made about the p_i probabilities and a large number of coalitions in the EU make the calculation more difficult than in our simple example above. In an enlarged EU of 15 members there are $2^{15} = 32\,768$ coalitions (i.e. there are that many possible outcomes) while there were 8 of them in the example. In addition, independence and homogeneity share the property that we are working with the mathematical expectations of an infinite number of acceptability vectors. It is not difficult to imagine what kind of process it would be to calculate the measures of influence of all 15 countries by classifying the 32 768 outcomes, even with a single acceptability vector. The latter problem is easy to handle by using the standard methods of probability calculus, but for the former we need cooperative game theory.

In the 'yes' or 'no' type of voting, the basic classification of coalitions is to divide them into majorities and minorities. If we take a sum of probabilities in (1) over the class of required majority we have a probability that a winning coalition is formed. This sum is usually referred to as a *power polynomial*, since all the three measures of influence can be calculated by using it. Let us denote the power polynomial with a given acceptability vector by $f(p_1, \ldots, p_n)$.

Intuitively, the easiest measure to understand is positive control, which can be calculated for country i simply by setting $p_i = 1$ (i votes 'yes' for sure) in the power polynomial. Country i's negative control can be calculated by setting $p_i = 0$ (i votes 'no' for sure) and taking the complement probability of the power polynomial (i.e. $1 - f(\cdot)$, the probability that a coalition is not winning). The most difficult measure to calculate is power. Again, it is possible to go through all majorities and count the ones where i is crucial. A much simpler method is to take partial derivates of the power polynomial $f(p_1, \ldots, pn)$. It turns out that the partial derivates are measures of power as defined at the beginning of this section. To clarify these ideas, we may write the power polynomial for our example (keeping the voting weights in mind) as follows:

$$f(p_A, p_B, p_C) = p_A p_B p_C + p_A p_B (1 - p_C)$$
$$+ p_A p_C (1 - p_B) + p_B p_C (1 - p_A) = p_A p_B + p_A p_C + p_B p_C - 2 p_A p_B p_C$$

Using the primitive acceptability vector, we can now check the calculations in the example. Positive control $(p_A = 1)$ for C is simply $1/4 + 1/2 + 1/2 - 2(1/4) = 3/4$ and negative control $(p_A = 0)$ $1 - (0 + 0 + 1/4) = 3/4$. Deriving the power polynomial with respect to p_C yields $f_C(p_A, p_B, p_C) = p_A + p_B - 2 p_A p_B$, and assuming the acceptability vector $(1/2, 1/2, 1/2)$ we have 0.5 power for C.

Generally, if we calculate the probability that one is crucial in the sense that she/he swings the coalition from losing to winning, we have two following well-known formulas. Let f_i be the ith partial derivative of the power polynomial f and M_i the class of minimum winning coalitions with respect to i (i.e. coalitions where i is crucial with respect to the outcome) and let S be a randomly chosen coalition. The independence assumption yields

$P_{ind}\{$'Voter i is crucial to the passage of a proposal'$\}$

$$= \int_0^1 \ldots \int_0^1 f_i(p_1, \ldots, p_n) dp_1 \ldots dp_n$$
$$= f_i(p_1, \ldots, p_n)$$
$$= \sum_{S \in M_i} \left(\frac{1}{2}\right)^{n-1}$$
$$= \beta_i' \tag{2}$$

where the subscript 'ind' stands for independence. The second equivalence is interesting. It shows that, after all, the independence assumption implies our primitive acceptability vector in the example above. That is why independence is often referred to as indifference. This property can be easily checked by taking a double integral of the formula $p_A + p_B - 2 p_A p_B$ in the example above. The third equivalence can be easily understood intuitively by thinking how one becomes crucial. We need an outcome where a minimum majority coalition is formed and i

belongs to that coalition. The sum formula in (2) is a probability that such an event will occur. What is important in the term $(1/2)^{n-1}$, describing the probability that a randomly chosen outcome will materialise, is that it is independent of the number of 'yes' votes (or 'no' votes) in the outcome. Thus each outcome has equal probability of occurring. In the literature, (2) is referred to as the Banzhaf power index (BI). Let n and s denote the cardinal numbers (cardinalities) of sets (coalitions) N and S respectively. The homogeneity yields

$P_{hom}\{$'Voter i is crucial to the passage of a proposal'$\}$

$$= \int_0^1 f_i(t, \ldots, t)dt$$
$$= \sum_{S \in M_i} \frac{(s-1)!(n-s)!}{n!}$$
$$= \Phi_i, \tag{3}$$

where the subscript 'hom' stands for homogeneity. (3) is referred to as the Shapley–Shubik power index (SSI). It is a more complicated measure than the BI. Intuitively speaking – as can also be seen in the second row of (3) – the homogeneity assumption turns the combinations (outcomes or coalitions) into permutations. The second row of (3) can be interpreted as a probability that the voters form a 'yes' vote coalition in the order of their probability of acceptance of each question (i.e. we choose a random order of voters) and i is the one who turns the 'yes' vote coalition into a winning one (see Shapley 1953).

Probabilistically, the main difference between the two indices is that under the homogeneity assumption there is a common standard t by which the ministers evaluate the Commission proposal, and thus the probabilities of the voters' decisions are correlated in a specific way (Straffin, 1988). For example, the event that 'voting behaviour of two independent voters is similar' has a probability 1/2 while it increases to 2/3 if the voters are homogeneous. When assuming independence, we suppose that on average each voter tosses a coin to decide whether to vote 'yes' or 'no'.[10] When assuming homogeneity, only a single coin is tossed; it determines whether a group of homogeneous voters accepts a proposal or not. However, knowing the result (i.e. the majority of 'yes' votes to be formed) does not tell us anything about individuals' voting behaviour. It is like a necessary condition for a certain kind of behaviour. The sufficient condition is that we know each voter's willingness to support the proposal. It defines an order of voters, and thus in general we take into account all possible orders of voters. Drawing whether a proposal is accepted or not and random orders together forms the homogeneity assumption.

One important difference, which also enlightens one of the basic differences between the independence and homogeneity assumptions, is that when assuming the former the number of 'yes' votes (or 'no' votes) is binomially distributed, and when assuming the latter it is uniformly distributed. This implies that under independence it is more probable to get approximately a '50–50' result than under homogeneity, which gives equal probability to all numbers of 'yes' votes (or 'no' votes) between zero and n, the number of voters.

Let us call the coalition of 'yes' votes *the supporting coalition*. Figure 5.1 presents density functions for the size of the 'yes' vote coalition measured by the voting weight under independence, denoted by I, and under homogeneity, denoted by H. The sum of voting weight in the supporting coalition is presented on the horizontal axis and the probability on the vertical axis. Figure 5.1 has been plotted by using the weights, etc. in an expanded EU-15. Also the density functions have been plotted by applying normal distribution approximations.[11] According to the central limit theorem, the distribution of the sum of random variables (here, voting weights) converges to the normal distribution if the variance of the variables does not exceed a certain limit: the smaller the variance, the faster the convergence. In the EU, it can be shown that the convergence is very fast and the approximation errors are no more than 10^{-3} in the EU of 15 members (see Widgrén, 1994b, and for the method Owen, 1982). The power measures and most of their properties can be illustrated by using figure 5.1. Assuming qualified majority voting, the SSI is the probability bordered by the rectangle (q_1, q_2, q_4, q_6) and the BI is the area (q_1, q_3, q_5, q_6). Probabilistically, they both are the probability that a supporting coalition with the voting weight little over required majority is formed minus the probability that a supporting coalition with the voting weight not too much under required majority is formed. Naturally, the voting weight that a country has affects the distance between q_1 and q_6. Figure 5.1 also tells us what we should look for in our results in sections 3 and 4. It is easy to see that power when measured assuming independence should increase while the majority rule decreases. Under qualified majority there should be no remarkable differences between the indices.

The difference between the independence and homogeneity assumptions can also be characterised by using conceptualisation of the communication among the voters (Straffin, 1988). According to Straffin, the homogeneity assumption is more appropriate for the analysis of the

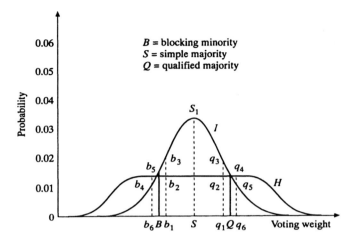

Figure 5.1   Homogeneity, independence and the size of the 'yes' vote coalition

voting bodies where there is considerable communication among the representatives. Interpreted in another way, it can be said that homogeneity (common standard in voting behaviour) can be reached by amending the original proposals, and thus they are likely to be more or less compromises after the bargaining process, which also increases the homogeneity between the originally heterogeneous voters. In other words, homogeneous voters negotiate whether a proposal is acceptable (t is high) or not (t is low). Homogeneity thus also takes into account the proposals for which the voting will never be taken. Naturally, one has power also in these questions.

It can also be thought that there are groups of voters who are originally more homogeneous than others, and thus there is a partition of the representatives into different homogeneous groups which are independent of each other. The independence assumption, by contrast, implies that there is no communication of any significance to speak of among the voters, and thus they do not negotiate to amend the proposal and the common standard is not likely to be reached. Roughly, one can imagine that the voters are independent when the draft proposal is given and their homogeneity increases if they do have a possibility of bargaining and revising proposals. It is worth noting, however, that the increased homogeneity can be reached by compromises between the member states, and thus the draft proposal may change significantly during the process.

This kind of illustration can also be used to characterise the different voting groups. It can be assumed that there is a group of voters, denoted by S, supporting the proposal in the sense of homogeneity, i.e. they have reached a compromise about the voting standard t, and another group, denoted by R, which opposes the proposal, i.e. having a voting standard $1-t$. In addition to this, there is a group of voters, denoted by U in which the voters are independent of each other and also of the homogeneous groups. This kind of set-up is a special case of the partial homogeneity and it yields

$P_{par}\{$'Voter i is crucial to the passage of a proposal'$\}$

$$= \underbrace{\int_0^1 \int_0^1 \cdots \int_0^1}_{} f_i(\overbrace{t,\ldots,t}^{s}; p_{s+1},\ldots,p_{s+u}; \overbrace{(1-t),\ldots,(1-t)}^{r})$$

$$\underbrace{dp_{s+1}\ldots dp_{s+u}dt} = \pi_i, \tag{4}$$

where n, s, u and r denote the cardinal numbers of sets N, S, U and R respectively and $f_i(\cdot)$ is the ith partial derivative of function (probability) f defined earlier. It is worth noting that the sum of BIs or any partial homogeneity indices is not one as it is for SSIs. That is why these indices are often normalised by forcing their sum to unity, but we do not intend to do that in this chapter because it ruins the probabilistic interpretation of the indices used. The mentioned so-called inconsistency property is due to the permutations and combinations. For example, if the order in which the voters form a 'yes' vote coalition is known, the voter who is crucial can also be defined uniquely whenever a majority is formed, but if only the outcome is known, there can be several crucial voters. Also for partially homogeneous voters forming a majority may become more difficult, and this status quo solution implies that there are no crucial voters. Particularly, when assuming a partial homogeneity with opposition as in (5), the distribution of the 'yes' vote coalition's size in figure 5.1 would concentrate more around the simple majority. Intuitively speaking, we may imagine that there is a 'cake' of total power which should be divided among the voters. Homogeneous voters can always share the whole cake while partially homogeneous or independent voters may hope too much (the sum of power indices exceeds one) or suffer from inefficiency losses (the sum of power indices is below one). We call voters who share the 'cake' properly *group–consistent*.

Power indices measure an individual's direct influence on the outcome. In addition to this, voters have control over decisions as members of different coalitions. In analysing the voting bodies with an asymmetric majority rule, it is interesting to decompose the idea behind the control since, as was noted earlier in this chapter, preventing and accomplishing decisions differs considerably in bodies like the Council of Ministers of the EU. Assuming homogeneity, the probability that the proposal is accepted on condition that one votes 'yes' can be written as follows:

$$P\{\text{a proposal is accepted} \mid i \text{ votes 'yes'}\} = \int_0^1 f(\underbrace{t,\ldots,t}_{i-1}, 1 \overbrace{t,\ldots,t}^{n-i})dt \quad (5)$$

where i is a positive integer smaller than n and assuming independence respectively by using indifference − an implication of the independence assumption as noted earlier in this chapter − and letting $t = 1/2$.[12] To analyse one's possibilities for pursuing negative control, i.e. the probability that a group decision rejects a bill one votes against, we use the complement probability of (5) on condition that $p_i = 0$ (see the example on p. 118) as follows:

$$P\{\text{a proposal is rejected} \mid i \text{ votes 'no'}\} = \int_0^1 f(\underbrace{t,\ldots,t}_{i-1}, 1 \overbrace{t,\ldots,t}^{n-i})dt, \quad (6)$$

where i is a positive integer smaller than n and assuming independence $P\{\cdot\}$ can be written respectively by letting $t = 1/2$. Turning back to figure 5.1 gives us a graphical illustration of control measures. Assuming a qualified majority, positive control can be defined to be the area right from q_1 between the distribution (H or I) and horizontal axis. It is the probability that i gets enough support and the majority is formed when its sure 'yes' vote is added. Similarly, the negative control is the area left from q_6 between the chosen distribution and the horizontal axis. It is the probability that the 'no' vote coalition can block the decision with i's sure 'no' vote.

When analysing power, one crucial question is: 'How concentrated is the power?'. To analyse the concentration of power, control measures are often used to make conclusions. The leading coalition is defined in cooperative game theory as an alliance of the m largest players (countries). The coalition is said to be weakly controlling if it can control the decisions by a probability higher than 0.95 and it is said to be controlling if the probability exceeds 0.99.[13]

3   The distribution of voting power

The new entrants' share of the population in the EU of 15 members is 5 per cent, but they get 11.5 per cent of votes. This is due to the apparent logarithmic relationship between the votes and population which favours the smallest members of the EU. Thus the expansion of the Community by the EFTA countries could potentially have significant consequences for the distribution of power.

In weighted voting, however, the relationship between power and voting weights is not necessarily straightforward. Let us define a concept which elaborates on this phenomenon. We refer to the ratio between normalised power index and voting weight as the *power coefficient* (PC), which can be interpreted as a measure for one's relative power. It tells us how effectively a voter can use his or her votes to exert power. The PC illustrates how important a voter strategically is. It has values over one if a voter has higher voting power than voting weight. S/he has then effectively more votes than the actual number would show. The usual well known result is that voters with a large number of votes tend to have higher PCs than voters with a small number of votes. This phenomenon can be illustrated by calculating the effective number of votes, which can be defined to be the actual number of votes multiplied by the PC.

When analysing the consequences of an enlargement of the EU (or any other institution where voting takes place), it would be interesting to investigate the changes in voters' relative positions. For this, we may use ordinal elasticies. Let us define a voting weight elasticity of power to be the ratio between the relative change in the power index and the relative change in the voting weight. Intuitively, the elasticities should be positive (i.e. loss of voting weight implies loss of power). As usual, it can be said that power is elastic if it exceeds one and inelastic if it lies below one. A voter loses relative power if the elasticity exceeds one and gains relative power if the elasticity is smaller than one. Negative elasticities indicate that a voter gains absolute power while his voting weight decreases. This phenomenon is often referred to as a paradox of new members.

Table 5.1 presents the Shapley–Shubik and Banzhaf power indices for qualified majority voting in the EC-9 and EU-12, and the voting weight elasticities of voting power in the enlargement of the 1980s. Table 5.2 shows the respective figures for an expansion of the EU by the three EFTA countries. It seems that both measures of power (SSI and BI) have approximately the same level in the EU-12 or in the EU-15, but before the accession of the Mediterranean countries the Banzhaf index gave higher estimates.

Widgrén (1994b) has shown that in the EU-12 it seems that there is no clear relationship between PCs and voting weights, but the new entries make the PC an increasing function of voting weight.[14] The countries with the largest power coefficients lose most in relative terms, and the reverse holds true for the small countries. However, the slope of the

Table 5.1   Voting power in the Council of Ministers of the EU-9 and EU-12 and the voting-weight elasticities of power

Member state	Shapley–Shubik index			Banzhaf index		
	EU-9	EU-12	$\epsilon_{\Phi,\omega}$	EU-9	EU-12	$\epsilon_{\Phi,\omega}$
Germany	0.179	0.134	1.07	0.207	0.139	1.39
Italy	0.179	0.134	1.07	0.207	0.139	1.39
UK	0.179	0.134	1.07	0.207	0.139	1.39
France	0.179	0.134	1.07	0.207	0.139	1.39
Spain	...	0.111	...	...	0.118	...
Netherlands	0.081	0.064	0.89	0.113	0.073	1.50
Portugal	...	0.064	...	...	0.073	...
Greece	...	0.064	...	...	0.073	...
Belgium	0.081	0.064	0.89	0.113	0.073	1.50
Denmark	0.057	0.042	1.12	0.082	0.049	1.71
Ireland	0.057	0.042	1.12	0.082	0.049	1.71
Luxembourg	0.010	0.012	−0.84	0.020	0.019	0.21

relationship between voting power and voting weight does not differ significantly from one. It can thus be argued that the enlargement of the Community by the EFTA countries equalises the fluctuations in the PC, and the effective number of votes do not differ remarkably from the real ones despite the slightly increasing relationship. There are, however, no differences higher than 0.5 votes between the actual and effective votes (Widgrén, 1994b). After all, in the EU Council of Ministers voting weights seem to be at least satisfactory proxies for member states' power. This is, indeed, exceptional for a body where weighted voting takes place. It even seems that there is a dose of brainwork behind the determination of voting weights and the choice of majority rule.

The elasticities in tables 5.1 and 5.2 also show this interesting difference between the enlargements analysed. It seems that old members' voting power is more elastic with respect to the voting weight in the enlargement of the 1980s when we assume independent voters than when we assume homogeneous voters, but for the accession of the EFTA countries this does not hold true. Thus in the 1980s voters lost more independent power proportionate to their voting weight than in an expansion of the EU by small EFTA countries. Intuitively, this can be interpreted by arguing that the Mediterranean countries made it more necessary for the Community to reach compromises since the independent power (Banzhaf index) decreased almost to the same level as the homogeneous power. If the independent power is higher than the homogeneous power a country has a higher probability of being crucial without communication with

Table 5.2   The distribution of voting power in the EU Council of Ministers after the entry of Austria, Sweden and Finland and the voting-weight elasticities of power for the old members

Member state	Shapley–Shubik index	$\epsilon_{\Phi,\omega}$	Banzhaf index	$\epsilon_{\Phi,\omega}$
Germany	0.119	1.02	0.113	0.93
Italy	0.119	1.02	0.113	0.93
UK	0.119	1.02	0.113	0.93
France	0.119	1.02	0.113	0.93
Spain	0.093	0.96	0.093	0.90
Netherlands	0.056	1.00	0.059	0.92
Portugal	0.056	1.00	0.059	0.92
Greece	0.056	1.00	0.059	0.92
Belgium	0.056	1.00	0.059	0.92
Sweden	0.044	...	0.048	...
Austria	0.044	...	0.048	...
Denmark	0.033	0.90	0.036	0.84
Finland	0.033	...	0.036	...
Ireland	0.033	0.90	0.036	0.84
Luxembourg	0.021	−2.00	0.023	−1.39

other countries (see section 2). A country has an incentive to push its own views through without significant admissions. In contrast, if the homogeneous power is higher there is an incentive to seek cooperation and compromises. While we may call a voting body where independent power is high competing, the one with high homogeneous power could be called conciliatory. The results in tables 5.1 and 5.2 show that the Mediterranean enlargement turned the Community from a competing towards a conciliatory direction. Hence a single country's prospects[15] of influencing decision making without compromises notably decreased.

In the enlargement of the EU by the EFTA countries the loss of power for the old members would be 12 per cent when measured by the SSI. In the 1980s the expansion of the Community by Greece and the Iberian countries yielded a 24 per cent loss of voting power for the previous members of the Community. For the most important decisions unanimity was needed more often in the 1970s than in the latter half of the 1980s. It is interesting, however, that the loss of voting power for the members in the EU-9 is almost exactly the same whether we compare the majority or unanimity voting in the EU-9 to the majority or unanimity voting in the EC-12. This does not hold true for the step from the EU-12 to the EU-15, since the loss of power in unanimity voting would be one-fourth for the old members, due to the new entrants' small size.

Table 5.3   Voting power in the EU Council of Ministers before and after
the entry of Austria, Sweden and Finland: simple and double majority rules

Member state	Shapley-Shubik index		Banzhaf index		Shapley–Shubik index	
	Simple majority		Simple majority		Double majority	
	EU-12	EU-15	EU-12	EU-15	EU-12	EU-15
Germany	0.135	0.116	0.336	0.365	0.144	0.134
Italy	0.135	0.116	0.336	0.365	0.115	0.108
UK	0.135	0.116	0.336	0.365	0.115	0.103
France	0.135	0.116	0.336	0.365	0.115	0.103
Spain	0.107	0.091	0.268	0.285	0.104	0.087
Netherlands	0.063	0.055	0.160	0.174	0.061	0.052
Portugal	0.063	0.055	0.160	0.174	0.059	0.048
Greece	0.063	0.055	0.160	0.174	0.059	0.048
Belgium	0.063	0.055	0.160	0.174	0.059	0.048
Sweden	...	0.043	...	0.138	...	0.046
Austria	...	0.043	...	0.138	...	0.046
Denmark	0.038	0.032	0.100	0.103	0.057	0.044
Finland	...	0.032	...	0.013	...	0.044
Ireland	0.038	0.032	0.100	0.103	0.056	0.044
Luxembourg	0.023	0.021	0.061	0.069	0.055	0.042

Table 5.3 presents the power indices for the EU-12 and the EU-15 when
a simple majority and a double majority rule are used. It is surprising
that the SSI gives almost exactly the same distribution of power in simple
majority as in qualified majority voting. It is even more surprising that in
double majority voting the smallest countries seem to gain somewhat.
Double majority rule has been analysed in detail in Widgrén (1994a),
which shows that countries with a population smaller than 7 million
would gain if double majority was used instead of a qualified or simple
majority rule. The independence assumption gives much more power to
each member in a simple or double majority game when compared to
qualified majority voting. If we normalise the BI the distribution is,
however, almost identical to the distribution of the normalised index in a
qualified majority game.

We can base our interpretation of this phenomenon on subjective
probabilities and on the phases of the decision making process. In the
first phase, a draft proposal is given and voters can be considered
independent since there has been no communication of any significance
to speak of between them. As noted earlier in this chapter, power indices
can be interpreted as players' prospects from participating in voting
games. The result in table 5.3 shows that a decrease in a voting rule

implies that independent prospects (i.e. without compromises) become more optimistic, but also that they become unrealistic in the sense of group consistency (see section 2). Hence on the basis of table 5.4 we may argue that voting power increases but also that voters seem to over-estimate their abilities during the early phases of the decision making process. This leads to more stringent competition since the decision making moves to the direction of 'may the best proposal win', while the independent power increases. In the EU Council of Ministers the independent power seems to exceed the homogeneous power when the voting rule is larger than the blocking minority and smaller than the qualified majority (see figure 5.1). Another question which arises is a question of increased risk of being outvoted in simple majority voting (see section 4).

The results concerning the loss of power do not support the hypothesis that the increased role of majority voting in the 1980s was a consequence of the fear of power losses for the members of the EU-9. It seems also that the distribution of power does not give any reason to claim a move from a qualified to a simple majority rule for any of the current Community members. Although the move from a qualified to a simple majority rule increases voting power for each member, it also increases significantly the risk of losing. It also seems that under the qualified majority rule independent and homogeneous power are in balance.

4   Decision making control

Tables 5.4 and 5.5 show the probabilities of blocking decisions and of ensuring acceptance of proposals for the leading coalition (i.e. a coalition with m largest countries) when assuming qualified majority. It can be seen that the decision making can be weakly controlled by the five largest countries, assuming independence; when assuming homogeneity, a qualified majority is needed to control decisions.

The negative control can be pursued by small coalitions with 2–3 members.[16] The probabilities in tables 5.4 and 5.5 show two basic characteristics of EU decision making. First, proposals have hurdles to pass without significant compromises and second, negative national control has dominance. The immediate consequence of these properties is that they limit the competence of the EU to the issues where member states can reach high homogeneity and make compromises. Also while main-taining the current decision making rules (i.e. voting weights and majorities) the high national control indicates that the Community cannot take new members with very different views from the average 'Community standard'. To get homogeneous ministers member states have to be

Table 5.4 The leading coalition's control over decision making in the EU-12

n	Homogeneity		Independence	
	Prob. of accompl.	Prob. of preventing	Prob. of accompl.	Prob. of preventing
1	0.35	0.78	0.17	0.97
2	0.41	0.90	0.28	1.00
3	0.48	1.00	0.46	1.00
4	0.59	...	0.71	...
5	0.74	...	0.91	...
6	0.86	...	0.98	...
7	1.00	...	1.00	...

similar. The third consequence of a high national negative control is that the decision making can be ineffective. There is a danger that significant decisions cannot be made before a wide homogeneity is reached (see section 5). A very important consequence of this third implication is that the decision making system in the EU in practice secures the role of the subsidiarity principle. The decision making process makes it too difficult, and above all too ineffective, to make decisions regarding the areas where there is not enough homogeneity between member states.

It can be seen in tables 5.4 and 5.5 that after a certain limit the measure of control increases faster under the independence than under the homogeneity assumption. The technical explanation for this lies in the probability model behind the indices. Assuming independence implies

Table 5.5 The leading coalition's control over decision making in the EU-15

n	Homogeneity		Independence	
	Prob. of accompl.	Prob. of preventing	Prob. of accompl.	Prob. of preventing
1	0.35	0.77	0.13	0.98
2	0.39	0.87	0.23	1.00
3	0.45	1.00	0.38	1.00
4	0.54	...	0.60	...
5	0.64	...	0.82	...
6	0.72	...	0.92	...
7	0.83	...	0.98	...
8	1.00	...	1.00	...

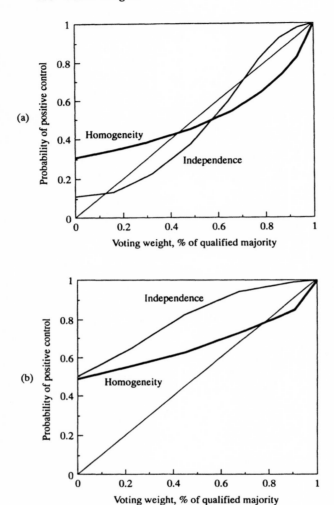

Figure 5.2   Leading coalitions' share of majority and control in the EU-15
a   Qualified majority
b   Simple majority

that the support for the leading coalition exceeds the limit needed for a blocking minority more readily than under the homogeneity assumption.

Intuitively, it is quite clear that a negative control decreases when voters negotiate and amend proposals. The conclusion that control increases faster under the independence than under the homogeneity assumption implies that the negative part of control has dominance. For compromises, member states have to give more of their negative control than they gain positive control. For the EU Council of Ministers, it seems that the dominance of negative control holds for coalitions of more than three to four largest members.

Another side of this phenomenon is shown in figure 5.2a and 5.2b. This presents the positive control as a function of the leading coalition's votes as a share of majority. Figures 5.2a and 5.2b are quite similar regardless of whether we investigate the EU-12 or the EU-15, which is why we present only the latter. The first common feature is that in qualified majority voting independent voters have higher positive control if the size of the leading coalition exceeds 60 per cent of that majority. Beyond this limit, a leading coalition cannot gain positive control by compromises. Simple majority voting changes the figures remarkably. To gain positive control, there is no need for compromises. Also the control is much more concentrated, i.e. the control curve lies above the 45 degree line, and the two largest countries could control decisions by a probability of 0.8.

The main conclusion of the measures concerning decision making control is that the qualified majority rule together with a voting weight determination which favours small countries ensure high national control for both the large and small members. The control is based on its negative side, i.e. on blocking decisions. Moving towards a simple majority, although it has a negligible effect on voting power, would change the control measures significantly. In simple majority voting, the control would be based on its positive side and in the sense of higher control the compromises would become useless. This also holds for double majority voting.

5   Policy change

The conclusions made in sections 3 and 4 were based on the assumption that voters behaved similarly regarding voting distributions (i.e. they were all either independent or homogeneous). Typically, this kind of analysis concentrates on a voting body itself, not on voters or particular questions of voting. The analysis is said to be abstract.

We have argued in this chapter (see Straffin, 1988) that voting assumptions can be interpreted as consequences of different levels of communication among the voters. This illustration can be used to model certain qualitative cooperation structures in a voting body. The cooperation structures may arise from differences in preferences, and thus they may alter from vote to vote, e.g. regarding the issue of voting. In this chapter, however, we do not intend to analyse different issues of voting,[17] but rather a more general setting which also arises from different preferences. On the basis of our analysis we can make conclusions about the magnitude of possible policy shifts after the three EFTA countries have joined the EU.

Our analysis in this section is based on partial homogeneity (see section 2). We simply assume that the Mediterranean countries (Spain, Portugal, and Greece) form one homogeneous group and the new entrants another one. Intuitively, it is reasonable to believe that these groups have common interests and that they are thus among themselves more homogeneous than all member states. It has also been assumed that Germany, the Netherlands, Belgium, Denmark, and Luxembourg will have deeper communication with the group of new entrants. Partial homogeneity is used to model this setting so that the Southern and the Northern coalitions are considered as in opposition to each other. This is quite a realistic situation in many issues of voting in the EU (see Widgrén, 1993b; Hamilton, 1991). However, it is worth noting that also inter-coalition cooperation is still permitted.[18]

Table 5.6 shows the partial homogeneity power indices for the EU-12

Table 5.6   Voting power in the EU Council of Ministers before and after the entry of Austria, Sweden and Finland in two set-ups

Member state	New entrants vs Mediterranean countries			New entrants and 5 Northern members vs Mediterranean countries		
	EU-12	EU-15	Group	EU-12	EU-15	Group
Germany	0.147	0.107	I	0.132	0.101	F
Italy	0.147	0.107	I	0.112	0.115	I
UK	0.147	0.107	I	0.112	0.115	I
France	0.147	0.107	I	0.112	0.115	I
Spain	0.118	0.091	A	0.130	0.118	A
Netherlands	0.074	0.057	I	0.074	0.054	F
Portugal	0.074	0.056	A	0.039	0.063	A
Greece	0.074	0.056	A	0.039	0.063	A
Belgium	0.074	0.057	I	0.074	0.054	F
Sweden	...	0.051	F	...	0.040	F
Austria	...	0.051	F	...	0.040	F
Denmark	0.052	0.034	I	0.051	0.032	F
Finland	...	0.036	F	...	0.032	F
Ireland	0.052	0.034	I	0.058	0.033	I
Luxembourg	0.019	0.022	I	0.021	0.017	F

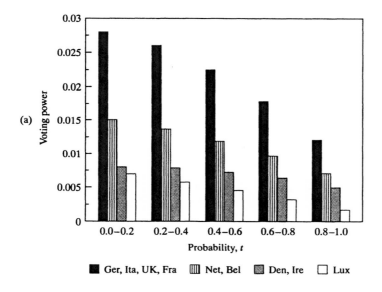

(a)

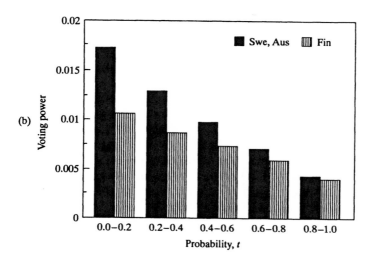

(b)

Figure 5.3 Power profiles in the EU-15 when the EFTA entrants and the Mediterranean countries vote as opposites
a   **Indifferent countries**
b   **EFTA entrants**

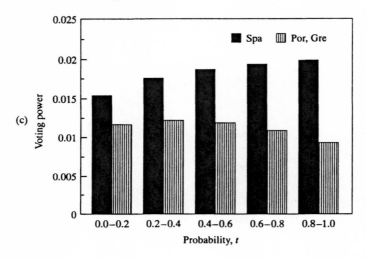

(c)

Figure 5.3 (*contd*)
c   **Mediterranean countries**

and the EU-15. As was mentioned earlier, it has been assumed that there are two homogeneous groups, the first of which contains the new entrants (case 1) or the new entrants supported by Germany, the Netherlands, Belgium, Denmark, and Luxembourg (case 2), and the second of which contains the three Mediterranean countries. It has also been assumed that there lies a group of individual voters between the opposite groups. In table 5.6 F stands for the 'For' group, i.e. members in this group favour a certain proposal with the probability t, A stands for the 'Against' group, i.e. members in this group favour proposals with the complement probability $1 - t$ and finally I stands for an indifferent country.

Table 5.6 and figures 5.3 and 5.4 reveal two interesting results. First, it seems that there are no significant gainers except the Mediterranean countries in case 2. It is counter-intuitive that they gain, although their opposition becomes stronger in terms of votes. Deeper analysis shows, however, that this result is intuitively reasonable (see figures 5.3 and 5.4). The second conclusion concerning the indices in table 5.6 is, once again, that proposals have remarkable difficulty in passing. The homogeneous cooperation may even decrease the voting power of countries in the 'For' group, while for the opposition the reverse may hold. This is due to the high negative control which has already been noted earlier.

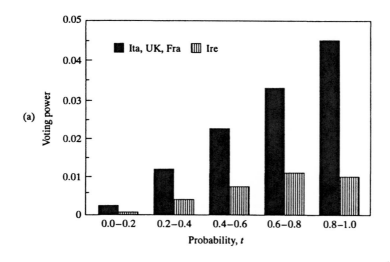

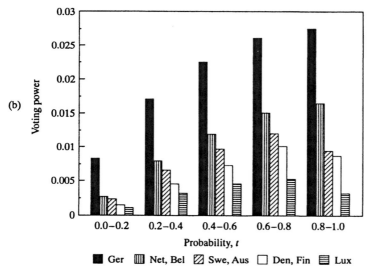

Figure 5.4   Power profiles in the EU-15 when the EFTA entrants support and the Mediterranean countries vote as opposites
a   Indifferent countries
b   EFTA entrants with support

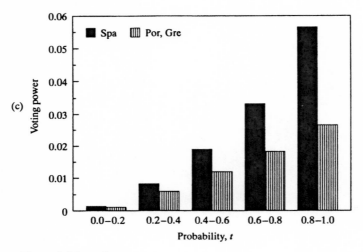

(c)

Figure 5.4 (*contd*)
c   **Mediterranean countries**

Let us now define a distribution of each voter's own power with respect to voting probabilities and let us call this distribution *a power profile*. The easiest way to calculate the profiles is to take the integrals in (4) for separate intervals with equal length. For example, we may take integrals from zero to 0.2, from 0.2 to 0.4, and so on to the final interval from 0.8 to 1. The five integrals should sum up to the partial homogeneity power index. They thus define its distribution with respect to t.

The purpose of the profiles is to reveal what kind of power different voters do have under different set-ups.[19] By analysing these profiles we can reveal what kind of voting behaviour an individual needs to be powerful or, less normatively, what kind of proposals an individual has the best chances to influence. If an individual has most of his power in questions that he supports with a small probability, this can be interpreted as blocking power. In contrast, if an individual's power is based on questions that he supports with a high probability, it can be interpreted as power to promote the passage of decisions. If the former type of distribution holds for both sides, the semi-coalition structure can, on the other hand, be interpreted as unstable, but then significant decisions cannot be made. On the other hand, low intensities to push through proposals increase stability. If the latter type of setting holds true for both sides, the semi-coalition structure can be stable but there is also more potential for significant decisions by making package deals. Figures 5.3 and 5.4 present the power profiles for the EU-15 in cases 1 and 2.

In the EU-12 it seems that the Mediterranean countries wield the more influence the tighter the opposition policy they pursue, if we assume that the other members behave homogeneously. Although the Mediterranean countries do not form a blocking minority they seem to have a high enough possibility to have an additional member to support their views and to form a blocking minority coalition. If, however, the other members behave independently, the need for cooperation to pursue a policy they prefer decreases. It is interesting that in a set-up where Germany, Denmark and the Benelux behave homogeneously, Spain becomes as powerful as Germany.

Figures 5.3 and 5.4 show an interesting result concerning new entrants' possibilities for changing the direction of policies pursued (see also Widgrén, 1993b). It seems that the new entrants have a significant risk of being outvoted when trying to push through policies they prefer. The Mediterranean countries do not have a need to pursue a tight opposition policy against the new entrants. Figure 5.4 presents a set-up where the new entrants collaborate with five other members (Germany, the Netherlands, Belgium, Denmark and Luxembourg) and they together form a homogeneous group. The profiles change significantly for all groups. The 'For' group, including the three former EFTA countries, seem to have much higher incentives to push through the policies they prefer, and for the opposition it seems that it would be reasonable to pursue a tight opposition policy. As regards the influence on the direction of policies in the EU, Sweden, Austria and Finland cannot make significant policy shifts without collaborating with other countries.

6   Conclusions

In this chapter we have investigated the change in the balance of power in the EU Council of Ministers when it is expanded by three former EFTA countries and when voting rules are assumed to alter.

The decision making process in the EU strongly favours small countries. It was shown in this chapter that the new entrants would get 12 per cent of the total power in the EU Council of Ministers. Relative to their share of the population in the EU of 15 members, the share of power is over twice higher; the new entrants would have a strong position in EU decision making. However, the loss of power for the current members is smaller than in the enlargements of the Community in 1973 or in the 1980s. It can also be argued that the Mediterranean enlargement in the 1980s changed the EU decision making more than the EFTA entrants. In the 1980s, the need for compromises increased significantly. Strengthening the role of qualified majority voting was a necessary reform to reach a balance between compromises and competition. This balance does not change due to the EFTA entrants.

The conclusion concerning control was twofold: first, it seems to be very difficult to promote the passage of proposals, while for preventing decisions the reverse seems to hold true and second, accomplishing a decision seems to be more difficult in an expanded EU the more independently the voters act. However, old members do not lose their control in the expansion of the Union, but there will be three new members with a significant control position regarding preventing decisions. It can also be argued that high national control over decisions implies more power to the officials in preparatory bodies. Significant decisions will need a deep homogeneity between the member states which can be reached only by negotiating and by preparing proposals properly. This implies that there is a danger that decision making will be ineffective; national control and need for deep homogeneity are together an effective life insurance for the subsidiarity principle.

As far as decision making efficiency is concerned, the current qualified majority rule gives too much negative control to member states. One cannot, however, argue that the new entrants create the inefficiency problem; it already exists. In terms of negative control, the increased inefficiency due to the new entrants could be eliminated by reducing the majority requirement by 3 votes. In general terms, avoiding the problem of easy blocking and inefficiency requires lower majority rules; this would decrease member states' negative control over decisions significantly. However, it is surprising that the balance of voting power remains almost unchanged if the decision making rule is lowered from qualified to simple or double majority. The latter even improves small countries' positions.

It was shown that negative control was the main element for new entrants to have an effect on policies pursued. Thus it is unlikely that there will be a significant policy change. That is why the new entrants, and also the other members, should concentrate on their most important interests. The Mediterranean countries maintain their key role, and it is profitable for them to deepen their cooperation. However, the Northern members' incentive to try to push through proposals that they prefer will also increase.

If common policies create positive externalities for member states, lower majority rules should be used to improve efficiency and Union capabilities. As regards national influence, improving efficiency is not a matter of power distribution. Double majority voting is an exception, as it increases small countries' and Germany's power, although the reason for such a proposal is, without doubt, based on entirely different arguments. Since in the current context lower majority rules give more weight and power to the supranational Union and its Commission and less weight to national interests, the improvement of EU decision making efficiency is a matter of centralisation and not a matter of distribution of national influence.

NOTES

The author is grateful for valuable comments to Richard Baldwin and Matti Pohjola as well as to the conference participants.

1 The relation between the voting weight w and population p can be described by the regression equation $\log w = 0.0063(\log p)^{2.465}$ with $R^2 = 0.972$. The criterion for this particular equation was to fit the estimates for the numbers of votes to the actual votes.

2 In this chapter we concentrate on a simple and a qualified majority. They seem to be the relevant alternatives in the EU Council of Ministers. We thus do not concentrate on voting power as a function of voting rule (see Nurmi, 1992).

3 This approach can also be criticised. It can be argued that voting behaviour should not affect the measures of power (see Holler and Packel, 1983).

4 Note that negative control is a conditional probability. There are four outcomes where C votes 'no' and four outcomes where C votes 'yes'.

5 It is worth noting, however, that the vector (1/2, 1/2, 1/2) is an implication of a wider range of acceptability vectors, as is shown later in this chapter.

6 These joint probability distributions (jpds) are different from the usual ones that assign probabilities directly to events. Each acceptability vector describes the n probability distributions that assign probabilities to the vote 'yes' and vote 'no' events for each of the n voters. The jdps discussed here assign probabilities to each possible acceptability vector. The jdps thus assign probabilities to probability distributions.

7 Since we assumed that the voting is simply 'yes' or 'no' type, the list of 'no' vote coalitions is the same. That is why for the measures of influence there is no difference in analysing 'yes' vote or 'no' vote coalitions.

8 See Owen (1982) for a fuller explanation of this. Intuitively, it should be quite clear. It is also interesting that the sum of this kind of terms is always one no matter whether p_is are probabilities or not. We can even choose complex numbers for p_is and the property holds true (Owen, 1964).

9 A class of coalitions is no more than a set of coalitions. In mathematics, the sets of sets are usually referred to as classes of sets.

10 For an unbiased coin this illustration holds true only for simple majority voting. For weighted majority voting we also need a weighted coin.

11 Actually, the exact distributions are unknown since we are analysing weighted voting. In the case of a symmetric voting game (one person, one vote), the theory tells us that the distributions should be uniform under homogeneity and binomial under independence.

12 Slightly modified versions of these probabilities can be used to analyse the concentration of power (Leech, 1987a, 1987b; Pohjola, 1988). It is then assumed that a coalition of the m largest players votes for the proposal and the probabilities are calculated for these alliances by letting $m = 1, \ldots, p$, where p is the largest number of players needed for a majority.

13 The choice of these particular limits is, of course, arbitrary. Here, as usual in control analysis, we use the analogy to significance levels in statistics.

14 For a more detailed discussion about the PCs, see Widgrén (1994b).

15 Power indices can also be interpreted by using subjective voting probabilities when an individual voter is assessing her/his prospects from participation in the game (Weber, 1988).

16 For example, subsystems are such coalitions (see Schoutheete, 1990). The role of the Franco–German axis, the Benelux countries, Mediterranean and Nordic countries have been analysed in Widgrén (1993a, 1993c, 1994a, 1994b).

17 For voting power in trade policy and social regulation, see Widgrén (1995).

18 Technically, the probability model which gives t and $1 - t$ probabilities for the two homogeneous groups to support a random proposal ensures that.

19 Partial homogeneity makes profile analysis interesting since analysis differs from individual to individual. Homogeneity and independence imply similar and symmetric profiles (see Widgrén, 1995).

REFERENCES

Banzhaf, J., 1965. 'Weighted voting doesn't work: a mathematical analysis', *Rutgers Law Review*, **19**, 317–43

Bolger, E., 1979. 'A class of power indices for voting games', *International Journal of Game Theory*, **9**, 217–32

Brams. S. and P. Affuso, 1985a. 'New paradoxes of voting power on the EU Council of Ministers', *Electoral Studies*, **4**, 135–9

1985b. 'Addendum to "New paradoxes of voting power on the EU Council of Ministers" ', *Electoral Studies*, **4**, 290

Brams, S., A. Doherty and M. Weidner, 1991. 'Game theory and multilateral negotiations: the Single European Act and the Uruaguay Round', C.V. Starr Center for Applied Economics, *Economic Research Reports*, **91–45**

Dehousse, R., 1992. 'Integration v. regulation? On the dynamics of regulation in the European Community', *Journal of Common Market Studies*, **30(4)**, 383–402

Dubey, P., A. Neyman and R. Weber, 1981. 'Value theory without efficiency', *Mathematics of Operations Research*, **6**, 122–8

Hamilton, C.B., 1991. 'The Nordic EFTA countries' options: Community membership or a permanent EEA-accord', in *EFTA Countries in a Changing Europe*, Geneva: EFTA

Holler, M. and E. Packel, 1983. 'Power, luck and the right index', *Zeitschrift für Nationalökonomie*, **43**, 21–9

Hosli, M., 1993. 'Admission of European Free Trade Association states to the European Community: effects on voting power in the EC Council of Ministers', *International Organization*, 47, 629–43

Johnston, R.J., 1982. 'Political geography and political power', in M. Holler (ed.), *Power Voting and Voting Power*, Würzburg-Wien: Physica-Verlag

Leech, D., 1987a. 'Ownership concentration and the theory of the firm: a simple game theoretic approach', *Journal of Industrial Economics*, 35, 225–40

1987b. 'Ownership concentration and control in large US corporations in the 1930s: an analysis of the TNEU sample', *Journal of Industrial Economics*, 35, 333–42

1987c. 'Corporate ownership concentration and control: a new look at the evidence of Berle and Means', *Oxford University Papers*, 39, 534–51

Nicholl, W. and T. Salmon, 1990. *Understanding the European Communities*, Oxford: Philip Allan

Nurmi, H., 1992. '*A priori* distribution of power in the EU Council of Ministers', *Politiikka*, 2/1992 (in Finnish)

Owen, G., 1964. 'Tensor composition of games', in M. Dresher, L. Shapley and A. Tucker (eds.), *Advances in Game Theory, Annals of Mathematical Studies*, 52, Princeton: Princeton University Press

1972. 'Multilinear extensions of games', *Management Science*, 18, 64–79

1977. 'Values of games with *a priori* unions', in R. Hein and O. Moeschlin (eds.), *Essays in Mathematical Economics and Game Theory*, Berlin: Springer-Verlag, 76–88

1982. *Game Theory*, New York: Academic Press

Pohjola, M., 1988. 'Concentration of shareholder voting power in the Finnish industrial companies', *Scandinavian Journal of Economics*, 90, 245–53

Schoutheete, P. de, 1990. 'The European Community and its sub-systems', in W. Wallace (ed.), *The Dynamics of European Integration*, London, Pinter, 106–24

Shapley, L.S., 1953. 'A value for *N*-person cooperative games', in H. Kuhn and A. Tucker (eds.), *Contributions to the Theory of Games, Annals of Mathematical Study*, 28, Princeton: Princeton University Press

Shapley, L.S. and M. Shubik, 1954. 'A method for evaluating the distribution of power in a committee system', in M. Shubik (ed.), *Game Theory and Related Approaches to Social Behavior*, New York: Wiley

Stålvant, C.-E., 1990. 'Nordic cooperation', in W. Wallace (ed.), *The Dynamics of European Integration*, London: Pinter

Straffin, P. 1988. 'The Shapley–Shubik and Banzhaf power indices as probabilities', in A.E. Roth (ed.), *The Shapley Value, Essays in Honor of Lloyd S. Shapley*, Cambridge: Cambridge University Press

Straffin, P., M.D. Davis and S. Brams, 1982. 'Power and satisfaction in an ideologically divided voting body', in M. Holler (ed.), *Power Voting and Voting Power*, Würzburg-Wien: Physica-Verlag

Wallace, H., 1990. 'Making multilateral negotiations work', in W. Wallace (ed.), *The Dynamics of European Integration*, London: Pinter

Weber, R., 1988. 'Probabilistic values for fames', in A.E. Roth (ed.), *The Shapley Value, Essays in Honor of Lloyd S. Shapley*, Cambridge: Cambridge University Press

Widgrén, M., 1993a. 'A game theoretic analysis of the Nordic coalition's role in the decision making of the EU Council of Ministers', in J. Fagerberg and

L. Lundberg (eds.), *European Economic Integration: A Nordic Perspective*, London: Avebury

1993b. 'Voting power in trade policy and social regulation of an expanded EC: a partial homogeneity approach', ETLA, *Discussion Paper*, **433**

1993c. 'National power in the decision making of the EU Council of Ministers' (in Finnish with English summary), *The Research Institute of the Finnish Economy*, ETLA, Series C, **64**

1994a. 'Voting rule reforms in the EU Council: needs, means and consequences, ETLA, *Discussion Paper*, **483**

1994b. 'Voting power in the EC and the consequences of two different enlargements', *European Economic Review*, **38**, 1153–71

1994c. 'The relation between voting power and policy impact in the European Union', CEPR, *Discussion Paper*, **1033**, London: CEPR

1995. 'Probabilistic voting power in the EU Council: the cases of trade policy and social regulation', *Scandinavian Journal of Economics*, **97(2)**

6 Migration in the integrated EU

RICCARDO FAINI

1 Introduction

Very few issues can stir controversies and arouse divisive passions as much as migrations. The literature on the topic is enormous. It has attracted contributions from all the fields of social science, including economics. Seldom, however, is the economist's assessment of an issue so much at odds with the common perception of the problem. Economists typically argue that free labour movement is conducive to economic efficiency. Existing barriers to labour mobility are responsible for a substantial loss in world-wide GDP (Hamilton and Whalley, 1984). However, the call for free labour mobility falls on deaf ears among policy makers. In 1990, a French Minister, addressing his national Parliament, pleaded for the maintenance of border controls within the EU, citing migrations as one of the main unresolved issues.

This chapter tries to assess the outlook for migrations in the EU. It makes four points: (1) Even the full abolition of intra-EU border controls will not lead to a significant expansion of migrations by EU residents. In the past, Southern European countries used to be the prominent source of migrant labour for Northern European markets. Today, there is mounting evidence pointing to a dramatic fall in the propensity to migrate from Southern European countries. (2) The presence of a large number of (often illegal) non-EU migrants in many European countries, particularly in Southern Europe, is often cited as a reason for concern. Given the alleged large remigration propensity of non-EU migrants, it is argued that unlimited labour mobility within the EU would lead to a substantial reallocation of the existing stocks. We argue that the size of this phenomenon may, however, be quite limited. (3) Migrations from the East have not been relatively large, so far. This can be explained by large migration costs and the belief that the transition toward a market economy is likely to be successful. However, any shift toward a more pessimistic assessment of future prospects in

143

the East could trigger substantial migrations. (4) A unified EU will have to tackle the issue of a common migration policy. Only if countries can agree on common procedures for the admission and employment of non-EU residents will unrestricted labour mobility in the EU become a real possibility.

The chapter is organised as follows. In section 2, we briefly assess the institutional context for labour mobility in the EU. We review both EU policy and inter-governmental agreements. We then turn in section 3 to the issue of labour mobility by EU residents. Section 4 is devoted to an analysis of migrations flows by non-EU residents. We then assess the outlook for East–West migrations. Section 5 discusses some of the problems which arise in the formulation of a common European migration policy and section 6 concludes the chapter.

2   The regulatory framework for labour mobility

The Treaty of Rome provides in Articles 3 and 8A for the free movement of people and workers within the Community.[1] It does not specify whether this freedom should apply to all people (and presumably all workers) or to EU citizens only. Any attempt to restrict labour mobility of third-country citizens within the EU would clearly impinge on the freedom of movement of EU citizens as well. Yet, it is virtually undisputed that policy decisions regarding the admission and the employment of third-country citizens should largely be left to EU national governments. The main issue is whether the Community, in particular the Commission, should have any competence in these matters. Some governments (in particular, France) argue that migrations of third-country nationals are mostly a security matter and thus should not concern the Community. In 1985, however, the Commission issued a regulation (85/381) instructing national governments to inform the Commission itself about any change in their migration policy and providing for some mild form of coordination. Five countries (Germany, France, the Netherlands, Denmark and the UK) appealed to the European Court of Justice. Their appeal, however, was rejected by a Court decision (9 July 1987). The Court ruled that EU institutions should retain some competence on migration policy to the extent that the latter may 'directly affect the establishment or functioning of the common market' (Article 100, Treaty of Rome). There are indeed several ways that migration policies can affect the common market. For instance, illegal migration and employment of non-EU citizens as well as lack of labour market protection for non-EU workers may strengthen the competitive position of a country, and distort the pattern of trade and competition within the EU. The European Court of Justice ruling means that Community institutions are empowered to issue regulations on these matters.

Paradoxically, one result of the decision was to strengthen the tendency for EU member countries to conclude inter-governmental agreements which lie beyond the mandate of EU institutions. Two main initiatives should be mentioned. In 1989, the European Council in Madrid paved the way for a new initiative aimed at defining a 'Convention on the Crossing of External Frontiers' of the then EC. The ultimate purpose of this Convention is to remove the obstacles to the full abolition of internal border controls. To this end, the Convention acknowledges the need for 'conducting effective controls, in line with common criteria, on persons at the external borders of those States and ... implementing a common visa policy'. Despite these ambitious targets, the progress made in the Convention has been quite modest. The Convention provides for a tougher posture *vis-à-vis* illegal immigration (through tighter border controls, compulsory expulsion of illegal migrants, sanctions against carriers), and for the possibility of reciprocal recognition among EU countries of short-term (less than 3 months) visas. It leaves to national governments all decisions regarding longer-term visas. Approval of the Convention is currently stalled because of the long-standing dispute between Spain and the UK on the status of Gibraltar.

The Schengen Agreement, concluded between the founding members of the EC (with the exception of Italy) (14 June 1985), is more substantive. First of all, the abolition of internal borders was no longer considered a distant aim, but was supposed to become effective for the signatories of the agreement by December 1993; there were however conspicuous reservations that the agreement would be fully implemented by that date.[2] To support unrestricted labour mobility in the Schengen area, the agreement provided again for tougher border controls (not too dissimilar from the ones envisaged in the Convention on the Crossing of External Frontiers), for the mutual recognition among signatories of short-term visas (this being now a commitment rather than a simple possibility as in the Convention) and again left long-term visa policy to the member countries. The Schengen Agreement also contained several provisions to strengthen cooperation on judiciary and security matters. The list of countries willing to join the agreement quickly grew longer and now includes Italy (since 1990), Spain and Portugal (since 1991) and Greece (since 1992). Only Denmark, Ireland and the UK, among the EU member countries, have until now adamantly opposed the spirit and the provisions of the agreement. Community institutions were initially also opposed to this initiative on the ground that it involved only a limited number of member countries and bypassed Community channels. They have lately taken a more positive attitude, now seeing the Agreement as an important step to showing that unrestricted labour mobility can work.

To sum up, the key distinction in the regulatory framework is between provisions affecting the mobility of EU citizens and those dealing with third-country citizens. As stipulated in the Treaty of Rome, all obstacles to the free movement of people across member states should be abolished. After 1 January 1993, even the transitional period of accession for Spain and Portugal came to an end: no restrictions are left within the Community on EU citizens. Non-EU nationals pose a different problem: member countries strive to retain full power in the decisions regarding their entry and employment. In the remainder of the chapter, we evaluate the migration outlook for both EU and non-EU nationals.

3   Migrations from Southern Europe

Migrations are a recurring phenomenon in European history. During the 1950s, there was little movement of labour across European borders, but the creation of the Common Market coincided with an impressive recovery in migration flows. From 1958–62, on average 332,000 Italians headed North each year mainly toward France, Germany and the Benelux countries. Greece, Portugal and Spain also provided a massive contribution to the flow of migrants. Migrations continued unabated during the 1960s, a new turning point came in 1974, when the deep recession in Northern Europe led to a dramatic drop in labour flows from Southern Europe (Molle, 1990).

Typically, in the literature, the collapse in migrations is attributed to the fall in labour demand in receiving countries and the stricter controls implemented after 1974 (Salt, 1991). It was indeed during this period that many countries in Northern Europe introduced programmes both to encourage existing migrants to return to their own countries and to discourage new migrations. If we believe in this interpretation, we should then expect migrations from Southern Europe to resume once economic recovery in Northern economies was solidly under way. But, even after traditional receiving countries had definitely come out of the recession, migrations did not resume. Table 6.1 reports the stock of foreign population living in Belgium, France and Germany. Two facts stand out. First, aggregate migrations from traditional sources did not recover. The record increase in the stock of foreign population in Germany after 1988 is accounted for by the political and economic upheaval in the East. Second, the number of Southern European citizens living in these three

Table 6.1   Stock of foreign population, 1981–90

| | Belgium | | | | | |
	1981	1983	1985	1987	1988	1990
Total	885.7	890.9	846.5	862.5	868.8	904.5
Italy	276.5	270.5	252.9	241.1	241	241.1
Spain	57.8	56	51.2	52.8	52.6	52.2
Greece	21.4	21	19.3	20.4	20.6	20.9
Portugal	10.5	10.4	9.5	12.2	13.5	16.5
% S. Europe	41.35	40.17	39.33	37.86	37.72	36.56
	Germany					
	1981	1983	1985	1987	1988	1990
Total	4629/8	4534.9	4378.9	4630.2	4489.1	5241.8
Italy	624.5	565	531.3	544.4	508.7	548.3
Spain	177	166	152.8	147.1	126.4	134.7
Greece	299.3	292.3	280.6	279.9	274.8	314.5
Portugal	109.4	99.5	77	79.2	71.1	84.6
% S. Europe	26.14	24.76	23.79	22.69	21.85	20.64
	France					
	1975	1982	1990			
Total	3342.4	3714.2	3607.6			
Italy	462.9	340.3	253.7			
Portugal	758.9	767.3	645.6			
Spain	497.5	327.3	216			
% S. Europe	49.94	38.63	30.92			

Source: Own calculations on SOPEMI data.

receiving countries, declined both in absolute and relative terms. For instance, the share of Italian, Spanish, Greek and Portuguese citizens in the total foreign population fell from 26.1 per cent in 1981 to 20.1 per cent in 1990. In France, it declined from 38.63 per cent in 1982 to 30.92 per cent in 1990. Overall, there is little sign that economic recovery in Northern Europe brought a resumption in migrations either from the rest of the world or from Southern Europe.

An alternative, or perhaps complementary, explanation of the fall in the number of migrants from the Southern border of Europe stresses the role of supply factors. According to this explanation, when in the 1980s conditions in Northern Europe did again favour a recovery in migratory flows, supply of potential migrants from traditional sending countries in Southern Europe had essentially dried up. Two main reasons account for the fall in supply. First, the decline in the level of income differentials between Northern and Southern Europe could explain the increasing reluctance of the Southern population to move north. The evidence in this respect, however, is somewhat mixed. As shown in figure 6.1, the gap between *per capita* income in Italy and in the main receiving countries tends to fall and thus could account for the fall in migrations. But there is little evidence that a similar phenomenon took place for the other Southern European countries. On the contrary, there is significant evidence that the 1980s brought a substantial widening in the level of income disparities between Northern and Southern Europe (figure 6.2). Furthermore, existing econometric evidence does not point to a quantitatively large role of income differentials in determining migrations.

Alternatively, the fall in supply may be predicated on a decline in the propensity to migrate. According to this approach, the propensity to move abroad is a declining function of income in the sending country, even after controlling for wage differentials. The approach is fully developed in Faini and Venturini (1994); here, we shall only illustrate the gist of their arguments. Suppose that the utility of a potential migrant is a function of both his income level and the location where he happens to live. Suppose also, in line with much of the migration literature, that potential migrants have an imbedded preference for living in their own country. Cultural, linguistic and social factors may account for this preference. Formally, the migrants' utility function can be represented as: $U(w_i, f_i)$, where w_i and f_i denote respectively the wage rate and the amenities in region i. Suppose finally that only two locations

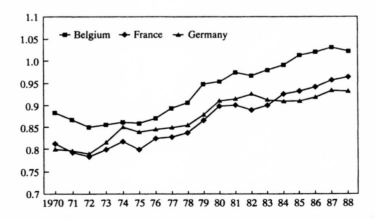

Figure 6.1   International income differentials with Belgium, France and Germany, Italy's income in the numerator, 1970–88

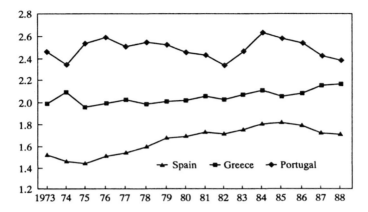

Figure 6.2   International income differentials with Spain, Greece and Portugal, Germany's income in the numerator, 1970–88

are available (North (N) and South (S)). A resident in S will migrate if and only if:

$$U(w_n, f_n) > U(w_s, f_s) \tag{1}$$

Given our assumptions, we have $w_n > w_s$ and $f_n < f_s$. Obviously, for someone to be willing to migrate, the wage differential should be large enough to offset the non-monetary costs of migrations.

(1) is too general for the purpose of empirical analysis, but can be used to assess the effect of higher income in the origin country on the propensity to migrate. Let us take a first-order-Taylor expansion of the left-hand side of (1) around w_s and f_s. The migration condition becomes then:

$$\frac{U_w(w_s, f_s)}{U_f(w_s, f_s)} > \frac{f_s - f_n}{w_n - w_s} \tag{2}$$

where U_i $(i - w, f)$ denotes the marginal utility of w and f, measured at (w_s, f_s). Consider now the case where income grows in S while the right-hand side of (2) is unchanged. The change in the marginal rate of substitution between w and f will be equal to:

$$\frac{d}{dw_s} \frac{U_w}{U_f} = \frac{1}{U_f^2} (U_{ww} U_f - U_w U_{wf}). \tag{3}$$

Under typical conditions of normality in consumption the expression on

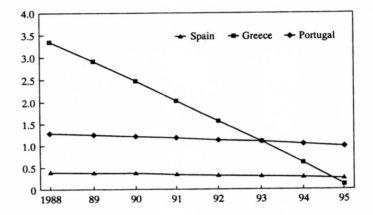

Figure 6.3 Migration rates from Spain, Greece and Portugal, per thousand of population, 1988–95

the right-hand side of (3) will be negative, indicating therefore that the marginal rate of substitution between w and f will fall following an increase in w. As a result, the probability that the migration condition (2) is satisfied will decline, and aggregate migrations will decrease.

The explanation for this result is simple. In this model, migration is an inferior good, i.e. staying at home is a normal good. When income grows in the origin country, people will be willing to consume more of the home country's amenities and will therefore have less propensity to migrate. The model predicts that, for a sufficiently high level of income, migration will then be a declining function of income.

Faini and Venturini (1994) offer considerable empirical support for this prediction. They focus on the case of Greece, Portugal, Turkey and Spain. They find that for all these countries further increase in income would lead to a substantial drop in the emigration rate. Their estimates can be used to simulate the impact of income growth on the migration rate (figure 6.3). Income is assumed to grow at an average annual rate of 2 per cent. We see that even moderate *per capita* income growth should lead to a significant drop in migrations.

Further evidence in this respect comes from an analysis of Southern Italian migrations. Figure 6.4 shows the absolute value of migrants from Southern Italy to Northern Italy and to foreign destinations. The striking feature is the fall in the propensity to migrate during the 1980s. Income differentials between Northern and Southern Italy cannot account for this evolution given that the gap between the two regions widened substantially during those years. Unemployment fluctuations do not help

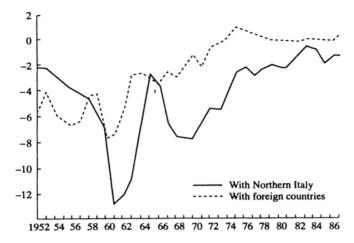

Figure 6.4   Southern Italy's net migration rate, 1952–86

either: the rate of unemployment showed a declining and an upward trend in Northern and Southern Italy respectively during the 1980s. Based on econometric evidence, Faini (1989) argues that rising income levels provide a more convincing explanation of the drop in migrations from the Italian Mezzogiorno.

4   A migration-diversion effect?

Not only has the propensity to migrate out of Southern European countries registered a substantial decline, but these countries have recently become the destination of a large and increasing number of non-EU migrants. Table 6.2 shows the rapidly rising stock of foreign population in Italy, Spain and Portugal. In all of these countries, the number of foreign residents has virtually doubled since 1980. They still account for a smaller proportion of total population than in Northern Europe, but the gap is steadily diminishing.

The rising stock of foreign population in Southern Europe is often cited as a source of concern not only for these countries, but also for Northern Europe. It is argued that increasing migrations toward Southern Europe reflect both lax migration policy there and tighter controls in Northern Europe. According to this argument, non-EU migrants (mostly from Third World countries) were induced to move to the Southern rim of Europe not because the latter represented their first choice, but because of the increasing difficulty of getting access to the more palatable labour markets in the North. According to this view, therefore, the abolition

Table 6.2   Foreign residents in Southern Europe, 1980–8

Year	Italy	Spain	Portugal
1980	298.7	181.5	58.1
1982	358.9	200.9	68.2
1984	403.9	226.5	89.6
1986	450.2	293.2	86.9
1987	572.1	334.9	88.1
1988	645.4	360.0	95.0

Source: SOPEMI (1991)

of internal borders in Europe will have two deleterious consequences: (a) it will allow migrants from poor countries to use Southern Europe as a staging post before heading to the North, (b) even if Southern European countries succeed in implementing tougher admission controls (this seems, for instance, to have been the case in Italy since 1990), it could lead to a substantial reallocation of (mostly illegal) migrants across Europe.

These fears may be largely unwarranted. There are good reasons indeed to believe that Southern Europe, and Italy in particular, has become an increasingly attractive destination on her own. First, as mentioned earlier, the declining income gap between Italy and Northern Europe (figure 6.1) was reflected in a rising income differential between Italy and the Southern Mediterranean countries (figure 6.5).[3] At the same time, there was no significant change in the income gap between, say, France

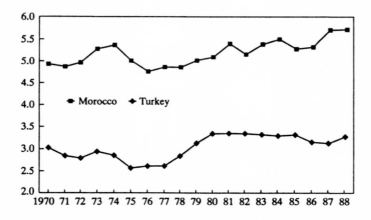

Figure 6.5   International income differentials with Morocco and Turkey, Italy's income in the numerator, 1970–88

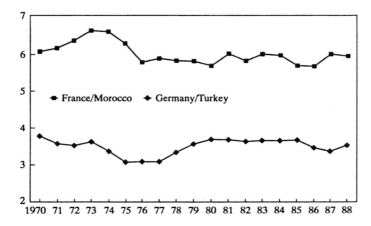

Figure 6.6   International income differentials with France/Morocco and Germany/ Turkey, 1970–88

and Morocco and Germany and Turkey (figure 6.6). Second, the growth pattern in Italy and, more generally, in Southern Europe during the 1980s, was characterised by a prominent role of the informal sector. According to a 1989 EC report (Commissione, 1989), the informal sector accounted for more than 10 per cent of GDP in Southern Europe and for less than 5 per cent in Germany, with France in an intermediate position. This pattern should have contributed to making Southern Europe more attractive to migrants, to the extent that their occupational composition is typically skewed toward the informal sector because of its lower skill requirement. In Northern Europe, on the contrary, employment growth was increasingly biased toward high skills and was therefore less conducive to migrations (Coleman, 1991). Third, employment growth was on the whole more sustained in Southern Europe during the 1980s than in most other EC countries. Finally, geographical proximity to the sending areas probably strengthened the propensity to migrate to Southern Europe.

In what follows, we try to discriminate between these competing hypotheses. We focus on migrations from Morocco. The choice of Morocco is dictated by the fact that this is a country where, during the 1980s, there was a significant shift in the geographical composition of migrants' destinations toward Southern Europe (table 6.3). By examining Moroccan migrations to Northern Europe, we attempt to assess whether the rise of new destinations in Southern Europe led to a migration-diversion effect. We also check whether the impact of employment

Table 6.3   Morocco's residents abroad, 1981, 1990 and 1992, 000

	1981	1990	1992
Italy	0.8	78.0	95.6
France	441.3	584.7	na
Belgium	110.2	141.6	na
Germany	39.4	67.5	na
Netherlands	83.4	156.9	na

Note: na   Not available.
Source: SOPEMI and Ministry of Interior, Italy.

growth in Northern Europe on migrations declined during the 1980s. We proceed in the following way. We first estimate a simple migration equation on Moroccan data:

$$M_i/POP = \sum_i a_{0i} + a_1 ln(w_i/w) + a_2 ED_i + \epsilon_i \qquad (4)$$

where M_i denotes migration from the sending country (Morocco) to area, i, POP is population in the origin country, w and w_i indicate *per capita* income in the sending and the receiving country respectively, while ED_i stands for employment growth in region i. (4) is estimated on pooled data for Morocco's migrants to their main destinations (France, Germany, Belgium, the Netherlands and Italy).

The model is estimated over the period 1965–87. We rely on a fixed-effect model where the intercepts (the coefficients a_{0i}) are allowed to differ across (destination) countries. We then check whether the countries' intercepts and the coefficient on ED show a structural break during the 1980s. Downward shifts in the coefficient on employment growth, ED are taken as an indication that the fall in migrations must, at least to some extent, be attributed to the change in the structure of labour demand in Northern countries, in particular to the shift toward higher skill requirements. We also interpret (negative) shifts in the intercept as suggesting that Northern European destinations have lost importance, possibly because either of stricter controls there or of the rise of alternative destinations.

The results are presented in table 6.4. We first consider (in column (1)) a restricted sample with only four destinations (Belgium, France, Germany and the Netherlands). The exclusion of Italy is dictated by the lower quality of available information on migration flows. We find rather strong evidence supporting the hypothesis that employment growth in

Table 6.4   Determinants of migrations, fixed-effect model

Dep. var.: M_i/POP

	Restricted sample (1)		Full sample (2)	
	Coeffic.	t-stat.	Coeff.	t-stat.
D_g	−1.52	1.33	−1.42	1.27
$D_g D_{74}$	0.04	0.78	0.03	0.74
D_b	−1.42	1.33	−1.32	1.27
D_n	−1.46	1.26	−1.36	1.20
$D_n D_{74}$	0.13	1.60	0.13	1.58
D_f	−0.55	0.51	−0.45	0.43
$D_f D_{74}$	−0.57	3.70	−0.57	3.68
D_{it}	—	—	−1.34	1.30
$\ln(w_i/w)$	0.90	1.42	0.85	1.36
$ED\ D_{70}$	0.083	2.93	0.082	2.91
$ED\ D_{80}$	0.014	1.46	0.014	1.49
ED_{it}	—	—	0.16	2.47
$(M/POP)_{-1}$	0.31	2.65	0.31	2.68
R^2	0.86		0.86	
DW	1.86		1.86	

Notes:

M_i	Migration to destination i (i = Belgium (b), France (f), Germany (g), Italy (it), the Netherlands (n)).
D_i	Intercept for country i.
POP	Population in the sending country.
$ED\ (ED_{it})$	Employment growth in the receiving country (Italy).
w_i	Wage in the receiving country.
w	Wage in the sending country.
D_{74}	Dummy variable (1 after 1974, 0 otherwise).
$D_{70}\ (D_{80})$	Dummy variable (1 before (after) 1980, 0 otherwise).

Northern countries during the 1980s no longer had a substantial impact on migrations. Indeed, employment growth, while a highly significant determinant of migrations in the 1960s and 1970s (the coefficient of ED D_{70} is significantly different from zero), no longer contributes to the explanatory power of the equation after 1980: the coefficient of ED D_{80} drops from 0.083 to 0.014 and loses significance. Adding Italy to the sample does not change the results (column (2)). There is however sufficient evidence to argue that, contrary to the findings for the other receiving countries, employment growth in Italy (ED_{it}) had a positive and statistically significant effect on migration even during the 1980s.[4] This finding can presumably be attributed to the prominent role in Italy of the informal sector. Overall, we conclude that part of the fall in migrations toward Northern European countries must be predicated on the increasingly dim employment prospects for potential migrants.

Turning to the pattern of countries' intercepts, there was no evidence of a significant shift at the beginning of the 1980s. The results change if we check for a structural break after 1974. The results in columns (1) and (2) show that, at least for France, there was a definite downward shift in the migration rate from Morocco (D_f D_{74} is negative and 'significant'). Whether this can be attributed to tighter controls in France or to the rise of new possible destinations remains, as argued earlier, ambiguous. For the other countries, there is little evidence of a structural break even after 1974.

A shortcoming of the previous approach is that the probability of migrating to a given destination is independent of conditions in other destinations. One could of course add the relevant explanatory variables describing all the alternative choices to the estimating equation, but would then quickly run into multicollinearity and degrees of freedom problems. A more palatable approach is to estimate a multinomial discrete choice model. There are two main advantages for such a framework: first, the probability of migrating to a given destination is constrained to lie between zero and one; second, the choices between alternative destinations become interrelated.

Estimation results of the multinomial logit model for Morocco are presented in table 6.5. The dependent variable is now the share of Morocco's migrants to a given destination. Consider first the restricted sample, exclusive of Italy (column (1)). Compared to the fixed-effect model, the coefficients are now less precisely estimated (presumably because of the reduced number of degrees of freedom), but point to similar conclusions: both wages and employment growth in the receiving country have a positive impact on the destination choice, but the impact of employment growth diminishes during the 1980s. The addition of Italy (column (2)) does not lead to any substantial change in either the size or the significance of the coefficients. We can use the Hausman–McFadden test to check whether the addition to the set of choices of a new destination (i.e. Italy) had an impact on the other alternatives.[5] The hypothesis is not rejected at comfortable significance levels. Taken literally, it would mean that the presence of an additional destination did not affect the relative probability of choosing between two existing alternatives. The result must at any rate be viewed with considerable caution to the extent that all coefficients are very imprecisely estimated.

To sum up, our results suggest that, even in the wake of the abolition of internal borders, there may not be a substantial reallocation of the

Table 6.5   Determinants of migrations, logit model

Dep. var.: M_i/M

	Restricted sample (1)		Full sample (2)	
	Coeff.	t-stat.	Coeff.	t-stat.
w_i	0.001	1.21	0.001	1.46
ED	0.85	1.30	0.84	1.30
$ED\ D_{80}$	−0.88	1.06	−0.87	1.06
Pseudo-R^2	0.10		0.10	

Notes:
M total migrations.
Other symbols see table 6.4.

existing stock of non-EU migrants. Yet, this does not imply that non-EU workers would not react to changing conditions across EU countries. There are in fact good reasons to believe that non-EU migrants may have a much higher labour mobility and may therefore have a greater propensity to relocate, if economic conditions so require. Presumably, non-EU residents will typically have weaker cultural and linguistic links with their place of residence and, as a result, be less reluctant to move. There is indeed some evidence for the US (Da Vanzo, 1983), but also for Sweden (Lundborg, 1992) that immigrants have a higher mobility than natives. The presence of a relatively large stock of more mobile workers should be welcome to the extent that it would allow European regions to adjust more easily to idiosyncratic shocks.

5   The rise of new sending countries

The results in sections 3 and 4 indicate that, following fuller EU integration and/or expansion to new members, larger intra-EU migrations, either because of a resumption of labour flows from Southern European residents or because of a reallocation of non-EU workers across Europe, should not be a cause of concern.

There is however an increasing fear, particularly in Northern Europe, that migrations pressures may rise from the new sending countries of Eastern Europe, following the political and economic upheaval there. Eastern European countries have switched from a condition of full employment to a situation of large and rising unemployment. Income differentials with Eastern Europe are enormous, substantially larger than those found for Southern Europe. Consider table 6.6. We find that, in

Table 6.6   Income differentials, 1990, relative to West Germany

	per capita GDP[1]	Hourly wages[2]
Germany	100	100
Hungary	43.9	9.9
Poland	32.4	5.7
Portugal	42.2	14.4[3]
Turkey	28.6	10.5

Notes:
[1] Summers and Heston (1991) data.
[2] Own calculations from ILO, *Yearbook of Labour Statistics*, and IMF, *International Financial Statistics*.
[3] Comparisons refer to 1988.

1990, wages in Poland and Hungary were only a fraction of those in West Germany. The differentials drop considerably if we focus on (PPP-corrected) *per capita* income data. Overall, it seems likely that migrations should rise, and, as argued for instance by Wyplosz (1993), the true paradox is why migrations from Eastern Europe remain so low.

Lack of adequate data precludes an econometric analysis of these issues. In what follows, we wish to stress one crucial difference between Eastern Europe and other poor countries, namely the fact that in the former group of countries there is a widespread expectation that, after years of slow growth because of the inefficiencies associated with the socialist regimes, economic conditions should definitely improve, at least in the medium run, and the East should fully recover her economic standing in the developed world. The presence of a relatively highly skilled workforce in the East is often cited as an indication of the growth potential in this area. Obviously, the anticipation of higher income in the future should not be enough to stem migrations, to the extent that Eastern European residents could still be willing to migrate to take advantage of more favourable conditions in the West, keeping open the option of returning to the East if conditions there improve. The conclusion, however, changes somewhat radically if we allow for the existence of migration costs.

To illustrate the gist of the argument, suppose that (risk-neutral) potential migrants in the East earn the wage w_e.[6] The wage in the West is w_w, with $w_w > w_e$. It is also assumed that migrations entail a fixed cost (say, α), but this is not sufficient to discourage migrations. Finally, we assume that conditions in the East may improve (substantially) with probability π. Let ρ be the discount rate. The asset value of being abroad is $U_w = w_w/\rho$, i.e. the present discounted value of the wage in the West. The analogous condition for those who stay in the East is

$\rho U_e = w_e + \pi(U^s - U_e)$, where U^s denotes the asset value of being in the East if things take a turn for the better there. Migration will occur if $U_w > U_e + \alpha$.

We have not considered so far the possibility that migrants may return to the East, if things improve there. Suppose therefore that $U_w < U^s - \epsilon$, where ϵ denotes a remigration cost: previous migrants will therefore find it optimal to return to the East if the favourable scenario materialises. The value of being in the West is now equal to:

$$\rho U_w = w_w + \pi(U^s - U_w - \epsilon). \tag{5}$$

Again, migration will occur if $U_w > U_e \alpha$. This implies:

$$w_w - w_e = (\rho + \pi)\alpha + \pi\epsilon. \tag{6}$$

(6) can account for the low migration rate from the East.[7] Consider the case where the probability of a successful transition in the East is quite high, namely $\rho + \pi$ is close to one. Suppose also that α, the initial migration cost, is worth three times the initial wage in the East.[8] Then, even if ϵ is equal to zero, an East–West wage differential of 300 per cent would not be sufficient to trigger migration from the East. We saw earlier how actual income differentials between, say, West Germany on the one hand and Poland and Hungary on the other are respectively 208 and 128 per cent. These are approximate figures, but they should provide a reliable order of magnitude. Admittedly, however, wage differentials are significantly larger.[9] From table 6.6, we see that the wage differentials of Poland and Hungary with respect to West Germany rise respectively to 901 and to 1650 per cent! We would need then very large moving costs to account for the fact that migrations have remained so low. Still, it is clear that migration costs can go a long way in explaining the low migration rate from Eastern Europe.

6   Conclusions

The completion of the internal market and the abolition of border controls within the EU should not lead to any substantial increase in migratory flows of EU citizens. This result is consistent with the common finding of a fairly low labour mobility in Europe (Eichengreen, 1992; Attanasio and Padoa Schioppa, 1991). What we show in this chapter is that the relative immobility of labour in Europe extends also to relatively poorer areas in Southern Europe which used in the past to be major sources of migratory flows toward Northern markets.

For non-EU nationals the issues are more complex. We have offered some evidence supporting the claim that there should not be a significant reallocation of non-EU workers, following the abolition of internal border controls in the EU. We have also stressed that this does not mean that non-EU workers will not relocate, if, say, economic conditions change within the EU because of idiosyncratic country shocks. But the mere existence of a sufficiently large stock of relatively mobile workers in the Union should be seen favourably, as it would facilitate the process of adjusting to regional shocks. We have also argued that high migration costs may to a large extent account for the relatively low migration rate from the East. However, a shift toward a more pessimistic assessment of future prospects in the East could lead to a sudden surge in the propensity to migrate.

What would happen in the wake of an EU enlargement to include EFTA countries? Our results do not provide an unambiguous answer to this question, unless we are willing to believe that what happens in the more developed part of the EU holds for EFTA as well. In such a case, we should conjecture that the fall in the propensity to migrate from Southern to Northern Europe holds also for potential migration toward EFTA. Similarly, EFTA countries should not be exceedingly concerned by the possible relocation across the EU of existing migrants. What happens in the East, however, is a highly conjectural question. We can only say that wage differentials are sufficiently large to induce large migration flows. If conditions in the East do not improve in the medium run, migrations will probably take place on a massive scale.

Finally, the presence of widely different regulations across EU and EFTA countries could provide potential migrants with an incentive to relocate simply to take advantage of the more favourable regulatory set-up. This consideration highlights the need for EU countries to harmonise both their admission and labour market conditions policy *vis-à-vis* non-EU citizens. As noticed earlier, progress on this front has been disappointingly slow, admittedly also because of the difficulty of finding a common approach to sensitive issues such as asylum and labour market policies. More generally, there are grounds for suspecting that a fully coordinated migration policy may be difficult to achieve to the extent that in a unified market individual countries may have an incentive to admit an excessive number of migrants. Indeed, while the benefits of admission, namely the higher probability that admitted migrants would be sufficient to meet the (uncertain) requirement of the domestic economy, would be fully captured by the country, its costs (the increase in unemployment, the rise in social tensions) would fall also on its neighbours.

NOTES

I am very grateful to Claudio Zanghi for superb research assistance. I would also like to thank Jaakko Kiander and Alessandra Venturini for useful comments and discussions. The responsibility for any remaining errors is my own.

1 '[T]he activities of the Community shall include ... (c) the abolition, as between Member States, of obstacles to freedom of movement for persons, services and capital' (Article 3, Treaty of Rome).

2 At the time of writing (June 1994) the implementation of the Schengen Agreement has been further postponed.

3 For other Southern European countries, however, the income differential with Turkey and Morocco does not exhibit any clear trend.

4 Notice that there were virtually no migrants from Morocco to Italy before the 1980s. It is not possible, as a result, to check whether the coefficient on employment growth for Italy changed significantly during that decade. Similarly, data for Belgium are available only from 1977. We cannot therefore test for a downward shift in the equation after 1974.

5 One often-cited limitation of the multinomial logit model is the so-called assumption of independence of irrelevant alternatives. Roughly, this means that in this model the probability of choosing between two alternatives does not depend on the other (irrelevant) alternatives. Hausman and McFadden (1984) have devised a test to assess whether this assumption is rejected by a given data set.

6 The argument has also been developed, in the context of a continuous time model, by Burda (1993). Our model draws shamelessly on Rodrik's (1991) analysis of the impact of uncertainty and partial irreversibility on investment.

7 Notice that U^s does not appear in the migration condition equation. This is because a larger value of U^s has a positive impact on the value of being both in the East and in the West, with the two effects cancelling out. However, a higher probability of a successful transition would discourage migration. The probability π would not matter only if migration costs were zero.

8 For the migration costs to be large enough, they must be defined broadly to include both monetary and non-monetary costs of moving abroad.

9 Data on *per capita* income refer to 1988 and may therefore be somewhat less than fully reliable. Data on wages refer to 1990.

REFERENCES

Attanasio, O. and F. Padoa Schioppa, 1991. 'Regional inequalities, migration and mismatch in Italy, 1960–86', in F. Padoa Schioppa (ed.), *Mismatch and Labour Mobility*, Cambridge: Cambridge University Press

Burda, M., 1993. 'The determinants of East–West German migration: some first results', *European Economic Review*, 37, 452–61

Coleman, D., 1991. 'Demographic projections: is there a need for immigration?', Turin: Giovanni Agnelli Foundation

Commissione della Comunità Europa, 1989. *Rapporto 1989 sull'occupazione in Europa*, Brussels: Direzione per gli Affari Sociali e l'Occupazione

Da Vanzo, J., 1983. 'Repeat migration in the United States: who moves back and who moves on?', *Review of Economics and Statistics*, **65**, 552–9

Eichengreen, B., 1992, 'Should the Maastricht Treaty be saved?', *Princeton Studies in International Finance*, **74**

Faini, R., 1989. 'Regional development and economic integration', in J. Silva Lopes and L. Beleza (eds.), *Portugal and the Internal Market of the EEC*, Lisbon: Banco de Portugal

Faini, R. and A. Venturini, 1994. 'Migration and growth: the experience of Southern Europe'. CEPR, *Discussion Paper*, **964**, London: CEPR

Hamilton, B. and J. Whalley, 1984. 'Efficiency and distributional implications of global restrictions on labour mobility: calculations and policy implications', *Journal of Development Economics*, **14**, 61–75

Hausman, J. and D. McFadden, 1984. 'Specification tests for the multinomial logit model', *Econometrica*, **52**, 1219–40

Layard, R., O. Blanchard, R. Dornbusch and P. Krugman, 1992. *East–West Migration: The Alternatives*, Cambridge, MA: MIT Press

Lundborg, P., 1992. 'Information quality and remigration in the Swedish labour market', Stockholm: Industrial Institute for Economic and Social Research, mimeo

Molle, W., 1990. *The Economics of European Integration*, Aldershot: Dartmouth

Rodrik, D., 1991. 'Policy uncertainty and private investment in developing countries', *Journal of Development Economics*, **36**, 229–42

Salt, J., 1991. 'Current and future international migration trends affecting Europe', 4th conference of European Ministers responsible for migration affairs, Luxembourg

Summers, R. and P. Heston, 1991. 'The Penn World Table (Mark 5): an expanded set of international comparisons: 1950–1988', *Quarterly Journal of Economics*, **106**, 327–68

Wyplosz, C., 1993. 'Migration from the East: the role of reform and capital mobility'. Paris: INSEAD, mimeo

Discussion

PENTTI VARTIA

Ricardo Faini's chapter 6 gives an excellent description of the present institutions and problems related to labour mobility within the present EU area. He points out that while obstacles to movement of EU citizens will be abolished, governments will want to retain power to determine the treatment of non-EU nationals. However, for the internal labour market to function properly, there is a need to have a common migration policy.

Chapter 6 addresses two main question. (1) Does abolition of intra-EU border controls lead to increased migration within EU countries? (2) Can we expect a substantial reallocation of the existing stocks of non-EU migrants that are already inside the EU area? Faini's answer to both questions is 'no'. However, the chapter gives some evidence that migration patterns from outside may change.

Section 3 of the chapter discusses the reasons for the drop in labour flows from Southern to Northern Europe in the 1980s. The traditional explanation for the decline in internal migration flows has been declining demand in the North, but the chapter points out that the drop may also be due to a decline in the propensity to migrate. This is an important conclusion for the future: if the propensity to move falls with rising incomes, then we can expect less migration from the South, both from EU and non-EU areas.

Faini also presents a model that explains the effect of rising incomes on the propensity to migrate. If I understand this correctly, wage levels in the model are in absolute terms. Thus in (2) we deal with the absolute, not relative wage differential. In this case, the conclusion of the model seems natural: if the income level is increased, the same absolute wage difference does not give as much incentive to move as earlier. Could the same conclusion be derived for any given relative wage differential?

In section 4 Faini asks why Southern Europe has become so attractive to non-EU migrants. To answer the question, he looks at empirical data for Morocco and two types of models: a regression model with wage differentials and employment growth as explanatory variables and a multinomial discrete choice model. He mentions geographical proximity as one reason for migration to Italy from Northern Africa, even if this variable is not included in the regression analysis. Distance is related to many costs: transport, psychological 'costs' and uncertainties related to living in a far-away country. Could the distance factor be integrated into the model? The country dummies point to a direction in which one could do this, by simply adding the distance.

According to some Nordic studies joining the EU would not have large effects on migration flows between these countries and the EC-12 (Alho *et al.*, 1992; Lundborg, 1990; ETLA *et al.* 1990). In the Nordic countries there is a feeling that immigration flows between the entrants and the old EC countries will be small. This view holds also for the non-EU migrants in the EC-12: existing stocks of non-EU migrants are not expected to remigrate to Nordic entrant countries. There is also the periphery problem. If firms move to the centre this will, of course, strengthen the outflow of labour from the periphery. On the other hand, there may also be some movement inwards of low-paid workers, as it is particularly their wages that would be increased in the Nordic countries. On the other hand, part of the educated labour force may flee high taxes and egalitarian wage polities. Net mobility may thus be unchanged, but there still may be flows in both directions. These studies thus emphasise the point that average wage levels and average unemployment rates do not give a full picture of the potential to migrate.

A major problem related to migration to the EU from outside the present member countries is, of course, potential labour flows from the Central and Eastern European countries (CEECs). Even if the EU immigration restrictions are tightened, emigration from Eastern Europe will increase, and this will be an important issue for many of the new entrants in years to come. The policy choice here seems to be that we have to accept either free trade or migration from the East.

Potential migration from ex-socialist countries is an important problem for the new entrants. For example, when Finland joins the EU, her long border with Russia will be also an EU–Russian border. From the Finnish angle harmonisation of obstacles to migration from non-EU countries is important, but I have the feeling that the Finnish government wants to have some control on the inward labour flows from Russia. Finland is closer than others, for example, to the densely populated St Petersburg region. Just as closeness is an important reason for a Southern African migrant to choose Italy, so is it a reason for Russians to choose the Nordic countries, particularly Finland. This aspect is particularly important for temporary workers. So far, official unemployment rates in Russia have been astonishingly low, given the large drop in output. Unemployment, however, is rising and this, together with large income differences, will increase the pressure to migrate.

REFERENCES

Alho, K., M. Kotilainen and M. Widgrén, 1992. 'Finland in the European Community – an assessment of the economic impacts' (in Finnish with English summary), The Research Institute of the Finnish Economy, ETLA, Series B, **81**, Helsinki

ETLA, IFF, IUI and IÖI, 1990. 'Growth and integration in a Nordic perspective', joint publication of the four Nordic Research Institutes, Helsinki

Lundborg, P., 1990. 'Konsekvenser av fri arbetsktaftsrörlighet mellan Sverige och EG' (Consequences of Free Labour Mobility Between Sweden and the EC), in *Svensk ekonomi och Europaintegrationen* (The Swedish Economy in European Integration), Stockholm

7 Trade effects of regional aid

PHILIPPE MARTIN and
CAROL ANN ROGERS

1 Introduction

One of the most serious points of disagreement during the negotiations over the Maastricht Treaty involved the regional aid policies, with their implied financial transfers. The poorest countries of the EU (Spain, Greece, Ireland and Portugal), led by Spain, threatened not to ratify the Treaty if the regional aid budget to finance public infrastructure investment in the EU's poorest regions was insufficient. The Commission sided with these countries, arguing that economic disparities in Europe would endanger the social and political cohesion of the EU and therefore the objective of trade and monetary integration set in the Single European Act (1986) and in the Maastricht negotiations.

This issue finds its origins in the admission of Greece (1981), Spain and Portugal (1986) to the then EC. Although the European Regional Development Fund (ERDF) was set up in 1975, the entry of these three countries increased the disparity between poor and rich regions in the EC and was at the origin, starting in 1989, of financial transfers of unprecedented scale. Trade integration was acceptable to these new entrants, who have lower *per capita* GDP levels than the EU average, only under the condition that it would not cause divergence of incomes from the EU level. These countries were concerned that the positive effects of European trade integration, such as the growth effects identified by Baldwin (1989), might not be shared equally by all European regions.

This concern is echoed in the new literature on economic geography (Krugman, 1989, 1991). In this literature, a core–periphery pattern emerges because of the interaction of economies of scale and transport costs, with manufacturing becoming concentrated in a few regions. When applied to the EU (see Krugman and Venables, 1990), these models suggest that trade integration could cause manufacturing to concentrate in northern Europe. Hence, European trade integration may lead to divergence in income levels.

In a related context, Bertola (1992) shows that if increasing returns can be exploited along geographical dimensions, then the geographical concentration of industry will increase. As a result, increased geographical inequality accompanies the gains from increased growth.

Some evidence has indeed raised concerns that *per capita* GDP in the poorest EU regions diverged from the EC average during the 1980s. For example, the mean income of lagging regions (regions with GDP/head less than 75 per cent of the EC average) fell from 67.9 per cent of the EC average in 1983 to 66.9 per cent in 1988. Neven and Gouyette (1994), using alternative methodologies to measure convergence, find that northern European regions converged strongly after 1985, at a time when southern European regions stagnated.

The divergence between a northern European core and a southern European periphery could be accentuated with the admission of Austria, Sweden and Finland. These countries should belong to the core because of their *per capita* income levels. They also move the core to the northeast because of their geographical position. Their entry could accentuate the disparity between rich and poor countries in the EU, the peripherality of southern European regions and the core–periphery pattern of European integration. The admission of new rich members of northern Europe comes after the admission of relatively poor members of southern Europe in the 1980s. Hence, enlargement has naturally contributed to an increased diversity and disparity of income between members. In the new geography models, regional economic diversity is precisely one of the elements that gives rise to industrial concentration in regions with an initial advantage. The three newest members would also all be net contributors to the regional aid policies budget. The enlargement of the EU makes it all the more important to analyse policies that are supposed to counteract possible divergence effects of trade integration between heterogeneous countries.

This chapter examines, both theoretically and empirically, the impact of EU regional aid policies on trade, industry location and welfare. In section 2, we review the evidence on the level of disparities in public infrastructure (transport, telecommunication, energy and education). We then describe the objectives and instruments of EU regional aid policies, which mainly consist of financing public infrastructure in the poorest regions: Portugal, the main recipient, receives transfers amounting to 3.5 per cent of its GNP. EU funding is strongly biased towards transport relative to the other types of infrastructure.[1]

In section 3, we set up a model similar to Helpman and Krugman (1985), in which trade is based on increasing returns and where we model infrastructure as facilitating trade both inside and between countries. In the absence of trade barriers, firms locate in countries rich in infrastructure. This is because a better infrastructure decreases the price of goods produced in the country and increases the demand for these goods. To take advantage of returns to scale, firms locate in the better infrastructure country. The Structural Funds policy, by decreasing the disparity in the levels of public infrastructure, implies a relocation of firms from rich to poor countries. If trade integration leads to divergence, in the sense of relocation from South to North, regional aid policies could be an instrument to reverse this undesirable effect. However, we show that the effectiveness of such policies decreases as the overall level of infrastructure improves in the EU. Relocation of firms has welfare implications, because the price index rises when production is relocated to a foreign country. In the context of this model, the regional aid policies can be interpreted as the price paid by the richest countries for the benefits of full trade integration.

In section 4, we test some of the implications of the model. We find that intra-industry trade, industry location and *per capita* GDP in Europe are empirically well correlated with the levels of education and telecommunication infrastructures. Transport infrastructure, on which EU regional aid programmes concentrate, is poorly correlated with either industry location or *per capita* GDP. Finally, we discuss the policy implications of these findings. Section 5 concludes the paper.

2   Infrastructure disparities in Europe and regional aid policies

In this section, we first review the evidence on the regional disparities in infrastructure among European regions. We then briefly describe the objectives and instruments of EU regional aid policies.

2.1   Infrastructure disparities in Europe

To assess the level of disparities in public infrastructure, we use data from two studies conducted for the Commission (Biehl, 1986; Biehl and Ungar, 1991), which calculate indicators of infrastructure endowment for the 168 level II regions of the EU. These indicators measure infrastructure in terms of its physical characteristics rather than in terms of its money value. In the case of roads, for example, the indicator measures the total surface of the regional road system. In addition, all indicators are expressed in relation to regional area (for roads, waterways and oil pipelines, for example) and/or to regional population (for schools, for example). They are thus adjusted for congestion. However, because of their measurement in purely physical terms, they are not adjusted for

Table 7.1   Relative infrastructure levels in EU countries, 1979–80 and 1985–6

	Transport-ation (1)	Telecomm-unication (2)	Energy (3)	Education (4)	Aggregate 1985–6 (5)	Aggregate 1979–80 (6)
Germany	143.0	108.1	88.2	134.7	116.4	116.7
France	109.7	128.1	179.2	90.7	122.9	124.1
Italy	90.8	73.7	83.7	106.6	85.4	81.7
Netherlands	259.2	128.3	180.1	73.7	144.9	134.9
Belgium	302.3	127.9	262.8	100.6	178.8	132.0
Luxembourg	266.3	188.6	334.5	92.9	198.7	217.4
UK	135.4	107.6	111.8	74.0	104.8	102.2
Denmark	193.5	149.0	62.0	117.1	123.8	128.8
Ireland	104.4	63.4	41.8	73.4	67.1	71.1
Spain	77.9	70.3	49.1	113.6	74.3	77.7
Greece	63.0	92.9	32.6	51.6	56.0	54.5
Portugal	51.3	34.1	37.2	34.6	38.7	40.0
EC	100	100	100	100	100	100

Source: Biehl (1986); Biehl and Ungar (1991).

quality. In table 7.1 indicators for transportation (with roads, railways, waterways, airports and harbours), telecommunication (telephones and telexes), energy (electricity networks, power stations, oil pipelines, oil refineries and gas network) and education (university education and vocational training facilities), together with an aggregate indicator,[2] are expressed for each country as a percentage of the EU average level. Hence, they give the relative position *vis-à-vis* the EU. The disaggregated data, for all categories of infrastructure, are available for 1985–6. For 1979–80, only the aggregate indicator of infrastructure was available. Note that the 1985–6 data set already contains data for the eastern part of Germany.

Table 7.1 indicates that the poor countries of the EU (Spain, Greece, Ireland and Portugal) have, not surprisingly, the lowest indices of public infrastructure. Italy also appears underequipped relative to the rest of the EU, except for education. The situation of the poor countries is not homogeneous. For example, Spain has an infrastructure in education which is above the EU average and Ireland appears to have a better infrastructure in transportation than the EU average. Among the rich countries, some are relatively poorly endowed in certain types of infrastructure. This is the case for energy in Germany and Denmark, and for education in France, the UK and the Netherlands. It is clear that the accession of Greece in 1981 and Spain and Portugal in 1986 dramatically

Table 7.2 Relative improvement or deterioration with respect to EC aggregate index of infrastructure, 1979–80 and 1985–6, per cent

Italy	+4.5
Ireland	−5.6
Greece	+2.7
Spain	−4.4
Portugal	−3.2

Note: The rates given in table 7.2 are: $(Ij_{1985-6} - Ij_{1979-80})/Ij_{1979-80}$, where Ij indicates the level of infrastructure of country j in per cent of the EC level.

widened the infrastructure disparity between the Community's richest and poorest regions, and these numbers indicate the long way the EU has to go in order to achieve real convergence in infrastructure.

Table 7.2 shows the rate of convergence of the infrastructure level of Italy, Ireland, Greece, Spain and Portugal relative to the EU indicator between 1979–80 and 1985–6. Italy, which has a lower infrastructure index than the EU average, has converged toward the EU average. With the exception of Greece, the relative position of the four remaining (poorest) countries has not improved between 1979–80 and 1985–6: Ireland, Portugal and Spain have diverged from EU levels of infrastructure. This divergence is especially troublesome for Portugal, which by Biehl's calculations is by far the most poorly endowed country. This divergence does not necessarily imply that the Community structural policies have failed: the 1985–6 data does not take into account the impact of the 1989–93 plan for regional aid, which was the most ambitious in terms of the sums involved (see below). These numbers, however, confirm that effective convergence (and not only improvement) of infrastructure levels in the poorest regions of the Community will require very important transfers.

In table 7.3, we compare the level of regional disparities inside the large countries such as Germany,[3] France, the UK, Italy and Spain on the one hand and between EU countries on the other. We find that regional disparities are larger or smaller than disparities at the country level, depending on the category of infrastructure. For energy, regional disparities are higher at the country than at the EU level (except for France). For telecommunication, except in the case of Germany, regional disparities are lower at the country than at the EU level. It should be

Table 7.3 Ratio of poorest endowed region infrastructure to country average, 1986

	Transportation (1)	Telecommunication (2)	Energy (3)	Education (4)
Germany	35.8	15.8	13.9	55.3
France	63	65.8	35.2	57.2
UK	75.1	66.9	24.6	67.7
Italy	25.0	40.0	15.6	48.5
Spain	19.6	41.5	29.2	45.9
EC	51.3 (Portugal)	34.1 (Portugal)	32.6 (Portugal)	34.6 (Portugal)

Note: In the EC row, the poorest EC country is indicated in parenthesis.
Source: Biehl (1986) and own calculations.

noted that the gap between the eastern and the western regions of Germany is the highest, by far, for telecommunication infrastructure; this exception would certainly not stand if the eastern part of Germany was excluded. In education, the level of regional disparities in all large EU countries is significantly lower than at the EU level. No clear pattern emerges for transportation.

2.2   The objectives and instruments of EU regional aid policies

In 1988, with the implementation of the Single European Act and partly in response to the admission of Spain and Portugal, a reform of the EC's structural interventions policy was decided.[4] This reform was implemented at the beginning of 1989, and its main element was to double the resources of the Structural Funds. In 1990, 25 per cent of the EC budget went to the Structural Funds; they are now the second largest expenditure item after price supports under the CAP, with 60 per cent of the Community budget. The total amount of funds allocated to regional aid between 1989 and 1993 was 63 billion ECU. The new policy identified five priority objectives. The geographical area, population, and volume of Community assistance allocated to each are listed in table 7.4.

A further aim of the 1988 reform was to concentrate the efforts of the Structural Funds policy on regions whose development is lagging behind the rest of the EU, the Objective 1 regions. For the 1989–93 plan, the Objective 1 regions are: the whole country for Greece, Ireland and Portugal; 10 regions for Spain; 8 regions for Italy; the overseas departments and Corsica for France and Northern Ireland for the UK. For the 1994–9 period, former East Germany, 1 region in Belgium, 2 in

Table 7.4   Basic data on the five priority objectives

Objective	Countries or regions concerned (1989–93)	Proportion of population concerned (1989) (%)	Amount of assistance from the Structural Funds (1989–93):	
			1989 prices (billion ECU)	%
Objective 1[a] Regions whose development is lagging behind	7 Member States (2)	21.5	38.3	60.5
Objective 2 Conversion of areas affected industrial decline	60 regions	16.5	7.2	11.4
Objectives 3, 4 Combating long-term unemployment and occupational integration of young people[c]	9 Member States (excluding Objective 1)		7.5 (excluding Objective 1)	11.8
Objective 5a Adjustment of agricultural structures [b]	9 Member States (excluding Objective 1)		3.4 (excluding Objective 1)	5.4
Objective 5b Development of rural areas	50 regions	5	2.7	4.4
Transitional measures and Community initiatives[c]			1.1	1.7
Assistance to former East Germany	The 5 new Länder		3.0	4.7

Notes: [a] Objective 1 covers all forms of assistance for eligible regions, including those under Objectives 3, 4 and 5a
[b] Greece, Ireland and Portugal: whole country; Spain: 10 regions; Italy: 8 regions; France: overseas departments and Corsica; UK: Northern Ireland.
[c] Objectives, 3, 4 and 5a and transitional measures do not relate to specific sections of the population.
Source: Commission of the European Communities (1992a).

the UK and 1 in Spain will be added to Objective 1 regions. Table 7.4 indicates that more than 60 per cent of Structural Funds go to these regions. The Objective 1 regions together will get 96.3 billion ECU over the next six years. 70 billion ECU of this will go to Portugal, Greece, Ireland and Spain. These countries will get an additional 15.5 billion ECU through the Cohesion Fund (created as a result of the Maastricht Agreement) for the four poorest countries. Projects to be considered for Cohesion Fund financing must concern transport infrastructure in the area of trans-European networks or environmental infrastructure.

Table   7.5   Relative   macroeconomic
importance of the Structural Funds, 1989–93

	% of region GDP
Italy (Mezzogiorno)	0.8
Ireland (entire country)	2.3
Greece (entire country)	2.9
Spain (70% of the country)	1.2
Portugal (entire country)	3.5

Source: Commission of the European Communities (1992a).

The numbers given in table 7.5 indicate the magnitude of the EU regional aid effort. These numbers take into account only the EU contribution. As the EU contribution must in most cases be matched by an equal amount of national contribution, the total contribution, which is called the Community Support Framework (CSF), is almost double the Structural Funds. Portugal is the most important recipient of regional aid, with aid totalling 3.5 per cent of its GDP.

Table 7.6 lists regional aid contributions by category of infrastructure. Except for Ireland, because the nature of regional programmes is not specified, it is difficult to assess the respective importance given by regional policies to each type of infrastructure. However, other EU documents indicate that within regional programmes, most of the Community funding goes to transport infrastructure. The conclusion from these numbers is that the two main categories of infrastructure financed by EU transfers are transport infrastructure and infrastructure linked to human resources. It should be noted that what is called here infrastructure in 'Human Resources' is not homogeneous, and is much larger than education infrastructure as defined in Biehl's (1986) data set. For example, this infrastructure category, in EU vocabulary, includes measures to combat long-term unemployment, training measures for young unemployed persons, employment incentives, in addition to education facilities *per se*. Hence, if we considered education infrastructure only in terms of facilities, the EU transfers on transport infrastructure would certainly look much more important than the EU transfers on education infrastructure. Finally, the new Cohesion Fund will be restricted to transport infrastructure, and there is thus a very strong concentration of EU funding on financing this.

Table 7.6   EC contribution, by category, 1989–93

Categories	Greece	Spain	Ireland	Portugal
Transport	10.4	14.9	21.5	
Telecommunication	6.9	1.9	0.7	41.1[*]
Energy	7.1	0.9	0.4	
Human resources	20.8	22.7	19.7	31.7
Industry	2.5	4.5	30.7	5.7
Agriculture	5.8	8.7	17.9	1.7
Regional programmes	45.5	39.4	**	15.6
Other (undefined)	0.9	6.9	9.0	4.1
Total	100	100	100	100

Source: Commission of the European Communities (1992b) and own calculations.
Notes: * For Portugal, data by infrastructure type are not available.
** Included in other categories.

3   Infrastructure, location and welfare in a model with increasing returns

We now present a simple model which focuses on the location impact of trade integration when countries differ in infrastructure levels. The model is a variant of Helpman and Krugman (1985). There are two countries, which we will call Germany and Portugal.[5] We describe the behaviour of German households and firms below. The countries are symmetric, so equations describing the behaviour of Portuguese households and firms can be derived analogously. Each German consumer chooses from a menu of goods to maximise the following utility function:

$$U = \alpha \ln D + Y. \tag{1}$$

D is a composite good made up of all of the differentiated products:

$$D = \left[\sum_{i=0}^{N} D_i^{1-1/\sigma} \right]^{1/(1-1/\sigma)}, \sigma > 1. \tag{2}$$

N is the total number of differentiated goods produced at home and abroad and σ is the elasticity of substitution among the products.

A typical German consumer chooses D_i and Y to maximise (1) subject to the budget constraint:

$$\sum_{i-1}^{n} \tau p_i D_i + \sum_{j=n+1}^{N} \tau \tau^* p_j^* D_j + p_y Y = I. \tag{3}$$

An asterisk refers to Portugal. Hence, $N = n + n^*$, where n^* is the number of differentiated goods produced in Portugal. I is German income.

Following Helpman and Krugman (1985), we have allowed in (3) for 'transport' costs in Samuelson's iceberg form, so that some of each of the differentiated goods melts away in transit: only $1/\tau$ of purchases of any German good is available for consumption, while only $1/\tau\tau^*$ of any Portuguese good is consumable.[6] We interpret these costs as directly related to the quality of countries' infrastructures. These costs are more general than simply transport costs: a reduction in τ, for example, is an improvement in Germany's infrastructure. With this interpretation, we impose these costs on both home and foreign purchases. A purchase of a good from Portugal incurs a cost τ^* in getting out of the country, and τ in reaching its destination in Germany.[7] Hence, the infrastructure costs are different from transport costs in the Krugman models, in that they affect not only trade between countries but also trade inside countries.

These costs raise the consumer price of a good i that is produced and consumed in Germany to $p_i\tau$, and raise the price of a good j that is produced in Portugal and imported in Germany to $p_j\tau\tau^*$.

At an interior solution, consumer demands are:

$$D_i = \frac{p_i^{-\sigma}\alpha p_y}{\tau(np_i^{1-\sigma} + n^*\rho^* p_j^{*1-\sigma})} \tag{4a}$$

$$D_j = \frac{(\tau^* p_j)^{-\sigma}\alpha p_y}{\tau(np_i^{1-\sigma} + n^*\rho^* p_j^{*1-\sigma})} \tag{4b}$$

$$Y = \frac{I}{p_y} - \alpha \quad (\alpha < I/p_y) \tag{4c}$$

where $\rho^* = \tau^{*1-\sigma}$. An individual consumer supplies one unit of labour inelastically. So $I = w$. The index D equals:

$$D = \alpha p_y \left[\rho \left(np_i^{1-\sigma} + n^*\rho^* p_j^{*1-\sigma} \right) \right]^{1/(\sigma-1)} \tag{5}$$

where $\rho = \tau^{1-\sigma}$. So the indirect utility function for the representative German household is:

$$V = \alpha \, ln \left\{ \alpha p_y \left[\rho \left(np_i^{1-\sigma} + n^* \rho^* p_j^{*1-\sigma} \right) \right]^{1/(\sigma-1)} \right\} + \frac{I}{p_y} - \alpha. \qquad (6)$$

The differentiated products are all produced with identical technologies that use only labour:

$$l_i = \gamma + \beta x_i \qquad (7)$$

where l_i is labour employed in the production of the ith variety and x_i is the quantity produced. There is a fixed cost γ which guarantees that each firm will specialise in the production of only one variety. Profits for a firm located in Germany are:

$$\pi_i = p_i x_i (p_i) - w [\gamma + \beta x_i (p_i)]. \qquad (8)$$

As in Helpman and Krugman, the demand elasticity perceived by the typical firm $= \sigma$. The choice of p_i that maximises profits therefore obeys the standard monopolist's rule:

$$p_i = \frac{w \beta \sigma}{\sigma - 1}. \qquad (9)$$

Without loss of generality, we can choose $\beta = (\sigma - 1)/\sigma$, so that $p_i = w$ for all i.

Good Y is produced under constant returns to scale. It takes a units of labour to produce one unit of Y. We assume that both countries will produce good Y in equilibrium. When x_y of this good are produced, profits in the constant returns sector are:

$$\pi_y = p_y x_y - w a x_y. \qquad (10)$$

Profits are maximised when $p_y = wa$. Suppose good Y is the numeraire, so $p_y = 1$. This ties down the wage rate, $w = 1/a$. Without loss of generality, we also choose $a = 1$, so that $w = 1$.

3.1 The equilibrium with free trade

Four equilibrium conditions determine x, x^*, n and n^*. Two further conditions guarantee labour market equilibrium and close the model. Demand for the outside good depends on income. $I = w = 1$, so individual demand for $Y = 1 - \alpha$, while aggregate demand $= L(1 - \alpha)$. Similarly,

$Y^* = L^*(1 - \alpha)$. Demands must equal supplies for the differentiated goods at home and abroad. Since firms in a given location are identical, (11a) and (11b) characterise equilibrium in the market for differentiated goods:

$$x = \frac{\alpha L}{n + n^* \rho^*} + \frac{\rho \alpha L^*}{n\rho + n^*} \tag{11a}$$

$$x^* = \frac{\alpha \rho^* L}{n + n^* \rho^*} + \frac{\alpha L^*}{n\rho + n^*}. \tag{11b}$$

Next, entry on both markets is free, and in equilibrium each firm makes zero profits. This determines the scale of production:

$$x_i = x = x^* = \gamma \, \sigma. \tag{11c}$$

In addition, the two equations that determine labour market equilibrium are:

$$L = L_x + L_y \tag{11d}$$
$$L^* = L_x^* + L_y^* \tag{11e}$$

where L_x and L_y are, respectively, the amounts of labour used to produce the differentiated goods and the outside good.

(11a–c) can be solved for n and n^*. The numbers of firms in each country are:

$$n = \frac{\alpha}{x} \left[\frac{L}{1 - \rho} - \frac{\rho^* L^*}{1 - \rho^*} \right] \tag{12a}$$

$$n^* = \frac{\alpha}{x} \left[\frac{L^*}{1 - \rho^*} - \frac{\rho L}{1 - \rho} \right]. \tag{12b}$$

Note that the total number of firms, $n + n^*$, is fixed and does not depend on ρ and ρ^*, hence does not depend on the levels of infrastructure. Location of firms in this model depends on two factors. Firms will locate in countries with large populations and relatively better infrastructure. The market size effect is similar to the one described by Helpman and Krugman (1985) and Krugman (1991). Firms will also tend to locate in the best infrastructure country. This is because poor infrastructure raises the price of goods produced in this country, and therefore reduces the demand for them. Hence, to exploit increasing returns to scale, firms will relocate in countries with better infrastructure. The equilibrium location described by (12) is stable, because labour is immobile and no agglomeration force is set in motion when firms relocate.

For positive numbers of firms to be located in both countries after trade integration, both n and n^* must be positive. This requires:

$$\frac{\rho^*(1-\rho)}{1-\rho^*} < L/L^* < \frac{1-\rho}{\rho(1-\rho^*)}. \tag{13}$$

Hence, countries must not be too different in size and infrastructure levels for both of them to produce differentiated goods. Note that, when countries are of identical size, and ρ and ρ^* are both close to 1, even small differences between ρ and ρ^* will drive all firms to concentrate in the country with better infrastructure. Hence, an overall high level of infrastructure in the EU makes concentration more likely.

The structure of trade will also be affected by differentials in infrastructure. The country with better infrastructure will run a trade surplus in differentiated products.

3.2   Regional aid

An improvement in Portugal's infrastructure (an increase in ρ^* or a decrease in τ^*) will have two effects. The first is a purely technological one: the price of all Portuguese goods will go down. This will affect positively both German and Portuguese consumers. For German consumers, only Portuguese imports will be cheaper, as their price is $\tau\tau^*$. For Portuguese consumers, both German imports and Portuguese goods will be cheaper, as their respective prices are $\tau\tau^*$ and τ^*.

The second effect is that German firms will relocate to Portugal. This is because the relative price between Portuguese goods and German goods has decreased for German consumers, as it is $\tau\tau^*/\tau = \tau^*$. For Portuguese consumers, the relative price is unchanged at $\tau^*/\tau\tau^* = 1/\tau$. Hence, demand by German consumers for Portuguese goods will increase relative to German goods. This will drive firms to relocate to Portugal to take advantage of economies of scale. German consumers will now have to pay the Portuguese infrastructure cost on the goods produced in firms relocated in Portugal.

Portuguese consumers gain while German consumers lose. The effects of regional aid on welfare can be seen from inspection of the indirect utility levels of German and Portuguese households: substituting the equilibrium values of n and n^* from (12a) and (12b) into the indirect utility functions gives:

$$V = \alpha \ln\left[\alpha\left(\rho L \frac{\alpha}{x}\frac{1-\rho\rho^*}{1-\rho}\right)^{1/(\sigma-1)}\right] + 1 - \alpha \tag{14a}$$

$$V^* = \alpha \ln\left[\alpha\left(\rho^* L^* \frac{\alpha}{x}\frac{1-\rho\rho^*}{1-\rho^*}\right)^{1/(\sigma-1)}\right] + 1 - \alpha. \tag{14b}$$

An increase in ρ^*, for example, raises V^* and reduces V.

The structure of trade will also be changed, as Portugal will now export more differentiated goods. Its trade deficit in differentiated goods will decrease.

The regional policy will drive firms to relocate to Portugal. This is exactly the objective stated by the Commission for regional aid policies in the EU. Note, however, that the efficacy of such policy decreases as the overall level of infrastructure in the EU improves. This can be seen from (13), which says that as the overall level of infrastructure improves in the EU (ρ and ρ^* are high), concentration in the larger or the richer countries (in terms of infrastructure) is more likely. If the objective of regional aid policies is to counteract this effect by increasing the range of parameters (L, L^*, ρ and ρ^*) for which full concentration does not occur, it follows that the efficacy of such policies decreases as the overall infrastructure level improves.[8]

Why would Germany agree to a regional aid policy that shifts industry away from Germany and makes its own consumers worse off? One possible explanation may be that Portugal can always mimic the relocational effects of regional aid by unilaterally undertaking policies that restrict trade.

If Portugal imposes a trade barrier on German imports, the numbers of firms in each country are:

$$n = \frac{\alpha}{x}\left[\frac{L}{1-\rho\gamma^*} - \frac{\rho^* L^*}{1-\rho^*}\right] \tag{15a}$$

$$n^* = \frac{\alpha}{x}\left[\frac{L^*}{1-\rho^*} - \frac{\rho\gamma^* L}{1-\rho\gamma^*}\right] \tag{15b}$$

where $\gamma^* = (1 + \theta^*)$ and θ^* is the cost to the German exporter of the Portuguese trade barrier. Note that the trade barrier affects Portuguese welfare in a similar way to a worsening of German infrastructure, by keeping industries in Portugal. The Portuguese trade barrier does not affect the relative price between Portuguese and German goods in Germany. For Portuguese consumers, however, the relative price between Portuguese and German goods is $1/\tau(1 + \theta^*)$, which decreases with increases in the cost of the trade barrier. (16) shows that Portuguese social welfare improves with increases in θ^* (or decreases in γ^*)

$$V^* = \alpha \ln\left\{\alpha\left[\rho^* L^* \frac{\alpha}{x}\frac{1 - \rho\rho^*\gamma^*}{1 - \rho^*}\right]^{1/(\sigma-1)}\right\} + 1 = \alpha. \qquad (16)$$

Because of the relocation effect, German welfare decreases with θ^*:

$$V = \alpha \ln\left\{\alpha\left[\rho L \frac{\alpha}{x}\frac{1 - \rho\rho^*\gamma^*}{1 - \rho^*}\right]^{1/(\sigma-1)}\right\} + 1 = \alpha. \qquad (17)$$

Hence, the regional aid programme can be interpreted as the price to be paid by the richest countries for the benefits of full European economic integration.

In this analysis, we have only considered the welfare costs for Germany of regional aid related to relocation of firms. We have abstracted from the direct cost of financing such programmes. Levying a lump sum tax to pay for these programmes would not change in impact of regional aid programmes on relocation in our framework, as the income effect of such costs would not affect the consumption of the differentiated goods. Martin and Rogers (1994) consider the effects on demand for differentiated goods.

4   Intra-industry trade, location of increasing returns activities and public infrastructure

In this section, we show that the location of increasing returns activities in Europe is well correlated with the level of public infrastructure, as predicted by the model.

In the context of the Helpman–Krugman models, countries for which trade with the EU is largely composed of similar differentiated goods should be countries where increasing returns industries are important. The percentage of intra-industry trade may therefore be a good indicator of the location of increasing returns industries. Table 7.7 lists the percentages of intra-industry trade with the EU countries in the

Table 7.7 EC countries' intra-industry trade
with the EC, 1988–90, per cent

Germany	75
France	82
Italy	63
Netherlands	77
Belgium–Luxembourg	76
UK	77
Denmark	63
Ireland	59
Greece	29
Spain	73
Portugal	42

Source: CEPR (1992).

Community. The countries for which trade is dominated by intra-industry trade are the same countries that earlier were shown to have infrastructure stocks above the EU average.

Simple regressions of intra-industry trade on the various infrastructure endowment indices are given in table 7.8. All regressions were run in logs.[9] These regressions suggest that intra-industry trade is well correlated with infrastructure levels, particularly with education and energy. Education infrastructure has the most significant coefficient in the last regression, which includes all four types of infrastructure. However, the small number of observations makes these results only suggestive.

Another way to investigate how public infrastructure affects the location of increasing returns activities is to assume that the share of industry (in contrast to services and agriculture) in the total labour force is a good proxy for the location of increasing returns activities. Obviously, we face an aggregation problem as not all industries exhibit increasing returns and not all agriculture and services exhibit constant or decreasing returns.

We use EU regional data (for 168 level II regions) for the shares of industry, services and agriculture in the total labour force and regional data on infrastructure from Biehl (1991). The data for sector shares are for 1987 and the data for infrastructure are for 1985–6. We had to drop 43 observations because not all of the regions were comparable in the two data sets. There are thus 125 observations. The results of these regressions are given in table 7.9. We also report specifications with *per capita* GDP (the mean of 1986–7–8) as an independent variable since the level of *per capita* GDP is usually strongly correlated with increasing returns industries (see Leamer, 1992; Loertscher and Wolter, 1980;

Table 7.8   Intra-industry trade regressions

Dependent variable	Coefficients				
	Transport	Telecommunication	Energy	Education	R^2
	+0.338 (2.69)*	—	—	—	0.419
	—	+0.335 (1.84)	—	—	0.252
% of intra-industry trade with EC	—	—	+0.282 (3.28)**	—	0.518
	—	—	—	+5.558 (3.03)*	0.479
	+0.112 (0.618)	−0.370 (−1.74)	+0.275 (2.36)*	+0.507 (3.02)*	0.801

Notes: * Significant at the 5% level; ** significant at the 1% level. The coefficients of the constants are not reported; *t*-values in brackets.

Balassa, 1986). Finally, as the official aim of the EU is to help convergence of *per capita* GDP levels in Europe, we regressed *per capita* GDP on the infrastructure levels. All regressions are run in logs.

The results of table 7.9 confirm the finding that education infrastructure is the most important determinant of industry location. The coefficients on education infrastructure are positive and significant at the 1 per cent level of confidence in all regressions – despite the strong collinearity among the right-hand side variables. Adding *per capita* GDP to the right-hand side reduces the coefficient on the education infrastructure index; however, it is still positive, significant, and quantitatively large.

For telecommunication infrastructure, the results are mixed. The coefficients are always positive but significant in only three out of six specifications. When *per capita* GDP is introduced into the regression, the coefficient loses its significance. This is because the relation between telecommunication infrastructure and industry share is different among regions with above-average infrastructure and among regions of below-average infrastructure (Spain, Italy, Portugal, Greece and Ireland). In the first group, the relation is negative and significant. In the second group, the relation is positive and significant. This is the only infrastructure type for which the relation we analyse is very different for the two groups of countries.

Table 7.9 Industry location and GDP/*per capita* regressions

Dependent variables	Transport	Telecomm-unication	Energy	Education	GDP/*per capita* at PPP	Popula-tion density	R^2
			Infrastructure coefficients				
	+0.045 (1.42)						0.016
	−0.034 (1.24)				+0.453 (4.89)**		0.178
		+0.174 (3.63)**					0.096
		+0.002 (0.02)			+0.391 (3.22)**		0.167
			+0.027 (1.11)				0.01
% of industry in total labour force			−0.040 (−1.55)		+0.465 (5.08)**		0.183
				+0.247 (5.36)**			0.189
				+0.177 (3.52)**	+0.254 (2.99)**		0.244
	−0.071 (−1.70)	+0.188 (3.00)**	+0.001 (0.03)	+0.222			0.248
	−0.062 (−1.50)	+0.104 (1.32)	−0.012 (−0.43)	+0.183 (3.54)**	+0.226 (1.74)		0.267
	−0.092 (−1.70)	+0.190 (3.01)**	+0.001 (0.001)	+0.211 (4.18)**		+0.022 (0.61)	0.251
	−0.069 (−1.24)	+0.107 (1.32)	−0.012 (−0.43)	+0.181 (3.39)**	+0.220 (1.63)	+0.006 (0.181)	0.267
	+0.192 (6.83)**						0.275
	+0.441 (12.82)**					0.572	
per capita GDP (at PPP)			+0.144 (6.57)**				0.260
				+0.272 (5.76)**			0.212
	−0.039 (−1.34)	+0.372 (8.52)	+0.058 (3.014)**	+0.169	(5.15)**		0.664

Notes: * Significant at the 5% level; ** significant at the 1% level. The coefficients of the constants are not reported; *t*-values in brackets.

Transport and energy infrastructure are not significant, and in five specifications out of six, transport infrastructure even appears with the wrong sign (but not significantly). This appears to be the most surprising result in table 7.9. However, the fact that the infrastructure indices that we use are not adjusted for quality may be especially important for transport and may partially explain this poor correlation.

Finally, we introduced a measure of market size in the regressions of the industry share. As in Helpman and Krugman (1985) and Krugman (1991), our model predicts that increasing returns industries will tend to locate in regions with large domestic markets. As the EU regions are not identical in terms of physical size, we used population density as a measure of the size of the regional market. The coefficient is positive, but small and not significant. More important, the coefficients on the infrastructure indices and their significance are not modified.

We have not reported the results for the shares of agriculture and services. The share of agriculture is negatively and very significatively correlated with each of the infrastructure endowments. These results can be interpreted as simply saying that agricultural regions are poor regions which are regions with low infrastructure. The results on the share of services in the total labour force do not point to any clear pattern or interpretation.

Per capita GDP is very well correlated with infrastructure, as shown in the last five rows of table 7.9.[10] This is particularly true for telecommunication and education, for which the effect is both significant and quantitatively large. For energy, the effect is significant but small. Transport infrastructure appears positive and significant in only one specification. In the specification with all four types of infrastructure, its coefficient is negative, although not significant.

One may ask if our results are distorted by simultaneity bias due to reverse causation. Indeed, in theory it is not clear whether *per capita* GDP levels are explained by infrastructure levels or whether infrastructure levels are explained by the levels of *per capita* GDP because of countries' resource constraints. However, direct reverse causation is ruled out, because the infrastructure indices were measured before the data we use for *per capita* GDP levels, which make infrastructure levels statistically predetermined relative to *per capita* GDP levels. However, serial correlation could bias the estimated coefficients that we find, so these results should be interpreted with caution.

The levels of public infrastructure cannot be considered as exogenous variables. Many other variables which explain the location of industry in Europe are certainly left out from these simple regressions (as the relatively low levels of R^2 suggest). These variables may not be independent of the level of infrastructure.

Given these limitations, the results on intra-industry trade and on the share of industry still point to the importance of education and telecommunication infrastructure for the location of industry in the poorest EU regions and suggests that transport infrastructure is not as important as is usually thought. The policy implications of these results can be summarised as follows. First, it may be possible to use transfers tied to infrastructure to encourage convergence in the share of industry in Europe and to encourage convergence in *per capita* GDP. Whichever is the aim of the EU regional policies, education and telecommunication should be given priority over transport and energy infrastructures. We note that the two infrastructures (education and telecommunication) that are the most important for explaining industry location and differences in *per capita* GDP levels are also the ones for which the degree of convergence at the EU level is the furthest from the degree of convergence reached at the national level.

In view of these policy implications, the concentration of EU regional aid on transport infrastructure (see section 3) might seem excessive, relative to spending on education and telecommunication infrastructure.

5 Conclusions

This chapter has shown, both theoretically and empirically, that one of the main factors determining real convergence in Europe, namely the location of industry, is the disparity in infrastructure. Trade integration between countries with large infrastructure disparities can lead to relocation of industry from poor to rich countries, and therefore to long-term divergence. A policy that improves infrastructure in the poor country can therefore counteract this effect. However, the effectiveness of such a policy decreases as the overall infrastructure level in the EU improves. Hence, the regional aid policies of the EU can be interpreted as the price to be paid by the rich countries for full trade integration. The main empirical result of this paper is that telecommunication, and even more education infrastructure, are strongly correlated with industry location and *per capita* GDP. Energy, and especially transport infra-structure, by comparison, seem relatively unimportant, and so the concentration of EU transfers on transport infrastructure might seem excessive. If this policy implication is confirmed by other studies, it would be interesting to question the reasons for this concentration. One simple reason might be that financing transport infrastructure has a direct, large and rapid macroeconomic impact on the economy of the recipient economy (see Commission of the European Communities, 1992a); the impact of improving education infrastructure certainly takes much more time.

NOTES

We thank Richard Baldwin, Matthew Canzoneri, Harry Flam, Martin Richardson and Jim Tybout for useful comments. Any errors are the authors' responsibility.

1 Delors' *White Paper* (1993) proposals of trans-European infrastructure networks will also have important implications for industrial location. For an analysis of trans-European networks, see Vickerman (1994).

2 For similar types of infrastructure (roads and railways, for example), the arithmetic mean is taken to give an index of each main category of infrastructure (transport, for example). Then, the geometric mean of these main indices is taken to give the aggregate infrastructure indicator. The two different procedures to aggregate the varieties of infrastructure reflect the different degrees of substitutability (high between roads and railways and low between transport and energy). For a more precise description of the data set, see Biehl (1986).

3 The poorest region in Germany is always in the eastern part. If the comparison excluded the eastern regions of Germany, the numbers would therefore be significantly higher.

4 For a detailed history and analysis of regional policies, see Tsoukalis (1993).

5 We call the two entities that are integrated 'countries'. When we analyse the impact of regional policies, one should rather think of these two entities as regions, as the EU regional policies are implemented at the level of the region.

6 These costs affect Portugal symmetrically: in Portugal $1/\tau^*$ of a Portuguese good is available for consumption, while only $1/\tau\tau^*$ of a German good is consumable.

7 As in Helpman and Krugman (1985), good Y is introduced to tie down the wage rate in each country. We rule out infrastructure costs on this good. If we include these costs in the model, countries will consume only domestically-produced amounts of Y. In general, both labour markets then will not be in equilibrium.

8 In another study (Martin and Rogers, 1994), we show that equalising the levels of infrastructure between two countries with different income levels may in fact produce industrial concentration in the high-income country if this policy comes with an overall improvement of infrastructure. We also analyse other types of regional aid policies and differentiate between infrastructure that facilitates trade inside the country and infrastructure that facilitates trade between this country and the rest of Europe. We find that the first type of programme will foster industrial relocation from the rich to the poor country, but that the latter type will foster relocation from the poor to the rich country.

9 Results for regressions run in levels were not very different. All coefficients tend to be less significant.

10 The results on *per capita* GDP are close to those of Biehl (1986), who used the 1980 data set.

REFERENCES

Balassa, B., 1986. 'Intra-industry specialization, a cross-country analysis', *European Economic Review*, 30(1), 27–42

Baldwin, R., 1989. 'The growth effects of 1992', *Economic Policy*, 9, 248–81

Bertola, G., 1992. 'Models of economic integration and localized growth', in report on the conference, 'A Single Currency for Europe: Monetary and Real Aspects', Banco de Portugal and CEPR (16–18 January), London: CEPR

Biehl, D., 1991. 'The role on infrastructure in regional development', in R.W. Vickerman (ed.), *Infrastructure and Regional Development*, European Research in Regional Science, vol. 1, London: Pion

Biehl, D. (ed.), 1986. *The Contribution of Infrastructure to Regional Development*, 2 vols, Luxembourg: Office for Official Publications of the European Communities

Biehl, D. and P. Ungar, 1991. 'Kapazitätsausstattung und Kapazitätsengpässe an Grossräumig Bedeutsamer Infrastruktur: Berichtung und Neuberechnung der Indikatoren', Goethe-Institut, Frankfurt-am-Main, mimeo

CEPR, 1992. 'Is bigger better? The economics of EC enlargement', *Monitoring European Integration*, 3, London: CEPR

Commission of the European Communities, 1992a. 'Community structural policies: assessment and outlook', Brussels: Commission of the European Communities

1992b. 'The Community's structural interventions', *Statistical Bulletin*, 3 (July)

Delors, J., 1993. 'The White Paper on growth, competitiveness and employment', Brussels: Commission of the European Communities

Helpman, E. and P. Krugman, 1985. *Market Structure and Foreign Trade*, Cambridge, MA: MIT Press

1989. *Trade Policy and Market Structure*, Cambridge, MA: MIT Press

Krugman, P., 1989. *Geography and Trade*, Cambridge, MA: MIT Press

1991. 'Increasing returns and economic geography', *Journal of Political Economy*, 99(3), 483–99

Krugman, P. and A. Venables, 1990. 'Integration and the competitiveness of peripheral industry', CEPR, *Discussion Paper*, 363, London: CEPR

Leamer, E., 1992. 'Testing trade theory', NBER, *Working Paper*, 3957

Loertscher, R. and F. Wolter, 1980. 'Determinants of inter-industry trade: among countries and across industries', *Weltwirtschaftliches Archiv*, 116, 180–92

Martin, P. and C.A. Rogers, 1994. 'Industrial location and public infrastructure', CEPR, *Working Paper*, 909, London: CEPR; revised version (1995), in *Journal of International Economics*, forthcoming

Neven, D. and C. Gouyette, 1994. 'Regional convergence in the European Community', CEPR, *Working Paper*, 914, London: CEPR

Tsoukalis, L., 1993. '*The New European Economy: The Politics and Economics of Integration*, 2nd edn, Oxford: Oxford University Press
Vickerman, R., 1994. 'Transport infrastructure and region building in the European Community', *Journal of Common Market Studies*, **32(1)**, 1–24

Discussion

HARRY FLAM

Philippe Martin and Carol Rogers' chapter 7 deals with a question of great concern to the poorer countries in the EU, namely the effects of stronger economic integration on the regional, or rather inter-country, allocation of industrial activity.

The reasons for this concern are not obvious if one uses the standard Heckscher–Ohlin model as a tool to judge the consequences of increased integration. The poorer countries are relatively abundant in labour and relatively scarce in physical and probably also in human capital. Given greater freedom for goods, services, capital and labour to cross national borders in the Community, one expects capital to move to the labour-abundant countries to take advantage of relatively cheap labour, and labour to move to the richer countries to earn higher real wages. In the end, this process will result in a new equilibrium, in which the returns to the various factors of production are more or less equalised.

The post-Second World War economic history of Western Europe seems to confirm these predictions: real wages and probably also returns to capital have converged greatly since the 1950s due to trade liberalisation (Ben-David, 1993). Furthermore, the economic history of the Community does not, I think, show any evidence of concentration of industrial activity. If anything, I think that the opposite is true, namely that the Community experience is one of the poor catching up and industrialising at a higher rate than the richer countries, where the share of industry is constant or even declining. The growth record of newly admitted members, particularly of Portugal and Spain, indicates that history will repeat itself on this score. Chapter 7 is, however, not built on the standard Heckscher–Ohlin model with constant returns, homogeneous goods and perfect competition. It uses the recent, generalised

Heckscher–Ohlin model with increasing returns, differentiated goods and imperfect competition, plus Samuelson's idea of modelling transportation costs between countries (locations). But instead of assuming a cost of transportation that is equal to some proportion of the product lost in transit, it is assumed that the level of infrastructure determines what proportion of a product is lost between production and consumption within the country. Production in one country and consumption of the same good in another leads to duplication of infrastructure costs. This is a novel, simple and quite useful way to model infrastructure.

A somewhat peculiar feature of the model when related to the reality it wants to depict is the assumption of an initial equilibrium in which factor prices are equalised. Location is wholly determined by the different levels of infrastructure (and by relative country size); better infrastructure means lower costs and more of the given total number of firms. In the new models of economic geography by Krugman (1989, 1991) that the authors refer to, locational choice is – more realistically – seen as a function of input costs, economies of scale and transportation costs. Given the concentration of population in the centre of the Community, one would think that while economies of scale dictate locational concentration of production in the centre, firms trade off high costs of transportation from the peripheral South with its low labour costs. Chapter 7 abstracts from labour cost differences, however, and concentrates on cost differences created by different levels of infrastructure.

Another peculiar feature of the model is that the number of firms and output per firm (economies of scale) by construction are unaffected by changes in infrastructure and consequent changes in real consumption. In a more general model, where the number of firms and output per firm are allowed to vary, one would expect total production of differentiated goods and economies of scale to increase following an improvement of Portuguese infrastructure, since real income in the Community is increased. Hence, there would not only be a redistribution of a constant total production of differentiated goods to Portugal from Germany but also gains from more efficient commodity 'distribution' inside Portugal. In particular, one must remember that Portugal is assumed to have a comparative disadvantage in production of differentiated goods. The transfer of resources from Germany to Portugal for the improvement of infrastructure will therefore not only be a redistributive measure, but also one that affects efficiency and in particular the distribution of the efficiency gains from exploitation of comparative advantage. Thus, Germany may lose for this reason also.

One may ask what reason Germany has for transferring resources to Portugal and thereby causing itself secondary welfare losses. Chapter 7 suggests that one reason is that Portugal could achieve the same end by introducing a trade barrier. This is not convincing – that would not be allowed by the rules of the Single Market – but the question is still valid. It seems to me that the Structural Funds and other redistributive schemes in the Community are based on the idea that Germany (the richer countries) will gain at the expense of Portugal (the poorer countries) from the Single Market and that the Structural Funds are partial compensation. I suggest above that this idea may be totally wrong: it is the poor that have more to gain and consequently they pay compensation.

The econometrics in section 4 of the chapter purport to show that the location of increasing returns activities in Europe is determined by the level of education and (to some extent) telecommunication infrastructure. The conclusion is that regional transfers will promote industrialisation and that the transfers should be biased towards education and telecommunication, and not transportation, as they are now. These conclusions seem plausible, but I am not convinced by the regressions. The authors themselves point out that 'it is not clear whether *per capita* GDP levels are explained by infrastructure levels or whether infrastructure levels are explained by the levels of *per capita* GDP'. They therefore do not regress GDP on infrastructure, but present correlations instead. For the same reason, one should not propose a one-way causation between GDP and the share of industry, or between the share of industry and infrastructure. High levels of GDP, industrialisation and infrastructure are in general very interdependent.

Even if it were true that education and telecommunication are more important for industry, one must consider that Portugal and the other poor countries in the Community at present have a comparative advantage in labour and resource-intensive activities. These may require a good transportation network. Welfare considerations may therefore dictate a bias towards transportation, even if industrial development may dictate a bias towards telecommunications.

REFERENCES

Ben-David, D., 1993. 'Equalizing exchange: trade liberalization and income convergence', paper presented to the European Workshop on International Trade, Rotterdam (10–15 June)
Krugman, P., 1989. *Geography and Trade*, Cambridge, MA: MIT Press
    1991. 'Increasing returns and economic geography', *Journal of Political Economy*, **99(3)**, 483–99

Part Three
Empirical issues

8 Regional effects of European integration

JAN I. HAALAND and VICTOR D. NORMAN

1 Introduction

European integration involves both lower trade costs and increased competition in product markets, and free movements of labour and capital. In practice, we are unlikely to see large-scale movements of labour, since language barriers, cultural differences and social adjustment costs remain high. Capital movements, on the other hand, could be very significant in response to even small differences in rates of return. An important issue, and the one we study in this chapter, is how product market integration and capital movements will interact.

We ask two questions. The first relates to the effects if the integration programme is successful: what will be the combined effect on the regional pattern of production in Europe of product market integration and capital movements? Will we see a tendency to general concentration of industrial activity in the northern EC area; will the effect be a sharper division of labour between the different regions; or what? The second concerns the effects if European integration is only partly successful. Suppose there are free capital movements, but only partial integration of product markets: will this (as has been feared in several EFTA countries) induce large-scale capital exports from North to East and South and, if so, could this have been prevented through complete product market integration?

Trade theory does not provide clear, unambiguous answers to these questions. If product markets are perfectly competitive, it says that the interaction between trade in goods and trade in factors depends critically on whether or not there are technology differences between countries (see Markusen, 1983; Markusen and Svensson, 1985, for detailed discussions of these issues). In a Heckscher–Ohlin world with the same technology everywhere, factor trade and goods trade will be substitutes, in the sense that trade in goods alone may suffice to equalise factor prices internationally. In a Ricardian world, the two could be complementary. As an example, suppose a country has a technological advantage in capital-intensive products. With free trade in goods, it will then export capital-intensive goods, and at the same time have a higher rate of return on capital than other countries. Free capital movements will cause an inflow of capital, which in turn will give increased production and exports of capital-intensive products.

Translated to the context of a fully integrated Europe, in which goods flow freely and product markets are highly competitive, these insights tell us that the end result *could* be capital movements to, and concentration of economic activity in, the centre of Europe (if the centre has a general productivity advantage); but it could also be that freer and more competitive product markets would provide little incentive for capital movements and geographic concentration (if there were insignificant productivity differentials). Other possibilities also exist, depending on the interrelationship between relative technologies and relative factor abundance. A number of different answers to the first question are thus possible.

Note that this question, while formally unconnected, is of considerable interest in relation to the new theory of trade and geography. In the literature on trade and geography (see Krugman, 1991, for an introduction), the questions are to what extent economies of scale and scope interact with factor mobility and intra-industry linkages to cause geographic concentration, and how changes in trade costs affect the degree and pattern of concentration. Our question is whether the interaction of trade in goods and factors alone – independently of possible scale economies – could have similar effects.

On the second question – the effects of capital mobility if product market integration is incomplete – theory provides somewhat clearer results. The context is one of imperfect competition. That means unexploited comparative advantage, and thus remaining factor price differences even with free trade and identical technology in all countries. Capital should then move to capital-scarce regions, or (as with perfect competition) to regions with a general technological advantage or a specific advantage in capital-intensive production.

A key factor here is the transactions cost for factors relative to goods. As shown in Norman and Venables (1993), in a Heckscher–Ohlin model, trade in a factor will replace trade in goods using that factor intensively if the unit transactions cost for the factor falls below the impact that the unit transactions cost for the goods has on the domestic price of the factor: if, for example, the cost of moving a unit of capital is t, the cost of moving a unit of a capital-intensive good is τ, and the effect on the domestic price of capital of a unit increase in the price of capital-intensive goods is s, then capital – rather than capital-intensive goods – will be traded if $t < s\tau$. The implication in the context of European integration is obvious: if capital movements are completely liberalised, so that t becomes much lower, but product markets are only partly integrated, so that τ remains high, we could experience a large-scale shift from trade in goods to capital movements.

It is effects of this type which have created concern in some EFTA countries. In general, EFTA countries are capital-rich; and it is felt that they do not have a technological advantage over the northern EC countries – if anything, they tend to have lower factor productivity. If product market integration is incomplete, therefore, it is feared that integration of capital markets could induce large-scale capital exports and subsequent deindustrialisation in the EFTA region.

To resolve the qualitative ambiguities and get some idea of the quantitative effects, this chapter uses a computable general equilibrium (CGE) model with imperfectly competitive product markets and perfectly competitive factor markets to simulate how capital mobility and product market integration interact in affecting the location of industrial production in Europe. Similar models have previously been used to study the general equilibrium effects of product market integration (Haaland and Norman, 1992; Gasiorek, Smith and Venables, 1991, 1992).

The model is calibrated to data for 1985; assuming initially significant product trade costs, segmentation of product markets along national lines, and factor price differences between the regions. It is used to simulate the effects of (a) capital mobility with no change in product trade costs or market structure, (b) capital mobility and a reduction in product trade costs, but no real integration of product markets, and (c) capital mobility, lower product trade costs, and full integration of European product markets. The last of these experiments sheds light on the interaction of market integration and capital mobility, i.e. the first question above. The first two experiments are intended to provide answers to the question of how capital mobility will affect industrial production in Europe if market integration is only partly successful.

The focus is on the broad pattern of regional relocation between three regions, which we have called EU South, EU North, and EFTA. The regions are defined not in terms of geography or institutional affiliation, but in terms of economic characteristics, so the labels are for convenience only. EFTA comprises previous and current EFTA members (Finland, Sweden, Norway, Austria, Switzerland, Iceland), but the region is assumed to be economically fully integrated with the rest of Western Europe. EU North comprises Britain, Denmark, the Benelux countries,

Germany, France, and Italy, while EU South comprises Spain, Greece, Ireland, and Portugal.

It would have been desirable to include the countries of Eastern Europe in the model, as an important question clearly is how capital movements to, and trade with, Eastern Europe will affect economic activity in Western Europe. We do not, however, have sufficient data to model an Eastern region properly, so we prefer to leave it out. In further work, however, the inclusion of Eastern Europe should be given high priority.

In section 2, the model and data are briefly presented. Section 3 presents and discusses the simulation results; some tentative conclusions are drawn in section 4.

2   Model and data

The model is a variant of one described in detail in Haaland and Norman (1992), so here we shall give only a brief, non-technical sketch of the model and indicate data sources and calibration procedure.

2.1   The model

The model distinguishes six world regions – the three European regions, the US, Japan, and the rest of the world. Initially, the European regions each consist of separate (but, for simplicity, identical) countries and submarkets. The US, Japan, and the rest of the world are modelled as fully integrated markets.

Each country produces 12 traded goods and one non-tradable, using three primary factors – capital and two types of labour (skilled and unskilled). The non-traded good and one of the traded goods are sold in perfectly competitive markets; the remaining products come from imperfectly competitive industries. The markets for capital and labour markets are perfectly competitive, and factors are initially not traded.

The goods are produced using primary factors and intermediate inputs. The production functions are two-level CES functions: quantities produced are CES functions of inputs of capital, labour and intermediates, and intermediate inputs are CES aggregates of goods. In the perfectly competitive industries there are constant returns to scale; in the rest, there are economies of scale (in the form of fixed costs).

Each imperfectly competitive industry consists of a number of identical subindustries. In each subindustry there are producers from all countries selling in all markets. All firms from a particular country in a particular industry are identical. Product markets are initially segmented along national lines, and products are differentiated. The individual firm,

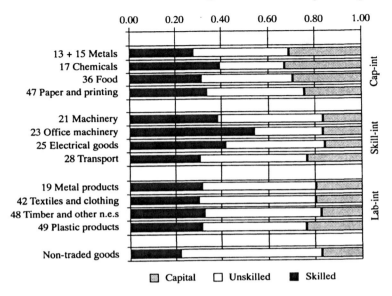

Figure 8.1   Factor cost shares

therefore, derives market power both from a monopoly on its particular product variety and from significant market shares; but its market power will vary from submarket to submarket. There is Cournot competition and free entry in all industries.

Final demand in each country is derived from a two-level utility function. At the top level (assumed to be Cobb–Douglas), income is allocated to each of the 13 product groups; at the bottom level (CES), we find demand for the differentiated products.

The model is closed by standard factor-market clearing conditions and national income–expenditure identities.

2.2   Data and calibration

The 12 traded goods in the model correspond to the two-digit NACE industrial classification. All other goods and services are lumped into one non-traded aggregate. Figure 8.1 lists the industries and gives factor cost shares for the goods. Cost shares and figures for production and trade are based on 1985 data from the EU and the OECD. Based on factor cost shares, we have grouped the tradables in three categories according to relative factor intensities. This is done to simplify reporting and interpretation of results – the industries are not aggregated in the model.

Table 8.1   Composition of production, 1985

	EFTA	EU North	EU South
Traded goods	0.265	0.254	0.331
Composition of tradables production: of which (%)			
Capital-intensive	44	45	56
Skill-intensive	27	31	20
Labour-intensive	29	23	23
Non-traded goods	0.735	0.746	0.669

For ease of exposition, however, in this chapter we only report figures for the aggregates.

Table 8.1 gives the pattern of production in 1985 in the three European regions and the aggregation of industries.

Of the tradables, 11 goods (NACE 17–49) are taken to be produced in imperfectly competitive industries. For these, concentration is measured by Herfindahl indexes, computed from national data on the size distribution of firms from the mid-1980s. Scale economies are based on estimates by Pratten (1987). The averages, over the industries in each main category, of the Herfindahl indexes and the assumed economies of scale, are given in table 8.2.

To calibrate the model, some parameters are specified exogenously, while the rest are determined in such a way as to make the model consistent with base-year data. The exogenously specified parameters are the top-level elasticities of substitution in cost and demand functions. On the demand side, all top-level elasticities are automatically unity by the choice of a Cobb–Douglas utility function. On the cost side, the elasticity of substitution between capital and both labour types is set at 0.8, while that between primary factors and intermediate goods is set at 0.3. The other parameters in demand and production then follow from base-year data. The procedure is described in Haaland and Norman (1992).

To be consistent with the data on production and trade, the model must be able to explain the almost universal dominance of home-market sales. The two most obvious explanations are real trade costs and a preference on the part of consumers for domestically produced goods. We follow the procedure of Smith and Venables (1988), by assuming real trade costs equal to 10 per cent of the value of trade, and assuming that home-market dominance beyond what that might explain to be explained by home-market preferences.

The new feature in this model version is international capital mobility.

Table 8.2   Scale economies^a and concentration, 1985

	Scale economies (%)	Concentration[b]		
		EFTA	EU North	EU South
Capital-intensive	7	0.13	0.08	0.08
Skill-intensive	10	0.24	0.26	0.33
Labour-intensive	5	0.12	0.09	0.06

[a] Scale economies: cost increase at $\frac{1}{2}$ initial output.
[b] Concentration: average Herfindahl index at subindustry level.

That calls for some specifics on calibration of factor markets. The general procedure is straightforward. First, initial factor prices are specified. From the factor cost shares and data on production, we then find factor use in each industry. Summing this over all industries, and assuming full employment, we obtain factor endowments in each region.

In previous model versions, no factors were internationally mobile, so the units of measurement of factors could differ from country to country. We therefore arbitrarily set all initial factor prices equal to unity, thus measuring factor endowments in (initial) domestic value terms. With internationally mobile capital, we obviously could not follow that route in the present version of the model: since capital must be measured in the same units across regions, we need internationally comparable initial rates of return. For labour, we could have proceeded as before. It is, however, easier to interpret some of the results – particularly results that relate to Heckscher–Ohlin-type comparative advantage – if the units of measurement are the same across regions. We therefore needed a set of internationally comparable factor prices to calibrate factor markets.

Unfortunately, we were not able to find a reliable and consistent set of data on factor prices, so we have had to rely on very rough estimates. Qualitatively, the picture is relatively clear: wage levels tend to be significantly higher in EFTA and EU North than in EU South; at the same time, the ratio of skilled to unskilled wages is lower in EFTA than in the EU. There are also indications of significant differences in rates of return, as illustrated by the OECD figures given in table 8.3.

It is clear from these figures that the rate of return has been lower in the EFTA countries, and in Denmark and Britain, than in other northern European countries. It also seems, based on the Spanish figure, as if the rate of return on investment is potentially higher in southern than in northern Europe.

The historical averages may exaggerate initial differences in marginal rates of return. In particular, the Scandinavian figures are likely to reflect

Table 8.3   Rates of return on capital in the business sector, average 1980–91, per cent

EFTA		EU North		EU South	
Finland	9.7	Germany	12.3	Greece	12.3
Norway	6.4	France	12.3	Ireland	8.3
Sweden	9.4	UK	9.7	Spain	16.5
Switzerland	9.0	Netherlands	15.7		
Austria	10.7	Denmark	9.6		
		Belgium	12.0		
		Italy	12.8		
Average	9.0	Average	12.1	Average	12.4

Source: OECD, Economic Outlook, **54** (December 1993).

highly distortive capital taxation in the 1980s. In setting up the model, therefore, we have used the much smaller initial factor price differences between the European regions given in table 8.4 (where all factor prices in EU North are normalised to 1, and the other regions are measured relative to EU North).

3   Simulation results

We now use the model to compare the effects of intra-European capital movements with varying degrees of product market integration in Europe.

3.1   Capital movements with incomplete product market integration

Our first simulation experiment concerns the effects of capital mobility if product markets are not fully integrated. We assume that the internal market in Europe, comprising all EU countries and all current and previous members of EFTA, is realised in the sense that capital and goods can move freely between countries. We further assume that real trade costs between national markets in Europe are reduced by 2.5 per cent of the value of trade. That is roughly the low Cecchini Report estimate of the cost reduction that will be achieved by elimination of national borders. We do not, however, assume that European markets are fully integrated – instead, segmented, national markets continue to exist, and firms are free to charge different prices in the different markets.

We compare the effects of this with a base case of no trade liberalisation and no capital movements, and with two reference cases – one with free capital movements but no trade liberalisation, and one with lower

Table 8.4   Initial factor prices

	Skilled labour	Unskilled labour	Capital
EFTA	0.90	1.20	0.95
EC North	1.00	1.00	1.00
EC South	1.10	0.90	1.05

product trade costs but no capital movements. The results are shown in table 8.5. All numbers are changes (in per cent) from the base case.

As can be seen, the partial integration case gives large-scale capital exports from EFTA, and corresponding capital imports to EU South. That causes similar relocation of capital-intensive manufacturing. Partial integration also involves a significant concentration of skill-intensive production in EFTA, and to some extent EU North, at the expense of EU South. There is a corresponding, but weaker, shift of labour-intensive production from EFTA and EU North to EU South.

If we compare the partial integration results with the two reference cases, we see that in the case of skill-intensive production, capital mobility and lower product trade costs both tend to shift production from EU South to EFTA; while in the case of capital-intensive production, trade liberalisation and capital mobility counteract each other.

The partial integration case involves a marked tendency to factor price equalisation. Since capital moves freely, the rate of return is, of course, automatically equalised. More interestingly, wages fall in the (high real-wage) EFTA region, and rise in the (low-wage) EU South. Note, however, that this is exclusively the result of capital mobility: lower product trade costs will raise real wages in all regions, and particularly so in EFTA and EU North.

On the question of whether partial product market integration is sufficient to prevent large-scale capital exports and deindustrialisation of EFTA, the answer seems to be 'no', but it helps a little. With no trade liberalisation, almost one-fifth of the capital initially employed in tradables production in EFTA will be exported, and EFTA industrial production will fall by 2.4 per cent. A reduction in product real trade costs will reduce capital exports only slightly, but it will reduce the loss of industrial production in EFTA by roughly one-third.

3.2   Complete integration

The second experiment concerns the effects of complete integration. We assume as before that capital can move freely within Europe, and that

Table 8.5   Effects of incomplete market integration

	EFTA			EU North			EU South		
	CM[a]	LTC[b]	PI[c]	CM	LTC	PI	CM	LTC	PI
Capital exports (& of capital in tradables)	18.4		17.6	−0.4		−0.3	−15.4		−15.2
Industrial production (% change)									
Cap.-intensive	−7.1	2.1	−5.5	0.2	−0.2	0.0	6.6	−0.4	6.8
Skill-intensive	2.8	1.3	4.6	−0.2	1.8	1.6	−3.3	0.5	−3.4
Lab.-intensive	0.8	−1.8	−0.2	−0.2	0.4	0.2	−1.2	3.0	0.6
Total	−2.4	0.7	−1.6	0.1	0.4	0.5	3.1	0.5	3.6
Real factor prices (% change)									
Capital	5.5	0.8	6.0	−0.1	0.4	0.3	−5.2	0.3	−4.8
Skilled labour	−1.3	0.7	−0.5	0.0	0.5	0.5	1.5	0.3	1.7
Unskilled labour	−1.3	0.7	−0.5	0.0	0.4	0.4	1.4	0.3	1.7
Real income (% of expenditure on tradables)	−0.1	2.0	1.9	0.0	1.5	1.5	0.4	0.9	1.3

[a] CM capital mobility, no trade liberalisation.
[b] LTC 2.5 per cent lower real trade costs for goods, no capital mobility.
[c] PI partial integration: capital mobility and 2.5 per cent lower real trade costs for goods.

real trade costs for goods are reduced by 2.5 per cent. Now we also assume that product markets are fully integrated, i.e. that the producer prices must be the same in all markets, and that only shares in the total European market give rise to market power.

Again, we have two reference cases. One of them is, as before, capital mobility with no trade liberalisation. The other is complete product market integration (including reduction in real product trade costs), but without capital mobility. The results are shown in table 8.6.

The effects on the industrial structure in Europe reflect two forces. One, similar to the case of partial integration, is a shift of skill-intensive production from EU South to EU North and (particularly) EFTA; and of capital-intensive and labour-intensive production from EFTA to EU South. The shift in capital-intensive production reflects capital exports from Northern to Southern Europe; the shifts in labour-intensive and skill-intensive production reflect initially unexploited comparative advantage.

Table 8.6   Effects of complete market integration

	EFTA			EU North			EU South		
	CM*a*	PMI*b*	CI*c*	CM	PMI	CI	CM	PMI	CI
Capital exports (& of capital in tradables)	18.4		18.2	−0.4		−0.3	−15.4		−15.3
Industrial production (% change)									
Cap.-intensive	−7.1	1.2	−5.8	0.2	1.2	1.5	6.6	0.1	7.0
Skill-intensive	2.8	6.5	9.0	−0.2	3.7	3.6	−3.3	3.8	0.5
Lab.-intensive	0.8	0.1	1.2	−0.2	1.0	0.9	−1.2	2.6	0.6
Total	−2.4	2.1	−0.3	0.1	1.8	1.9	3.1	1.3	4.4
Real factor prices (% change)									
Capital	5.5	1.2	6.7	−0.1	0.9	0.8	−5.2	1.0	−4.2
Skilled labour	−1.3	1.3	0.0	0.0	0.9	0.9	1.5	1.2	2.6
Unskilled labour	−1.3	1.1	−0.2	0.0	0.7	0.8	1.4	1.0	2.4
Real income (% of expenditure on tradables)	−0.1	3.0	2.9	0.0	2.8	2.8	0.4	3.0	3.4

a CM capital mobility, no trade liberalisation.
b PMI integration of product markets, 2.5 per cent lower real trade costs for goods, no capital mobility.
c CI complete integration: capital mobility, market integration, and 2.5 per cent lower real trade costs for goods.

The other force is the pro-competitive effect of market integration, which tends to shift resources from sectors which initially are highly competitive to sectors which initially have a low degree of competition. Recall from table 8.2 (p. 199) that the skill-intensive sectors are initially the least competitive ones. The competition effect will therefore tend to shift resources generally into the skill-intensive industries. That explains why skill-intensive production increases in all three European regions. It is the same effect which explains the general, but weak rise in labour-intensive production.

Once more, we also see a marked tendency to factor-price equalisation within Europe. Compared to the partial integration case, however, there will be a larger increase in real wages in EU South, and a smaller reduction in real wages in EFTA.

The most surprising result in table 8.6 is that there is hardly any interaction between capital mobility and market integration. Capital exports will be roughly the same whether or not product markets are integrated; and the effects on industrial structure and factor prices in the complete integration case are very close to the sum of the effects in the two reference cases.

On the question of whether complete integration will lead to concentration of industrial activity or increased inter-regional specialisation and trade within Europe, the answer seems to be that it will lead to neither. There is a weak tendency to increased industrial production in EU North; but the dominating effect in table 8.6 is the shift in industrial production from EFTA to EU South, brought about by capital exports from EFTA and capital imports to EU South. And as regards specialisation and trade, the results are mixed: increased capital-intensive production in the South will reduce trade (a Heckscher–Ohlin effect of capital movements), while increased skill-intensive production in EFTA will create trade (a Ricardian effect).

3.3   Sensitivity

To test the robustness of our results, we have carried out two supplementary experiments. One concerns the extent and degree of European integration, the other initial differences in rates of return on capital.

On the question of whether product market integration will dampen capital exports and deindustrialisation in the EFTA region, the results above seem to indicate that the answer is 'yes', but that the effect is relatively small. To study the question more closely, we have looked at an additional case, free capital mobility in all of Europe and partial product market integration in the EU regions only – i.e. with the EFTA regions outside the partially integrated product markets. That gives us four cases altogether – capital mobility only, and three cases with capital mobility and various degrees of product market integration. One extreme case is that of product market integration without EFTA participation; the other extreme is that of complete integration including both the EU and EFTA regions. The most important results for the EFTA region are given in table 8.7.

The results confirm the hypothesis that product market integration has little effect on the volume of capital exports from the EFTA region, but that it will dampen the deindustrialisation effect of capital exports. The degree of EFTA integration in European product markets seems also to have a significant effect on the composition of EFTA industrial production. If EFTA is outside an integrated product market, capital mobility gives general deindustrialisation, while capital mobility in the context of complete EU/EFTA product market integration gives a strong

Table 8.7   Effects of capital mobility and integration on EFTA, sensitivity
w.r.t. the degree of product market integration

	Capital exports	Industrial production	Skill-int. production	Unskilled real wage
Partial integration, EU only	18.4	−2.5	−1.6	−1.4
No product market integration	18.4	−2.4	2.8	−1.3
Partial integration, EU and EFTA	17.6	−1.6	4.6	−0.5
Complete integration, EU and EFTA	18.2	−0.3	9.0	−0.2

boost to skill-intensive industries in the EFTA region. Finally, the real wage adjustments following from capital exports become significantly smaller the more fully EFTA is integrated in EU product markets.

We have also looked at the sensitivity of results with respect to initial differences in the rates of return on capital. As should be expected, the results are highly sensitive to these differences. If, for example, we assume that same initial rate of return on capital in EU North and EU South, capital imports to EU South drop from 15.2 per cent of the tradables capital stock to 1.1 per cent. As the evidence on differences in rates of return between these two regions is inconclusive, this sensitivity calls for caution in interpreting some of the results. Initial rate-of-return differences between EFTA and the EU regions are much clearer, so the qualitative results on EFTA capital exports and industrial relocation from EFTA to the EU regions should be robust.

4   Conclusions and extensions

We ask two questions in this chapter. One is how the combination of market integration and capital mobility will affect the regional pattern of industrial production in Western Europe. The other is how integration and capital movements interact; in particular, whether market integration can prevent large-scale capital exports from the (previous) EFTA countries. We obtain clear, but perhaps surprising, answers.

On the first question, we find no marked tendency to industrial concentration in the 'heart of Europe' (EU North) as the result of integration; nor will integration lead to increased inter-regional specialisation and trade. Instead, we shall expect a substantial increase in industrial production in EU South, at the expense of EFTA; but at the same time a significant absolute and relative increase in skill-intensive production in the EFTA countries.

On the second question, we find remarkably little interaction between market integration and capital mobility. Initial (modest) differences in rates of return induce substantial capital exports from the EFTA countries, and substantial capital imports to EU South; neither partial nor full product market integration will prevent this. Those in EFTA countries who have seen EU membership as a means to prevent capital exports, will thus find no support in our analysis.

We want to stress, however, that these results are highly preliminary; and that the analysis should be extended in at least three directions before any definite conclusions are drawn.

The obvious and perhaps most important extension is to include Eastern Europe in the analysis. In some respects, such an extension is likely to strengthen our conclusions. That seems almost a certainty for capital exports from EFTA, and it is probable when it comes to skill-intensive industrial production in EFTA and EU North. In other respects, inclusion of Eastern Europe could give qualitatively different conclusions. The question of where northern capital exports will go is the obvious one.

Another, perhaps equally important, extension is to allow for industrial agglomeration or external economies of scale, along the lines of the 'new' trade and geography literature. What we have found is that the combined effects of market integration and capital mobility – independently of external scale economies or other industrial-clustering forces – will not produce industrial concentration in Europe. The incorporation of such forces in the analysis could clearly give agglomeration effects.

The third extension has to do with trade costs. One possible explanation for the lack of interaction between capital mobility and product market integration is that substantial real trade costs for goods remain even in the complete integration case, while we have assumed no trade costs for capital. Even in the complete integration case, it is thus cheaper to export capital and produce near the market than to move final goods. An obvious, and important, extension is therefore to introduce trade costs for both goods and capital, and model market integration as a reduction in these.

NOTE

The research for this chapter was funded by the Norwegian Research Council. We are grateful to Richard Baldwin and Carl Hamilton for comments on an earlier draft.

REFERENCES

Gasiorek, M., A. Smith and A.J. Venables, 1991. 'Completing the internal market in the EC: factor demands and comparative advantage', in L.A. Winters and A. Venables (eds.), *European Integration: Trade and Industry*, Cambridge: Cambridge University Press

1992. '1992: trade and welfare – a general equilibrium model', in L.A. Winters (ed.), *Trade Flows and Trade Policy After '1992'*, Cambridge: Cambridge University Press

Haaland, J. and V. Norman, 1992, 'Global production effects of European integration', in L.A. Winters (ed.), *Trade Flows and Trade Policy After '1992'*, Cambridge: Cambridge University Press

Krugman, P.R., 1991. *Geography and Trade*, Cambridge, MA: MIT Press

Markusen, J.R., 1983. 'Factor movements and commodity trade as complements', *Journal of International Economics*, 14

Markusen, J.R. and L.E.O. Svensson, 1985. 'Trade in goods and factors with international differences in technology', *International Economic Review*, 26

Norman, V. and A.J. Venables, 1993. 'International trade, factor mobility and trade costs', CEPR, *Discussion Paper*, 766, London: CEPR

Pratten, C., 1987. 'A survey of economics of scale', in *Research on the Costs of non-Europe, Basic Findings*, vol. 2, Brussels: Commission of the European Communities

Smith, A. and A.J. Venables, 1988. 'Completing the internal market in the EC: some industry simulations', *European Economic Review*, 32, 1501–25

Discussion

CARL B. HAMILTON

Haaland and Norman's chapter 8 now takes into account most of any comments on the original version. This is most welcome.

My remaining comments relate to factors outside Haaland and Norman's model. They deal with differences in institutions among countries, which in turn may affect the location of production in a world with free mobility of capital. It seems to me that in the Western Europe of the 1990s the prospect of more marked institutional differences between EU countries and other, applicant, countries is an important factor that must be taken into account by both private and public decision makers. Such institutional aspects are not covered in Haaland and Norman's chapter.

Firms serving the combined EEA–EU market shop around for institutional stability in conditions of production. For the former EFTA countries, this raised two problems which would have remained had there been a five-country (Finland, Sweden, Norway, Austria and Iceland) EEA Agreement. First, the EEA governments would have had a weak bargaining position in Brussels on behalf of their firms when proposals were put forward to change the EU's legal system: EEA firms would lack EU firms' protection against new 'hostile' directives coming out of Brussels, risking the firms' competitive position. This problem is likely to be significant for Norway, Iceland and Lichtenstein, the only parties left in the EEA Agreement and now having an even weaker bargaining position compared to the original 1193 EEA Agreement.

Second, firms seek to reduce exchange rate instability and, *ceteris paribus*, prefer lower to higher interest rates. Thus, for the individual EEA country the issue is not whether the EMU is good or bad for EU member countries but, instead, given that the EU countries decide to form an EMU, in that situation what should an EEA country do? In the context of the Haaland and Norman chapter, what will be the consequences for location of production if an EEA country in effect chooses to turn down an offer to participate in EMU? To firms when they shop around this is likely to be seen as a signal that the currency of the EEA country in question is likely to depreciate in the future, and is likely to have an inflation premium attached to its domestic interest rate. These two factors are not captured, or attempted to be incorporated in the Haaland–Norman model. However, in my view they will be decisive for the location of production within Western Europe.

9 Implications of EU expansion for European agricultural policies, trade and welfare

KYM ANDERSON and ROD TYERS

1 Introduction

One of the thorniest issues that arises when there are discussions on reducing governmental barriers to economic integration concerns agriculture. This is true whether the negotiations are intra-national (between states or provinces), minilateral (as with free-trade areas or customs unions involving a small number of countries), or multilateral (as with the GATT-based trade negotiations), and is certainly evident in past and present negotiations to expand the number of full or associate members of the European Union (EU). The issue arises because while virtually all countries have interventionist farm policies, the levels and types of assistance provided vary markedly between countries. In the case of EU expansion, the member countries of the current European Free-Trade Association (EFTA), for example, have provided substantially higher levels of support to their farmers than was the case in the EU-12. On the other hand, even the most advanced of the former socialist countries of Eastern and Central Europe provide levels of farm assistance that on average are substantially lower than those in the EU.

In seeking to examine the likely effects on European food markets and on economic welfare of EFTA member countries joining the EU later this decade, and of the more advanced East European countries' access to EU markets being extended for farm products, it is helpful to proceed in two stages: first, to examine the effects of integration assuming Common Agricultural Policy (CAP) prices are adopted by the new entrants, and second, in the light of those projections, to consider what modifications to agricultural policies are likely in the transition to, and following, enlargement.[1] The chapter begins in section 2 by using straightforward partial equilibrium theory to show the effects on farm trade and on the economic welfare of different groups of (a) the EFTA countries joining the EU-12 and lowering their agricultural protection levels to those of the EU, and (b) the enlarged EU allowing the Visegrad-4 economies of Central Europe (Hungary, the Czech Republic, Poland and Slovakia) completely free access to EU markets for farm products. The latter is included to help shed light on the opportunity costs and benefits associated with limiting that market access, and on one of the reasons for EU reluctance to widen eastwards.

Section 3 then draws on a multicommodity simulation model of world food markets to quantify the orders of magnitude that could be involved by the year 2000 in such integration initiatives, assuming the EU-12's CAP prices at the time of integration are the food prices which new entrants adopt. In the first case the reference scenario assumes that the EU-12 implements during the mid-1990s the CAP reforms announced in mid-1992, while all other countries continue their current policy trends. The alternative scenario involves EFTA countries lowering their domestic food prices to those in the EU-12 after the CAP reform has been fully implemented. This alternative scenario is then taken as the reference scenario in the second case, in which Central and Western European food markets are integrated. The use of a multicommodity model ensures that the supply and demand interactions between the various farm products are captured. Although it is not a full general equilibrium model and so misses the interactions with non-farm sectors, that is not a serious limitation for these goods, particularly for Western Europe where farm products account for a very small share of the production and trade of those economies[2] and where trade between the EU-12 and EFTA is already close to being free in most other products.

Given the assumption (qualified later in the chapter) that CAP prices are unaffected by these integration initiatives, food producer and consumer welfare in the EU-12 is unchanged. EU taxpayers *are* affected, however. When EFTA lowers its domestic food prices to CAP levels, some of the EU-12's surplus can be disposed of in EFTA markets at CAP instead of international prices, so lowering the budgetary cost of EU export subsidies and raising international food prices slightly. That is, expanding the EU to include the EFTAns in this way would mean a liberalisation of West European agricultural protection which would improve overall welfare both in the EU and (according to the empirical results) in EFTA, as well as improve the welfare of the rest of the world's farmers.

But the modelling results suggest that these positive effects of EU–EFTA food market integration could be more than offset by allowing Central European farmers preferential access to EU food markets. A complete integration of Western and Central European food markets at projected CAP prices would make Europe's farm policies more protectionist on average, and while that would benefit Central European farmers it would require a huge increase in the budgetary cost of the CAP to dispose of the transforming economies' export surplus.

After qualifying the empirical results in section 4, the final section 5 of the chapter examines the implications of the results for the prospects for EU enlargement and addresses the question of whether, and how, CAP protection levels are likely to change in response to the pressures for closer economic integration from the non-EU countries of Western and Central Europe. Clearly from the viewpoint of agriculture at least, EFTA's membership of the EU would be favoured by all but EFTAn farmers, whereas the CAP budgetary costs of allowing Central Europeans to join the EU are likely to delay an eastern enlargement. If and when EU–EFTA integration takes place, it could result in upward pressure on CAP prices, however, thanks to stronger protectionist sentiments from the EFTAn ministers of agriculture (and to a greater 'cheap-rider' problem because of the enlarged membership). On the other hand, new pressures for lower agricultural protection could come from the former socialist countries if their bids for EU membership are effectively ignored until well into the next century. To reduce the risk of that adding to existing external pressures for further reductions in CAP prices, Western Europe may well continue to give farmers in those former communist countries limited preferential access to EU markets.

2 Effects of integrating European agricultural markets: the simple analytics

Tables 9.1 and 9.2 provide the basic data necessary to analyse qualitatively the effects of European food market integration. The points to note at this stage of the analysis are (a) that 1990 agricultural protection levels on average were considerably higher in EFTA and much lower (close to zero) in Central Europe compared with the EU-12's CAP; (b) that all three country groups were slight net food exporters in 1990, that is, they were slightly more than fully self-sufficient in food at those protection levels (although not in all food product groups); and (c) that some EFTA countries in 1990 were net importers of temperate foods, Austria was almost exactly self-sufficient, and Finland was a net exporter of food.

In this and section 3 it is assumed that integration will involve the new entrants adopting the CAP prices of the EU-12. The assumption is unrealistic in the sense that in practice integration is likely to alter the political economy of CAP price-setting, but it is useful in that it allows one to see the effects of not altering CAP prices and thereby provides an

Table 9.1   Food price distortions and self-sufficiency, Western and Central Europe, 1990[a]

	Wheat	Coarse grains	Rice	Sugar	Dairy products	Ruminant meat	Non-ruminant meat	**Total**
Distortion coefficients								
EU-12								
–prod	1.75	2.22	2.78	2.27	4.00	2.33	1.54	**2.52**
–cons	1.54	1.89	2.33	1.92	2.50	1.89	1.33	**1.88**
EFTA								
–prod	8.33	4.00	1.00	3.33	6.67	3.70	2.78	**4.97**
–cons	2.22	2.56	1.00	2.38	2.78	2.63	2.33	**2.57**
CE-4[b]								
–prod	1.20	1.36	1.00	0.84	0.93	1.86	1.20	**1.23**
–cons	0.98	1.36	1.00	1.26	0.51	0.89	1.06	**0.92**
Self-sufficiency (%)[c]								
EU-12	126	103	90	94	105	102	102	**105**
EFTA	118	115	0	94	103	109	99	**105**
CE-4	101	94	13	97	101	113	104	**102**

Notes:

[a] The distortions shown are based on the producer and consumer subsidy equivalents but are expressed as the equivalents of domestic-to-border product price ratios. They include national government supports as well as those provided by the EU's CAP.

[b] CE-4 refers to Visegrad-4 (Hungary, The Czech Republic, Poland and Slovakia).

[c] The self-sufficiency numbers are the ratios of domestic production to consumption, expressed as a percentage.

Source: Tyers (1994, table 4 and appendix 2).

indication of the likely extent of pressure to change those prices, as discussed in section 5. The fact that the domestic-to-border price ratios for the three country groups shown in Table 9.1 are so different ensures that these effects of integration on European food markets will be non-trivial.

2.1   Effects of EFTA countries joining the EU-12 and adopting CAP prices

Since some EFTA countries are slightly more than fully self-sufficient in one or more temperate farm products at the high domestic prices currently in place, and others are slightly less than fully self-sufficient (see

Table 9.2 Net exports of food products by EFTA countries and the EU-12, 1990, $ million, 1990 US dollars

	Austria	Finland	Norway	Sweden	Switzer- land	Total EFTA	Total EU-12
Grains (SITC 04)	53	83	−150	81	−169	−102	5390
Other animal feeds (SITC 08 + 22)	−172	−102	−143	−169	−185	−771	−8334
Meats (SITC 01)	90	54	0	−76	−371	−303	−61
Dairy products and eggs (SITC 02)	64	187	80	20	190	541	3363
Sugar (SITC 06)	−33	−20	−118	−50	−26	−247	968
Total of above	2	202	−331	−194	−561	−882	1326

Source: USDA (1992, Appendix Tables 44 and 45).

table 9.2), both of these situations are depicted by the excess demand curves in parts a and b of figure 9.1, where it is assumed for diagrammatic simplicity that the same domestic price, P_f, operates for producers and consumers in both sets of EFTA countries. Part c of figure 9.1 depicts the EU-12's excess supply curve for those goods. The EU-12's food price level is lower than in EFTA (P_e rather than P_f) but still above the price in international markets (P_w) and sufficient to make the EU-12 more than fully self-sufficient in farm products.

Should EFTA's markets be integrated with the EU-12's and adopt the EU's domestic price level of P_e, this partial liberalisation would raise each of the EFTA countries' excess demand by Q_fQ_f. International food prices would rise, benefiting farmers outside Western Europe as well as countries with a comparative advantage in temperate farm products and the world as a whole. But whether economic welfare improves or worsens for the integrating countries is, as is well known from customs union theory, an empirical question. In the EFTA countries farmers would lose and food consumers (and most non-farm producers) would gain, but net economic welfare would increase unambiguously only for those EFTA countries that are net food exporters, by *adefg* in figure 9.1a (which is made up of the gain to EFTA consumers net of the loss to EFTA farmers, *cde-abc*, plus the export subsidy that is no longer needed, *abfg*).[3] In the case of EFTA countries that are net importers of these goods, it is clear from figure 9.1b that their net economic welfare increases only if the gain to consumers net of the loss to farmers, *hjqr*, exceeds the loss of import tariff revenue, *hmnr*. The reason for the ambiguity is that while EFTA's own distortion is being reduced, it effectively also worsens its

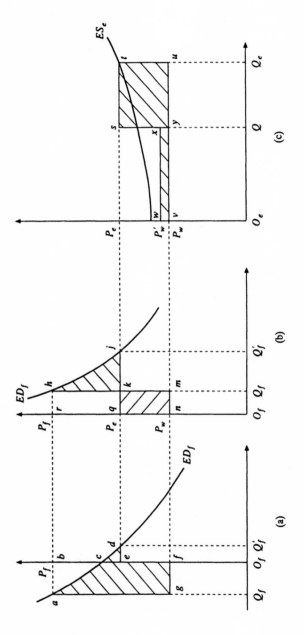

Figure 9.1 Effects of EFTA countries joining the EU's CAP
a Food-exporting EFTA countries
b Food-importing EFTA countries
c EU-12

terms of trade by paying P_e instead of P_w for its imports. Its net welfare is more likely to improve the larger the gap between P_f and P_e, the closer is this EFTA country to being self-sufficient in these goods, and the more elastic is its excess demand curve.

Economic welfare in the EU-12 is also likely but not certain to improve. In the situation illustrated in figure 9.1c it would gain *stuvwx*. This area has two components. The first is *stuy*, the gain from diverting some exports from the international market (where they had received P_w) to EFTA markets (where they receive P_e for QQ_e units which is the sum of O_fQ_f across all EFTA countries). The second is *vwxy*, which is due to the increase in the international price (resulting from the reduction in EFTA's net exports) received for the EU's remaining exports to the rest of the world. But if the new EU entrants from EFTA were to remain net exporters as a group, the first component (*stuy*) would not exist, and the second component (*vwxy*) would be offset by the transfer from the EU-12 to the new entrants that would be necessary to fund the export subsidy required to dispose of their remaining surplus, in which case the EU-12 could be worse off.[4]

Clearly, empirical analysis is necessary to determine not just the extent but even the direction of some of the effects of integrating Western Europe's agricultural markets. What is clear, though, is that such an integration would lower agricultural protection and thereby would be welfare improving for the world as a whole, for the EU and for the rest of the world's farmers, and – importantly from a political economy viewpoint – it would reduce the budgetary cost of the CAP.[5] But, before turning to some empirical results to illuminate its other effects, it is of interest to supplement the above analysis with a similar qualitative analysis involving an integration of Western and Central European markets for food products.

2.2 Effects of East European countries getting open access to West European agricultural markets

Some of the economies of Central and Eastern Europe and the former Soviet Union are net exporters and others are net importers of farm products at current domestic prices (indicated in table 9.7, p. 233), but in all cases those domestic prices when converted at equilibrium exchange rates are well below West European domestic prices (see table 9.1). Should all or a subset of the Central and East European economies in transition (for example, the Visegrad-4 countries) be given preferential, tariff-free access to West European agricultural markets at existing EU prices, the increase in their excess supply would reduce international food prices, more or less offsetting the increase caused by EU–EFTA integration. Whether this would represent an increase in distortions in world food markets depends on how low Central European prices are. If they are well below international prices, the distortionary cost of them remaining there may be greater than that from having them above international prices, at P_e. But if their domestic prices are close to or above P'_w (the international price following EU–EFTA integration), then the integrating of Western and Central European food markets would worsen world welfare (assuming that lesser distortions exist in non-agricultural markets).

The welfare effects for food-exporting and food-importing Central European economies can be seen in figure 9.2, where the excess supply curves are shown as ES_c. For diagrammatic simplicity it is assumed that the domestic producer and consumer prices prior to integration are the same, at P_c. The provision of free access to the high-priced West European markets clearly would benefit the food-exporting Central European countries' farmers more than it would hurt their consumers, the difference being represented by *abde* in figure 9.2a. However, such integration could harm food-importing Central European economies, as it would if *fgh-hkj* in figure 9.2b were negative. The latter is more likely the more import-dependent those countries are at the time of integration, the more inelastic is their excess supply curve, and the smaller the gap prior to integration between Western and Central European domestic food prices.

For Western Europe such an integration initiative is likely but not certain to increase the CAP budget, and hence worsen the West's economic welfare. On the one hand, if Central Europe were to be a net food exporter after integration, then additional CAP funds would be needed for export subsidies to dispose of (the equivalent of) its export surplus which, in terms of figure 9.2, is the sum of O_cQ_c' across the four Central European economies. The total transfer would be *abce* + *fgmk*, which is clearly less than the net gain to Central Europe of *abde* + *fgh-hkj*, the difference being *bcd* + *gmj* which is the net welfare cost of expanding Central Europe's excess supply beyond its pre-integration level. Furthermore, since the international price would fall because of the greater excess supply on international markets, Western Europe would also have to provide a larger export subsidy than previously for each unit of its own surplus sold to other countries.[6] This illustrates the general point that direct aid is less costly to the economies concerned than (what in this case is effectively) tied aid, the 'tie' being that Central Europe must add a price distortion to its food markets. And it is a reminder that the cliche 'trade is better than aid' applies to MFN, non-

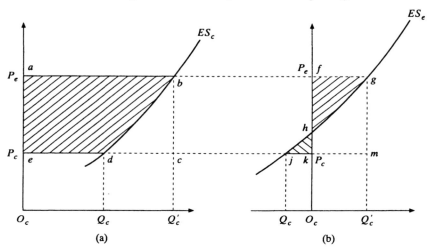

Figure 9.2 Effects of CE-4 countries joining an enlarged EU's CAP and being or becoming net food exporters
a Food-exporting CE-4 countries
b Food-importing CE-4 countries

discriminatory trade and not to the preferential, conditional trade being analysed here.[7]

If, on the other hand, Central European farm output were to grow sufficiently slower than domestic food demand in the next few years such that, even at CAP prices these countries as a group were net food importers, then integration could reduce the CAP budget and be a net benefit to Western Europe. Figure 9.3 illustrates this possibility. The raising of domestic food prices in Central Europe from P_c to P_e would still reduce Europe's excess supply and so depress international food prices a little (the fall from P'_w to P''_w in figure 9.3b), but this negative effect on the CAP budget would be more than offset by the positive effect of being able to dispose of some of the EU's surplus ($EE_e = Q_c'O_c$) at the high CAP price of P_e in Central Europe instead of at the world price. The net gain to Western Europe would be *fghj-hnmk*. In this circumstance consumers would lose more than farmers would gain in the Central European economies, the net loss being *abcd* in figure 9.3a. Even so, it is not inconceivable that Central European governments would be attracted to such an integration, either as a price to pay for a broad-based free trade agreement with the EU and/or to appease what may become (as it has in the West) a powerful domestic interest group, namely farmers.[8]

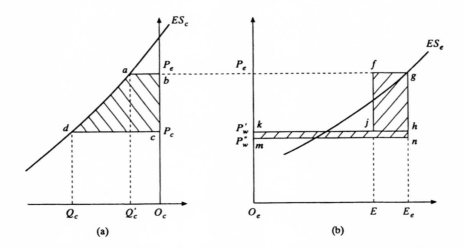

Figure 9.3   Effects of CE-4 countries joining an enlarged EU's CAP and remaining net food importers
a   Food-importing CE-4 countries
b   Food-exporting CE-4 countries

3   Effects of integrating European agricultural markets: empirical modelling

Clearly, not all of the directions of the budgetary and welfare effects mentioned above can be determined *a priori*, and in any case there is an interest in the orders of magnitude involved even for the effects of known sign. Such quantification requires information on the policy distortions in place in the three different groups of European countries identified above, as well as a model of world markets for the agricultural products of importance to Europe. Furthermore, the model needs to be able to project markets and policies into the future, since any such integration is unlikely to begin to occur before the latter half of the 1990s. One such model, documented in Tyers and Anderson (1992), has been updated and revised recently to allow a more detailed analysis of the effects of reforms in the various East European and former Soviet economies (see Tyers, 1994). A brief description of that model is given below, followed by a summary of empirical results generated from using it to simulate the above market integration scenarios.

3.1   The Tyers–Anderson world food model

The model used is a dynamic, multicommodity simulation model of markets for the major traded food staples. Seven commodity groups are included: wheat, coarse grain, rice, sugar, dairy products, meat and ruminants (cattle and sheep), and meat of non-ruminants (pigs and poultry). These seven commodity groups account for about half of world food trade, most of the rest being edible oils and beverages. It is not a general equilibrium model, in that it excludes markets for other tradable goods and services (including agricultural inputs and food processing and distribution services), for physical and financial factors of production, and for non-tradables. Currency exchange rates have thus to enter as exogenous parameters. This drawback is offset, however, by the model's detailed specification of farm product markets and other features which include the following:

- It is global in coverage, involving 35 countries or country groups spanning the world, so that both domestic and international effects of policy changes in one or more countries or commodities can be determined endogenously.
- It incorporates the cross-effects in both production and consumption between the interdependent markets for grains, livestock products and sugar.
- Its dynamic capacity is such that the model incorporates the effects of structural, policy, income, population and productivity changes for each year through to 2010, so that short-run as well as longer-run supply adjustments are incorporated (although for present purposes a long-run comparative static version of the model is used so as to see the net effect of market integration on prices, quantities and welfare following full adjustment).
- Food price and trade policies (other than the CAP in the present analysis) are endogenous in that international-to-domestic food price transmission equations are used to incorporate the two key features of each country's food policies, namely, the protection component, which drives a wedge between the international and domestic trend level of food prices faced by producers and consumers around which prices fluctuate from year to year, and the stabilisation or insulation component, which allows a country's trade fluctuations to limit the degree to which the domestic price of a good changes in response to shifts in domestic output or in its international price.

Production behaviour is represented by Nerlovian reduced-form partial-adjustment equations which are log-linear, resulting in constant supply elasticities. Allowance is also made for the effects of land set-aside policies, in the form of supply curve shifts (appropriately discounted to allow for 'slippage').

Direct human consumption is assumed to be characterised by income and price elasticities of demand which are set to decline slightly over time. The demand for livestock feeds is based on input–output coefficients for each livestock product, which again are assumed to change over time not only as the domestic price of feedgrain changes but also as the proportion of livestock output that is grain-fed alters.

The price transmission equations, which summarise a variety of government interventions in each country, are estimates from FAO and national time series price data for the past three decades. They indicate the extent to which a country's policies alter the domestic price in response to a change in the international price of food. They are reduced-form Nerlovian partial-adjustment equations which distinguish short-run from longer-run elasticities of price transmission. Separate elasticities have been estimated for producer and consumer prices. In general, even the long-run price transmission elasticities are less than unity, reflecting the prevalence of non-tariff protection instruments in many food markets.

The estimated welfare impact of a policy change has four components. The benefit to food consumers is the expected Hicksian equivalent variation in their income; the benefit to food producers is the expected net change in producer surplus; the government revenue effect is the expected net budgetary impact of producer, consumer and trade taxes and subsidies; and the storage benefit is the expected change in profits from stockholding. All benefits are evaluated assuming risk-neutrality.

Structurally, the model is a set of expressions for quantities consumed, produced, and stored, each of which is a function of known past prices and endogenous current prices. Simulations start from a 1990 base and can extend through to the year 2010, although in this chapter attention will focus on the effects of policy changes only to the year 2000.

The degree of policy distortions and of food self-sufficiency in the model's base period (the trend level for 1990) for the three country groups of interest in this study are summarised in table 9.1 (p. 212). In the case of the price distortions the averages for Western Europe are based on the producer and consumer subsidy equivalents published by the OECD (1992),[9] while the averages for Eastern Europe are necessarily more rudimentary estimates compiled by Tyers (1994) and based on data being analysed continually by the US Department of Agriculture (see, for example, Webb *et al.*, 1990), the World Bank and others. The production, consumption, storage, and trade data in the model, from which the self-sufficiency data are derived, are from the Australian National University's International Economic Data Bank and are based on FAO and USDA series.

Table 9.1 makes clear that in the model's base period (1990):

- EFTA countries on average are even more protectionist towards their farmers than is the EU-12, while the Visegrad-4 or CE-4 countries (Hungary, the Czech Republic, Poland and Slovakia), have domestic prices much closer to those in international markets.
- In all three country groups, producer price distortions are substantially greater than consumer price distortions.
- All three country groups are slightly more than fully self-sufficient in these foods as a group, given their levels of protection.
- The extent of both price distortions and self-sufficiency vary considerably across commodities for each of the country groups.

This last point, together with the fact that there are varying degrees of substitutability among these product groups in both production and consumption and varying extents to which livestock is grain-fed,[10] ensures that it is not possible to infer welfare effects of market integration from the weighted average price distortions and self-sufficiencies alone. For the same reasons, plus the fact that there are varying differences between producer and consumer price distortions, it is difficult to infer the effects of policy changes on government revenue. This underscores further the need for formal empirical modelling.

3.2   The reference scenario

Setting a reference scenario for the 1990s, against which to compare market integration scenarios by the turn of the century, is a non-trivial task. Except in the case of the transforming socialist countries, the model's assumed rates of growth of population and *per capita* income, and changes in exchange rates, are derived from the World Bank and Wharton Econometrics, while the assumed rates of farm productivity growth are extrapolations from the previous three decades. The reference scenario also assumes that food policy trends (as incorporated in the price transmission equations for each country and commodity) will remain unchanged in the 1990s except in the EU. It may well be that a Uruguay Round agreement is reached that leads to some agricultural protection cuts elsewhere before the end of the 1990s (in which case the qualifications in section 4 below become relevant), but at the time of writing the uncertainty about that possibility and the degree of liberalisation it might involve was too great to warrant its inclusion in the reference scenario.

For the EU-12, it is assumed that the unilateral reforms announced in mid-1992 will be implemented in the mid-1990s, and that compared with the model's 1990 base they will involve:

- A phased reduction of 35 per cent in the domestic prices of grains (regardless of what happens to international prices).
- Compensatory payments to grain producers on condition that 15 per cent of land is set-aside (which is modelled as a shift in supply curves so as to reduce grain output by 10 per cent, the assumption being that, as in the US, there is a one-third 'slippage' factor).
- A phased reduction of 15 per cent in the consumer and producer prices of beef (again irrespective of what happens to international prices).
- No change to sugar, dairy or other livestock policies.

Finally, for the transforming socialist countries of Eastern Europe and the former Soviet republics the reference scenario assumes low growth following declines in output and incomes during 1991–3, such that by the year 2000 these economies' food markets are the same size as in 1990. This conservative choice for the post-1993 rates of growth of population, income and farm productivity is deliberate, so as to reduce the risk of overstating the effects of integrating Western and Central European food markets.[11] It is also assumed that these countries continue to practise a considerable degree of insulation from food markets in the rest of the world.

Given all these assumptions, the model's reference scenario projects that real international food prices during the 1990s will trend downward slightly as they have in previous decades, and be nearly 8 per cent lower on average in 2000 than they were in 1990. It also projects that Western Europe's food export surplus will continue to rise despite some reform in EU policies, partly because of farm productivity growth continuing to outpace demand growth and partly because the unilateral reform is assumed to reduce protection of only a subset of foods (so that farm resources move to the unreformed industries such as dairying and non-ruminant meat).

3.3   EU and EFTA food market integration

How different would food markets be, and what would be the welfare effects, if all the EFTA countries were to join the EU and to adopt the

Table 9.3   Annual quantity and price effects of EFTA joining the EU-12's CAP, 2000

	Grains	Sugar	Dairy products	Ruminant meat	Non-ruminant meat	Total
International price (% differences)	2.0	0.7	2.5	1.3	1.1	**1.7**
EFTA's net exports (mmt difference)	−6.0	−0.3	−4.1	−0.3	−1.1	**−US$4.6 billion**
EFTA output (% difference relative to 1990)	−24.7	25.4	0.1	6.6	−18.2	na
EFTA self-sufficiency						
− 1990	115	94	103	109	99	**105**
− 2000	78	111	98	96	56	**84**

Source: Authors' model results.

na Not available.
mmt Million metric tons.

same domestic prices as those assumed for the EU in the reference scenario? The model is used to simulate that market integration by phasing it in during the mid-1990s, on the assumption that the non-farm aspects of EU–EFTA integration have no effect on food markets.[12] Pertinent differences between this and the reference scenario are summarised in tables 9.3 and 9.4.

Not surprisingly, the lowering of EFTA's agricultural protection to EU levels causes international food prices to be higher in 2000, by 1.7 per cent on average, and EFTA's net exports of farm products to be lower, by $4.6 billion (in 1990 US dollars), compared with the reference scenario for 2000. EFTA's output of only some farm products would be lower in 2000 than in 1990, however. Grain production would be 25 per cent less than a decade earlier, and non-ruminant meat output would be 18 per cent lower, but EFTA's production of dairy products would be maintained and its beef and sugar output would be higher than in 1990, by 7 and 25 per cent, respectively. Self-sufficiency would drop below 100 per cent in EFTA for all but sugar, and the aggregate level of food self-sufficiency would be 84 per cent, compared with 105 per cent in 1990 and 121 per cent in 2000 under the reference scenario without integration and

Table 9.4   Annual welfare effects of EFTA joining the EU-12's CAP, 2000, $ billion, 1990 US dollars

	EFTA	EU-12	Enlarged EU
Consumer welfare	7.9	0.0	7.9
Producer welfare	−29.7	0.0	−29.7
Government revenue	30.8	2.0	32.8
Net economic welfare	9.0	2.0	11.0

Source: Authors' model results

with continued protection growth. While that may seem a large drop, it certainly does not support the claim of the more extreme of EFTA's farm lobby groups that the agricultural sectors in EFTA countries would disappear if CAP prices were to be adopted.

The estimated welfare effects in EFTA and the EU of integrating their food markets and EFTA becoming part of an enlarged EU's CAP are shown for the year 2000 in table 9.4. The benefit to consumers in EFTA countries would be almost $8 billion per year (in 1990 US dollars) compared with the alternative of continued protection growth in EFTA, while farmers would be worse off by about $30 billion per year. The biggest beneficiary would be EFTA taxpayers: because EFTA would no longer have a farm surplus to be disposed of internationally with the help of export subsidies, and because the wedge between producer and consumer prices would be narrowed, the drain on government revenue in EFTA would be lower by $31 billion or an average of almost $1000 per person per year (not counting any contributions by EFTA country governments to the EU budget, which are not included in the model, and assuming the wedge between producer and consumer prices is paid for from the EU's budget). Thus the net benefit to EFTA countries is estimated to be $9 billion per year, *less* those countries' net contribution to the EU budget (at least part of which would be used to help fund the CAP). This net benefit would represent about 1 per cent of EFTA's GDP[13] – a massive contribution, given that agriculture's total contribution to GDP in these economies would be no more than 2 per cent when measured at CAP prices in the year 2000.

EU-12 farmers and consumers are unaffected directly in this scenario because of the assumption that the prices they face are unchanged. But government revenue in the EU-12 is enhanced by $2 billion per year (plus any direct contributions from EFTA), because under this scenario some of the EU-12 farm surplus can be sold to consumers in EFTA instead of on the lower-priced international market (saving $1.7 billion), and the rest that is sold in the latter market receives a slightly higher price than before and so requires a smaller export subsidy (saving $0.3 billion). The sales to EFTA account for about one-quarter of the value (at CAP prices) and one-seventh of the volume of the EU-12's net farm exports. In the rest of the world, food exporters would be slightly better off, and food importers slightly worse off, as a result of international food prices being 1.7 per cent higher because of EU–EFTA food market integration.

These results for agriculture differ in an important respect from those for other sectors. Generally, when a small set of economies integrates with a much larger set, most of the benefits – especially as a share of GDP – accrue to the former (EFTA in this case – see, for example, Haaland and Norman, 1992; CEPR, 1992). This asymmetry is less obvious in the case of agriculture because the cost to EU-12 of the CAP would be reduced by having access to EFTA markets for disposing of part of the EU-12's surplus of farm products. Moreover, according to the above estimates it would take a direct transfer of only $4 billion per year from EFTA countries to the EU budget to ensure that the EU-12 gained more than the new entrants from integrating Western Europe's food markets. Recall, though, that the above results are based on the assumption that *all* EFTA member countries join the EU *and* that they phase down their food prices to the reformed CAP levels of the late 1990s. To the extent that only some EFTA countries join the EU and/or that the common CAP price levels after integration are higher because of the new entrants' influence on the annual price-setting process (discussed in section 5), the economic benefits will be lower, or could even be reversed.

3.4 Effects of Western Europe providing Central Europe with preferential access to its food markets

It is unlikely that any of Europe's former socialist countries will become full members of the EU before the next century. However, the Visegrad-4 or CE-4 countries (Hungary, the Czech Republic, Poland and Slovakia) are hopeful of early consideration. In any case, it is of interest to consider what the effects would be if they were given preferential access to West European markets, if only as a measure of the cost to them of delaying CE-4 membership consideration, and of the cost forgone to the EU (the latter providing insights as to why some EU farmers are so strongly opposed to the granting of preferential market access to East European farmers). For this purpose, the previous scenario in which the EU-12 and EFTA countries' food markets are integrated is taken as the reference

Table 9.5   Annual quantity and price effects of CE-4 countries joining an enlarged EU's CAP, 2000

	Grains	Sugar	Dairy products	Ruminant meat	Non-ruminant meat	Total
International price (% differences rel. to reference in 2000)	0.4	−1.7	−11.6	−2.6	−1.6	**−2.0**
CE-4 production % difference rel. to reference in 2000)	12	14	69	46	34	na
CE-4 consumption (% difference rel. to reference in 2000)	24	−18	−17	−16	−9	na
CE-4 net exports (mmt difference rel. to reference in 2000)	−7.6	1.0	22.0	0.8	2.0	**US$9.6 billion**
CE-4 self-sufficiency in 2000						
− reference	97	97	100	114	102	**102**
− integration	86	135	202	200	150	**138**

Source: Authors' model results.

na Not available.
mmt Million metric tons.

scenario, against which is compared a scenario in which the food markets of the CE-4 countries are combined with the newly integrated Western European food markets. A consequence is that food prices in the CE-4 countries move up to those in Western Europe. In this scenario, the EU is assumed to fund the producer and export subsidies necessary to maintain those high domestic prices and to dispose of the additional surplus of the region, as if CE-4 was a full participant in the CAP.

The pertinent effects of this subsequent market integration are summarised in tables 9.5 and 9.6. The raising of CE-4 domestic prices causes international food prices to be lower in 2000, by 2 per cent (more than enough to offset the increase of 1.7 per cent that would result from EFTA's food market integration with the EU-12), and it causes Central

Table 9.6 Annual welfare effects of CE-4 countries joining an enlarged EU's CAP, 2000, $ billion, 1990 US dollars

	CE-4	Enlarged EU	Enlarged EU plus CE-4
Consumer welfare	−15.9	0.0	−15.9
Producer welfare	52.5	0.0	52.5
Government revenue	0.0	−47.4	−47.4
Net economic welfare	36.6	−47.4	−10.8

Source: Authors' model results

Europe's net exports of farm products to be higher, by $9.6 billion per year (in 1990 US dollars), compared with the reference scenario for 2000. The output of all farm products in CE-4 would be higher, but the production increases (and hence the international price decreases) would be concentrated in the livestock sectors: after full adjustment the annual output of pig and poultry meat would be up by a third, that of beef by a half, and that of dairy products by two-thirds, compared with a rise of only one-eighth for grain. The relatively higher prices of livestock products would curtail their consumption in CE-4 countries and lead to a greater direct grain consumption by people adapting to the relative price change, but most of the greater grain consumption (which is up by a quarter) would be as animal feed. About half of all CE-4 livestock output and a quarter of its sugar would be exported under this scenario, while self-sufficiency in grains would be somewhat lower (86 instead of 97 per cent). The aggregate level of CE-4 food self-sufficiency would be 138 per cent, compared with 102 per cent in 2000 under the reference scenario in which there is no preferential access to West European markets.

The estimated welfare effects in CE-4 and in the enlarged EU of integrating their food markets and CE-4 adopting the domestic price levels of the enlarged EU's CAP are shown for the year 2000 in table 9.6. The cost of the higher prices to consumers in the CE-4 countries would be almost $16 billion per year (in 1990 US dollars) compared with the reference scenario in which CE-4 prices stay close to international levels. Farmers in CE-4, on the other hand, would be better off by a little over $50 billion per year. Assuming the EU funds all the production and export subsidies required to sustain these higher prices in CE-4 and there is no transfer of government funds from CE-4 to the EU, there would be a net benefit to these Central European countries of almost $37 billion per year. However, this is possible only because of the assumed transfer from the EU to provide the necessary subsidies to CE-4 producers and exporters, which would amount to $47 billion per year.[14] The EU would also have to pay an extra $0.4 billion per year in export subsidies to dispose of its own excess supply on a slightly lower-priced international market. The net economic loss to Western and Central Europe combined is thus $11 billion per year from freely allowing CE-4 *de facto* participation in the EU's CAP. In other words, for every dollar this integration initiative would transfer to Central Europe's farmers, it would cost Central European consumers 30 cents and Western European taxpayers 91 cents, or a total of $1.21 (not including the resource costs of raising through taxes and then dispersing that money).

In the rest of the world, food exporters generally would be slightly worse off, and food importers slightly better off, as a result of international food prices being 2 per cent lower because of EU–CE food market integration. The net gain in the rest of the world would be less than the net loss in Europe (by a little under $1 billion per year), illustrating the possibility raised in section 2 that global economic welfare could be reduced by this integration initiative through increasing the distortions to world food markets.

4   Qualifications to the results

Several qualifications to these results are in order. First, we have assumed in the initial reference scenario that the EU but no other industrial countries reform their agricultural policies from the mid-1990s. If in fact we had assumed that a Uruguay Round agreement was reached that caused all industrial countries to reduce their agricultural protection levels by a similar proportion to the CAP reform (by around one-quarter),[15] the results would be different in two ways. One is that EFTA's agricultural protection levels would have declined instead of risen in the latter 1990s, which would reduce, by about one-third, the estimated gains from integrating the EU-12 and EFTA. The other impact on the results comes about because international food prices would be a further 3 or 4 per cent higher on average (Tyers and Anderson, 1992, ch. 7). This would reduce slightly further the welfare gains to Western Europe of integrating the EU-12 and EFTA food markets, as well as reduce the cost to Western Europe of allowing Central European farmers preferential access to EU markets. But it would do little to reduce the Central European farmers' demands for preferential access to those markets, especially if CE-4 governments had allowed little of the Uruguay Round-induced international price rise to be transmitted to their domestic markets.

Second, we have assumed that there are no supply constraints other than price on milk production and that there is no reform to EU dairy policy. In fact a small price reduction has been subsequently fore-shadowed, and production controls are in place and may be tightened. Our results suggest that if there were to be less dairy price support under the CAP by 2000, this could boost significantly the gain to Western Europe from its integration. The difference would be substantial both because the domestic price gap between the EU-12 and EFTA is largest for dairy products, and because (not unrelatedly) among the agricultural products the ratio of EFTA to EU farm production is highest for dairy products. And for similar but opposite reasons, the loss to Western Europe (and gain to Central Europe) from allowing access to Central Europeans would be substantially lessened if CAP milk prices were lowered.[16]

Third, if only some of the EFTA countries join the EU, the effects will of course be lower. For example, if Switzerland, Iceland and Liechtenstein stayed out of maintained high farm protection, the estimated effects of EU–EFTA integration would need to be reduced by about one-quarter. For this and the previous two reasons the above results concerning EU–EFTA integration might be considered upper-bound estimates. An offsetting influence, however, is becoming evident: farm lobby groups in EFTA are arguing that if EU membership is inevitable, their output should be encouraged as much as possible prior to integration (by way of higher domestic price supports), so as to establish a larger base on which to claim CAP benefits after joining.

Fourth, should there not only be no Uruguay Round agreement but also a lesser CAP reform in the 1990s, the gains to Western Europe and the rest of the world from EFTA joining the CAP would be less, and the costs to Western Europe (and the world as a whole) and gains to Central Europe from allowing Central European farmers access to the EU would be greater. (The latter could be offset by a quota restriction or tax on exports from Central to Western Europe, of course.)

And fifth, what if, instead of Central European economies growing slowly over the rest of the 1990s (as we assume), they were to expand rapidly?[17] On the one hand, if their productivity growth were to be concentrated in agriculture, Central Europe's excess supply of farm products would be greater, which would raise the costs to the EU and the world – and raise the benefits to Central Europe – of its preferential access to EU food markets. On the other hand, if the growth were spread across all sectors, it is possible that the region's excess supply of farm products would be smaller than we project in the reference scenario for 2000, which would lower the estimated costs and benefits of providing preferential access. This possibility is not unreasonable for both demand and supply reasons. On the demand side, incomes and hence food consumption would be growing faster, while on the supply side, being relatively densely populated and relatively well endowed with skilled industrial workers, these economies might strengthen their comparative advantage in manufactures and experience a de-agriculturalisation in the medium-to-longer term (even though in the short-to-medium term it is likely that agriculture will be the faster-growing sector, for reasons spelled out in CEPR, 1990, Hamilton and Winters, 1992 and Anderson, 1993). This double-edged qualification is a reminder that there is necessarily a wide confidence band around any projection for Central Europe over the next decade.

5   Summary and implications of the results for European agricultural policies and integration initiatives

From the points of view of West European taxpayers and EFTA's consumers, the adoption of CAP prices in EFTA and food market integration with the EU-12 would be a good thing: according to the above results, government revenue would be $33 billion higher and consumer welfare $8 billion higher per year in Western Europe. The net welfare benefit to EFTA is estimated to be $9 billion per year or around 1 per cent of their GDP. The benefit to the EU-12 would be smaller but still non-trivial at $2 billion per year, most of which would result from being able to dispose of some of the EU's farm surplus in EFTA markets instead of in the lower-priced international market. Welfare in the world as a whole would increase as a result of such a cut in EFTA's farm protection, and in particular farmers outside Western Europe would benefit. Farmers in EFTA are opposed to such integration, however, which is understandable given the loss they would incur (almost $30 billion per year if they were not compensated, according to table 9.4).

Despite their relatively small numbers (or in fact partly because of it – see Anderson, 1994a), the political power of farmers in EFTA is such that they will have to be appeased before closer integration eventuates. At least three possible avenues may be considered. One is to copy Sweden, which has already begun unilaterally to reduce its agricultural protection in anticipation of joining the EU and has chosen to provide generous direct compensation to farmers.

A second possibility is that the eventual accession agreement will include some raising of CAP prices, which would erode some of the economic gains to Western Europe (and to food exporters in the rest of the world) from EU–EFTA food market integration – or could even *reverse* the direction of the net welfare effects shown in section 3.3. For reasons discussed below such an explicit increase in agricultural protection seems improbable, and in any case may be acceptable to the EU-12 only if EFTA countries covered the extra budgetary cost each year of higher CAP prices not only in their own countries but also in other member countries, which would amount to a politically prohibitive expenditure.

A third possibility is that *after* the EFTA countries integrate into the EU there is a shift in the centre of gravity in the annual CAP meetings which set agricultural prices for the subsequent year. It would most likely shift in a more protectionist direction, for four reasons. One is simply that the newly admitted Nordic and Alpine farm ministers will be more protectionist than the average EU-12 minister, judging from current protection levels in the two groups of countries. The second reason is that, with the addition of several new members, the EU's cheap-rider problem would increase significantly: each country would have more incentive (a) to seek price rises for the products for which their excess supply is relatively large and (b) to cooperate less in policing acreage set-asides, production quotas and other farm supply constraints. The third reason is that the current budgetary restraint on further CAP expenditures would be lessened considerably, partly because EU–EFTA integration would involve significant direct financial contributions to the EU budget but also because that integration would cause EFTA to absorb some of the EU-12's surplus and thereby would substantially reduce the budgetary cost of the CAP's export subsidies. And the fourth reason is that external pressures from the US and the Cairns Group to reduce CAP prices would be less following the reduction in Western Europe's average level of farm protection. Even if a Uruguay Round agreement is reached which requires cuts in assistance, the extent of liberalisation involved in an EC–EFTA integration may well be more than sufficient to satisfy that accord (Anderson, 1994b).

Likely though some upward movement on CAP prices would be in those circumstances (and even more so if there is no Uruguay Round agreement to prevent protection increases), it is evidently still insufficient to reduce EFTA farmer opposition to full integration with the EU. Therefore generous national compensation packages (such as direct income supplements, re-training subsidies, payments to set-aside land or curtail milk production) seem inevitable in EFTA countries if integration is to proceed. Hopefully national governments in EFTA countries have already begun evaluating the efficacy of different forms of compensation, and will choose less wasteful and more equitable means than those adopted in the past by other industrial countries.

Even if some EFTA countries (for example, Switzerland) choose to stay out of the EU, their agricultural policies, and the EU's CAP, will continue to be under pressure to reform from internal forces such as Western Europe's non-farm exporters, its finance ministries, and increasingly better-informed consumers, taxpayers and environmentalists,[18] as well as from external forces such as the US, the Cairns Group, and other actual or potential food exporters,[19] most notably via the GATT-based multilateral trade negotiations.

But as Hamilton and Winters (1992) have stressed, one of the most pressing external forces on Western Europe's agricultural policies is likely to come from neighbouring Central and Eastern Europe, depending on how the latter countries are treated by the West. On the one hand, in the absence of EU membership most of the European economies in transition would benefit from a reduction in Western Europe's agricultural protection (including several that are currently net food importers, for reasons explained in Anderson and Tyers, 1993 and Anderson, 1993). In this situation the other external advocates for reducing Western Europe's agricultural protection in the multilateral trade negotiations, notably the US and the Cairns Group, would be supported by Europe's former communist countries. The extent of this support would be greater the more the transition economies become net exporters of farm products – which in turn increases the budgetary cost of the CAP in so far as it depresses international food prices and hence raises the export subsidies necessary to dispose of Western Europe's food surpluses.

On the other hand, should Western Europe allow Central and East European farmers preferential access to its food markets to reduce this external opposition to the CAP, the budgetary cost of the CAP could escalate much more. Even if just the Visegrad-4 countries in Central Europe were to be given access, it would raise Western Europe's farm subsidy payments by nearly a third (from $150 billion to $198 billion per year, according to the simulations reported above, based on the assumption that the EU fully covers the budgetary cost of supporting producer prices and disposing of the export surplus of these economies in transition). Yet the projections in table 9.7 show that even with the assumption of slow farm productivity growth and no more price reforms, the other transforming socialist economies would also by the turn of the century be large agricultural producers: the Balkan states would be producing and exporting almost as much food as the four Central European economies, and farm output of the former Soviet republics would be more than twice that of all Central and Eastern Europe. It is the enormity of the possible excess agricultural supply from many of these economies (especially if their domestic food prices were to rise towards CAP levels) that worries EU farm groups, and has led the latter

Table 9.7 Food production and self-sufficiency in Western Europe, Central and Eastern Europe, and the former Soviet Union, assuming CAP reform and EFTA countries joining the EU, 2000[a]

	Production (mmt)				
	Grain	Sugar	Dairy products	Meat	Food self-sufficiency (%)
Western Europe	*207*	*22*	*165*	*42*	*110*
EU-12	194	20	149	40	113
EFTA	13	2	16	2	84
Central/Eastern Europe (EE)	*100*	*4*	*38*	*10*	*102*
CE-4	50	3	26	6	102
Balkan states	50	1	12	4	103
Former Soviet Union (FSU)	*210*	*10*	*109*	*18*	*91*
Russia	111	4	56	9	87
Ukraine	51	5	25	4	115
Baltic states	6	0	7	1	147
Other Western republics	12	1	11	2	75
Kazakhstan	25	0	5	1	130
Central Asian republics	5	0	5	1	37
Total EE+FSU	*310*	*14*	*147*	*28*	*95*

Source: Authors' model results.
Notes:
[a] This reference scenario, as in section 3.4 above, assumes EU-12 CAP reform and EFTA adopting EU domestic food prices in the mid-1990s, plus slow productivity and income growth after 1992 and no further price and trade policy reform in the former communist economies.
mmt Million metric tons.

to vigorously oppose the provision of even the slightest degree of access to EU markets from the East.[20]

Thus a quite likely possibility is that Europe's economies in transition will be given just sufficient preferential market access to West European markets, via association accords, to make them prefer to support rather than oppose EU agricultural protection. If this is all that is done to help agriculture in the transforming economies and (partly as a result) those economies' non-farm sectors grow relatively faster than agriculture, a larger number of the transforming economies could become net food importers over time. Ironically, as the discussion of figure 9.3 above suggests, food market integration with such economies may then well be looked on favourably instead of unfavourably by the EU. This is because, in the event that those transforming economies were net food importers at CAP prices, then the EU could dispose of some of its excess supply at a higher price (at the expense of Central Europe's consumers and economy as a whole, but to the benefit of what is becoming an ever-more powerful interest group, namely Central European farmers). In that event the forces of agricultural protection would have triumphed once again. Such possibilities underscore the economic importance of the EU implementing the CAP reform announced in mid-1992 and, with its GATT partners, concluding the Uruguay Round with an agreement to reverse the long-term upward trend in agricultural protectionism in Europe and elsewhere.

NOTES

Helpful comments from Richard Baldwin and Richard Snape, and financial support from the Australian Research Council, the CEPR and the Yrjö Jahnsson Foundation are gratefully acknowledged.

1 It is reasonable to start with CAP prices as the anchor because the EU-12's agricultural production and consumption levels are more than 10 times those of EFTA countries as a group, and even the farm output levels of the four Central European economies in transition are less than one-fifth those of the EU-12.

2 In 1990, agriculture contributed only 3 per cent of Western Europe's GDP, and agricultural net exports amounted to less than 3 per cent of total merchandise exports of the region. Even in the Visegrad-4 economies agriculture contributed in 1990 only 12 per cent of GDP and less than 3 per cent of exports (except for Hungary, where net agricultural exports were just under 20 per cent of total exports).

3 If the EFTA country were to remain a net exporter at P_e (or even at P_w), it would benefit even more from lowering its domestic price, for the benefit would include all the area under the excess demand curve between a and d and above the international price line (not just a part of it), plus a transfer from the EU-12 to finance the export subsidy required to dispose of any remaining surplus. Throughout the analysis in this section we ignore the general fiscal transfer that relatively affluent EFTA countries would have to make each year on becoming EU members.

4 See n. 3 above. It would be possible for the new EU entrants to compensate the present EC-12 members so that both groups of countries were better off (for example, by forgoing the transfer needed to finance the new entrants' export subsidy), *provided* the EU-12 was a net exporter of these goods. If the EU-12 was a net importer, however, it would suffer a terms of trade deterioration from the increase in P_w and so would require even larger compensation from the new entrants.

5 That CAP budgetary pressures are an important influence on policy decisions is clear from the fact that they led to the introduction of milk quotas in 1984 and 'stabilisers' in 1988.

6 If East–West market integration were to be accompanied by a proposal to

lower the domestic price or otherwise reduce production in the West (for example, by imposing production quotas or land set-asides in the enlarged EU), this would lessen the above effects. However, even if there was a cut in the domestic price sufficient to ensure that the increase in East European net exports was fully offset by a decrease in the EU's own surplus (so that the international price stayed at P'_w), there would still be a transfer of EU government revenue to Eastern Europe equal to the difference between domestic and border prices times the volume of exports from the East.

7 One situation where trade could be almost as good as aid (in terms of the cost of transferring an ECU from West to East), is the following. If the EU were to offer Central European farmers quota-restricted access to its markets and an export tax was imposed on those quota sales to the EU equal to the difference between the domestic prices in West and East, then domestic prices in the East would be unchanged. This would then simply be a transfer to the treasuries of Central Europe from the CAP budget (as the equivalent volume of EU produce would need to be exported to the rest of the world with the help of an export subsidy if EU prices were unchanged).

8 A possibility not analysed here is that the EU simply offers quota-restricted access to Central European farmers, and the rents from those exports to the EU are taxed by the Central European governments. In that extreme case, there would be no direct price or quantity effects in Central Europe, just a transfer from EU to Central European treasuries.

9 For the EU these include the effects of national government policies in addition to those of the CAP.

10 It needs to be kept in mind that a high consumer price for feedgrain reduces effective assistance to the livestock sector, the extent of which depends on the degree to which stock are grain-fed.

11 Clearly there is an interest in the differences between this and a more optimistic scenario for these economies in transition, but that is the subject of another study (Tyers, 1994).

12 This may seem unrealistic, but in fact most of EFTA's other tradables sectors are much more integrated into EU markets than is the case for agriculture, and in any case agriculture contributes only about 2 per cent of EFTA's GDP when measured at CAP prices.

13 This is comparable with estimates for Finland by Alho, Kotilainen and Widgrén (1992) of 1.5 per cent of GDP, and by Törmä and Rutherford (1993) of just under 1 per cent, using a CGE model.

14 This compares with the reference scenario's (CAP plus national government) transfer payments in Western Europe of $150 billion, and is consistent with the fact that in this integration scenario CE-4's food output is almost a quarter that of Western Europe. It is almost as large as the boost in CE-4 farmer welfare. Recall, though, that the boost to livestock producer welfare is eroded by higher feedgrain prices.

15 In fact over time that is looking an ever less realistic upper limit on any Uruguay Round reform; as of mid-1993 it looks more likely that it will involve an assistance reduction of less than one-sixth, phased over the rest of this decade (Anderson, 1994b).

16 Needless to say the loss to Western Europe and the gain to Central Europe would be less still if Central Europe's milk (and other) output were to be supply-constrained by effective production quotas or export taxes.

17 In an earlier study undertaken when analysts were more optimistic about medium-term growth prospects in Eastern Europe, Hamilton and Winters (1992) assumed much higher farm (and non-farm) productivity and income growth rates than the modest rates assumed in the present study.

18 Studies pointing out the adverse environmental effects of agricultural support policies include Lutz (1992) and Anderson (1992).

19 Most developing countries, including the former communist countries, would gain from reduced agricultural protection in the more advanced industrial countries, even if they are currently net importers of food. This is partly because some would become exporters at the higher international prices that would result from cutting protection, and partly because others would be net food exporters but for their own anti-agricultural policies, and so would nonetheless gain so long as they transmitted some of the international price rise (following protection cuts abroad) to their domestic market (Anderson and Tyers, 1993).

20 The study by Rollo and Smith (1993) downplays this risk that exports from the East would undermine the CAP. But the empirical estimates they use to support their claim assume away the problem by setting exogenously (at only double their 1989 level) the volume of farm exports they expect to emerge from the East. Their assumed doubling of exports implies either a very inelastic excess demand curve for these countries, given that exports accounted for only about 2 per cent of Central European food production (at least in 1990 – see table 9.1, p. 212), or the presence of an export tax so that domestic prices in Central Europe are not allowed to rise to CAP levels.

REFERENCES

Alho, K., M. Kotilainen and M. Widgrén, 1992. 'Finland in the European Community – an assessment of the economic impacts' (in Finnish with English summary), The Research Institute of the Finnish Economy, ETLA, Series B, **81**, Helsinki

Anderson, K., 1992. 'Agricultural trade liberalization and the environment: a global perspective', *The World Economy*, **15(1)** (January), 1–24

1993. 'Intersectoral changes in transforming socialist economies: distinguishing initial from longer term responses', in I. Goldin (ed.), *Economic Growth and Agriculture*, London: Macmillan

1994a. 'Lobbying incentives and the pattern of protection in rich and poor countries', *Economic Development and Cultural Change*, **41(1)** (October)

1994b. 'US–EC farm trade confrontation: an outsider's view', ch. 10 in G. Anania, C.A. Carter and A.F. McCallan (eds.), *Agricultural Trade Conflicts and GATT*, Boulder, CO and London: Westview Press

Anderson, K. and R. Tyers, 1993. 'More on welfare gains to developing countries from liberalizing world food trade', *Journal of Agricultural Economics*, **44(2)** (May), 189–204

CEPR, 1990. 'Monitoring European integration: the impact of Eastern Europe', CEPR, *MEI*, **1** (October), London: CEPR

1992. 'Is bigger better? The economics of EC enlargement' *Monitoring European Integration*, **3**, London: CEPR

Haaland, J.I. and V.D. Norman, 1992. 'Global production effects of European

Integration', in L.A. Winters (ed.), *Trade Flows and Trade Policy After '1992'*, Cambridge: Cambridge University Press

Hamilton, C. and L.A. Winters, 1992. 'Opening up international trade in Eastern Europe', *Economic Policy*, 7(14) (April), 78–116

Karp, L. and S. Stefanou, 1993. 'Domestic and trade policy for Central and East European agriculture', IATRC, *Working Paper*, 93–7 (June), Berkeley: University of California

Lutz, E., 1992. 'Agricultural trade liberalization, price changes and environmental effects', *Environmental and Resource Economics*, 2(1), 79–89

Munk, K.J., 1992. 'The development of agricultural policies and trade relations in response to the transformation in Central and Eastern Europe', paper presented to the IATRC conference, St Petersberg, Florida (13–15 December)

OECD, 1992. *Agricultural Policies, Markets and Trade: Monitoring and Outlook*, Paris: OECD

Rollo, J. and A. Smith, 1993. 'The political economy of Eastern Europe's trade with the European Community: why so sensitive?', *Economic Policy*, 8(16) (April), 140–81

Törmä, H. and T. Rutherford, 1993. 'Integrating Finnish agriculture into the EC', *Research Report*, 13, Helsinki: Government Institute for Economic Research

Tyers, R., 1994. 'Economic reform in Europe and the former Soviet Union: implications for international food markets', IFPRI, *Research Report*, 99, Washington, DC: International Food Policy Research Institute

Tyers, R. and K. Anderson, 1992. *Disarray in World Food Markets: A Quantitative Assessment*, Cambridge: Cambridge University Press

USDA, 1992. *Western Europe Agriculture and Trade Report*, ERS, *Situation and Outlook Series* (December), Washington, DC: United States Department of Agriculture

Webb, A.J., M. Lopes and R. Penn, 1990. 'Estimates of producer and consumer subsidy equivalents: government intervention in Agriculture', ERS, *Statistical Bulletin*, 803 (April), Washington, DC: United States Department of Agriculture

Discussion

HANNU TÖRMÄ

The research topic of Anderson and Tyers' chapter 9 is contemporary and most interesting; it is a pity that these results were not available when EFTA countries voted on EU membership. People really need scientific guidance on difficult decision matters such as this, and economic models can be used to sketch out at least the rough magnitude of expected changes of policy reforms.

Despite the high quality of the authors' work, I would like to comment on four matters. First, the multicommodity simulation model of world food markets used in chapter 9 remains a black box; the authors should have explained in more detail the working of their model. The multicommodity character is reasonable, but what are the main mechanisms that produce the results?

Second, in the reference scenario of EFTA joining the EU, it is assumed that EFTA countries will continue their current agricultural policy. Is this reasonable? At least in Finland there would have been strong pressures to reduce agricultural support if EU membership had not materialised. Would it have been a better alternative to assume that EFTA countries would proceed according to the proposals of GATT in reducing their farming subsidies?

Third, the authors base their findings on a partial equilibrium model, which means that it is quite possible that important feedbacks will be forgotten. Agricultural policy change, such as adopting CAP prices, affects the whole economy. It seems wrong to use the magic words 'ceteris paribus'. Changes in agriculture will cause effects in food processing industries, which together will pass on many effects to the other sectors of the economy. Effects on chemical industries are probable, since as agriculture declines the demand for fertilisers and pesticides will decline, too. Would a general equilibrium framework have been better? This would require a numeric computable general equilibrium model of the world economy, with agricultural policies modelled in it. The task would be huge, but such a model could be built given enough resources.

Fourth, EFTA is not a homogeneous area with respect to agriculture. Harvesting conditions, farm sizes and financial structures differ between, for instance, Finland and Sweden. Sweden has rationalised agriculture much more heavily than Finland; in Sweden, farmers supported membership while Finnish farmers opposed it. My opinion is that calculations concerning EFTA do not represent Finnish reality. It seems to me that the authors have presented a picture that is unrealistically bright.

We have built a one-country static numeric general equilibrium model for Finland (GEMFIN, see Törmä and Rutherford, 1993). The chapter 9 results for EFTA of the output effects of EU membership have been compared to our new results for Finland (Törmä, Rutherford and Vaittinen, 1995) in table D9.1.

Table D9.1 Output effects of agriculture in the case of EU membership, percentage change compared to 1990 bench mark

Commodity	EFTA (year 2000), chapter 9	Finland (long run), our study (1994)
Grains	−25	−41
Sugar	+25	na
Dairy products	0	−25 (milk and beef)
Ruminant meat	7	−31 (pork)
		−19 (poultry and eggs)
Non-ruminant meat	−18	
Total	na	−21
Food processing industries	na	−8

na   not available.

As can be seen from table D9.1, the future of at least Finnish agriculture is more gloomy than the EFTA average predicts.

REFERENCES

Törmä, H. and T. Rutherford, 1993. 'Integrating Finnish agriculture into the EC's Common Agricultural Policy', *Reports from the Government Institute of Economic Research*, 13
Törmä, H., T. Rutherford and R. Vaittinen, 1995. 'What will EU membership and the value-added tax reform do to the Finnish food industry – a numeric general equilibrium analysis', *Discussion Papers from the Government Institute of Economic Research*, 88

10 The economic consequences of EU enlargement for the entrants: the case of Finland

KARI ALHO

1 Introduction

The accession of Austria, Finland and Sweden into the EU was prompted by a series of changes that took place in Europe in the 1980s and early 1990s. This process started in 1985, when the then EC launched its internal market programme. As exports to the EC made up 60 per cent of their total exports, the EFTA countries felt that the internal market programme could pose a severe threat to them in the form of trade diversion. This prompted the EFTA countries to reach an agreement on the formation of the European Economic Area (EEA), which after many ups and downs came into being at the beginning of 1994. In effect, the EU internal market was enlarged to encompass the EFTA countries as well, but with the exclusion of Switzerland.

Initially, the EFTA governments sought to ensure access to the Single Market for their firms without having to join the EU. During the EEA process, the end of the East–West confrontation in Europe sparked off a new political orientation in the EFTA countries, most of which have traditionally pursued neutrality in their foreign policies. Simultaneously, Finland and the other EFTA countries started to feel that under the EEA they would only have rather limited power to influence European cooperation and EU decision making with respect to the enforcement of the Single Market measures and their future development, which is particularly vital to them. The reduced risks in foreign policy and overcoming this 'influence deficit' were decisive factors behind the application for full membership in the EU by Austria, Sweden, Finland and Norway.

On 12 June 1994, Austria decided with a clear majority to join the EU at the beginning of 1995. On 16 October 1994, Finnish voters said 'yes' to joining the EU. On 13 November, Sweden followed, but the Norwegians

240

refused to enter the EU – for the second time – in the referendum on 28 November 1994.

As a further stage of integration, membership in the EU will entail changes in the external conditions of the economy, such as reduced foreign trade barriers, but the most significant change is that new sectors of the economy will be integrated into the international economy. The scope of the previous EU–EFTA integration was limited to free trade in manufacturing. Accordingly, agriculture, which the EFTA countries on average pursue quite extensively under fairly harsh climatic conditions, remained outside the realm of the integration process, as did the service industries or the sheltered (non-tradable) sector.

This chapter studies the economic consequences of moving from EEA to EU membership. As we shall see, the gains are likely to be significant, at least in the case of Finland. The long-run gains will stem mainly from three factors: the restructuring of agriculture, the attendant liberalisation of related industries such as food processing and other sheltered sectors and participation in EMU.

It could be argued that most of these gains could be secured without EU membership, so that it is misleading to ascribe them to membership alone. The fundamental reason that this point of view is incorrect has to do with the so-called 'rent-sharing' feature of the EFTA economies. The small EFTA countries are marked by a great deal of social cohesion, centralised special interest organisations and pressure groups covering the whole society. The net result has been what might be called 'rent-sharing'. That is, a complex system of import protection, production subsidies and welfare provisions have directly shared out the economic benefits of rapidly rising productivity in EFTA's export oriented industrial sectors. For instance, price support schemes have maintained farmers' incomes in most EFTA countries with much less shrinkage than might have been expected given the adverse farming conditions in the alpine and arctic regions. The result of this system is that the EFTA countries, or certainly the Nordic countries, have an unusually compressed income distribution.

Given this complex system of distortions and income supports, it is quite unlikely that a single component – such as agriculture price supports – could be liberalised without an external impetus such as EU membership; such a liberalisation would have upset the equilibrium of national rent-sharing. As a matter of fact, the actual terms of accession allowed the Finnish government to substantially offset losses to the farmers with direct income support schemes so that the reduction in producer prices will to a large extent be compensated by channelling extra direct income support payments. In this sense EU membership will not destroy the rent-sharing arrangement; it will merely force a transformation in it.

Similarly, EFTA participation in EMU is also likely to provide the external stimulus needed to redress another part of the Nordic rent-sharing arrangements. Powerful trade unions have at times managed to secure wage settlements that might have threatened the competitiveness of EFTA firms, thereby leading to job losses in times of recession. Devaluations, which were used to offset such effects, were essentially part of rent-sharing arrangements. While this tactic worked in the 1960s and 1970s, by the 1980s it was widely seen as essentially an engine of inflation.

While the Finnish and Swedish governments forsook this type of policy making in the late 1980s and early 1990s, the foreign exchange markets were not convinced of the credibility of this switch. As a consequence, the market has demanded a substantial interest rate premium on Nordic currencies. Only a formal participation in EMU would eliminate this interest differential, thereby lowering long-term costs of capital in Finland and Sweden.

The aim of this chapter is to consider the likely economic effects that membership in the EU could have for the EFTA countries, especially Finland. At ETLA an extensive study, Alho, Kotilainen and Widgrén (1992), has been completed on this issue. The main finding of this study was that there existed the potential for a sizable long-term welfare gain for Finland from EU membership. The long-run welfare gain was estimated to be of the order of 4 per cent in relation to GDP. But in order to exploit this opportunity, a marked capacity and willingness to adjust will be required, as some changes are going to be of the inter-industry type, resisted by the forces striving to preserve the rent-sharing equilibrium. This may slow down the adjustment towards a more efficient production structure.

The chapter has three sections after the Introduction. Section 2 discusses the economic differences between EEA and EU membership. Section 3 presents an analysis of these differences and their quantitative impact on the Finnish economy, the prime attention being focused on three main areas: sheltered sector restructuring, participation in EU agricultural policy and participation in EMU. Section 4 presents a summary and concluding remarks.

2   Differences between EEA and EU membership

The starting point for analysing the changes that membership in the EU would imply for the EFTA countries is the EEA Agreement, which is then treated as the baseline scenario, see table 10.1.[1]

Table 10.1   Major differences between EU membership and the EEA

Area	EEA	EU membership
Foreign trade	Free-trade agreement with the EU and national trade policy towards third countries	Customs union with the EU and common external trade policy
Mobility of factors	Free with minor exceptions to the EU rules (on secondary houses)	Free, with no permanent national exceptions
Agriculture	Not covered	Participation in CAP, coupled with a nationally financed subsidy scheme for arctic agriculture
Sheltered sector	Intensified competition through, for example, opening of public procurement, and indirect pressures caused by increased factor mobility	As in EEA, but magnified in sectors linked to agriculture and due to EMU
Macroeconomic policies	Not covered, freedom of exchange rate adjustments and likely real interest rate differential *vis-à-vis* the German mark	EMU, no exchange rate changes and uniform interest rates
Taxation	Not covered	Harmonisation of indirect taxation
Budgetary items	Total payment by the EFTA5 of 500 million ECU (over a 5-year period) to an EU Cohesion Fund	A net payment of 2 billion ECU (in 1995) to the EU by the EFTA-3 new member countries
Institutions	Commitment to the internal market legislation, but with virtually no influence on it	Full commitment and influence on EU decision making

2.1   Trade policy changes

As the EEA links the EFTA countries to the EU internal market programme, full membership will not imply major changes in foreign trade. The EEA simplified border formalities facing Finnish goods; however, some border controls will still be necessary: the EU is a customs union while the EEA is still merely a free-trade agreement.

Under the EEA, the rules of origin thus apply to EFTA exports to the EU, but not any more as a member.

On the import side, as a member Finland will be obliged to adopt the EU's Common External Tariff (CET). This implies that in some industries the imports of intermediate goods and some final consumer goods will face higher – or lower – barriers than previously, although on average there will not be an appreciable difference in external tariffs. According to Alho, Kotilainen and Widgrén (1992) on the effects of EU membership on the Finnish economy, the net gains in foreign trade were evaluated to be quite minor in their totality. The same is likely to hold for the other EFTA economies as well. In foreign trade, the abolition of border formalities under full membership between EFTA and the EU and elimination of the rules of origin were estimated to lead to a rise in export earnings of the order of 1.5 per cent in relation to Finnish exports to the EU. This same estimate was reached by Flam (1994). The barriers in imports from the EU are reduced owing to lower administrative costs.

Some of the import barriers towards third countries will in contrast, rise. The net effect of these changes will be small. The EFTA-3 new members will also have to adapt to the anti-dumping duties imposed by the EU. However, their impact cannot be assessed beforehand, as they are uncertain and will be applied only in the future.

2.2   Mobility of factors

The EEA had already dismantled the remaining barriers in capital flows between the EFTA countries and the EU with a minor exception on secondary homes, the foreign purchases of which require the permission of the national authorities. However, the reaction of foreign direct investment (FDI) and domestic investment to EU membership was a central economic argument in the referendum debate in both Finland and Sweden. Since full membership will redress the influence deficit that exists under the EEA, Finnish and Swedish firms are likely to stay in the home country. The positive interaction between EU membership and the gateway position with respect to the Baltic countries and Russia is also likely to attract some additional inward investment to Finland.

2.3   Agriculture

The scope of integration is going to deepen and be even dramatically widened as a result of EU membership. The EFTA entrants have to adopt the Common Agricultural Policy (CAP) of the EU, coupled with the reduction in agricultural support implied by the GATT agreement.

To give an idea of this adjustment pressure, in 1994 EU average agricultural prices were roughly 40–50 per cent lower than those in Finland. The gap was even wider in the 1980s, and narrowed to this size to a large extent as a consequence of the considerable weakening of the Finnish Mark in 1991 and 1992. The recent strengthening of the Mark has again widened the gap between the price levels. In the Accession negotiations, it was agreed that there will be an immediate reduction of producer price levels from the beginning of EU membership instead of a gradual phase-in of the reductions desired by the Finnish government.

The country will be divided into three regions. The northern region, lying roughly north of 62 degrees of latitude, as a compensation for the inferior conditions of 'arctic' agriculture, will be subject to a permanent and direct national subsidy scheme. In this region also the less favoured agricultural regions' (LFA) support will be paid out of national and EU sources, so that one-third comes from the EU. In the middle region between the northern and the southern region of crop-growing the LFA support will be paid by EU and national sources. The southern part of the country, covering 15 per cent of crop-growing area, will receive no LFA support, but the bulk of environmental support, half of which is to be financed by the EU, will be channelled to this region. The Finnish government is entitled to pay national transfers to this region after a period of 2 years of membership if overwhelming adjustment problems occur.

The Finnish government is entitled to pay diminishing transitory subsidies, totalling some 6 billion FIM in 1995, over a period of 5 years, alleviating the immediate transition to EU producer prices. In the first year the total national support will be some 12 billion FIM and the EU transfers (those due to the CAP reform LFA and environmental support) will be permanently some 3 billion FIM annually. In addition, the EU will contribute almost 0.5 billion ECU over a period of 4 years towards compensation of losses related to value of inventories and other costs of the change in the price system. Adjustment support for the foodstuff industry, the total sum being 1.4 billion FIM, can be financed from national sources. The quotas, for example, for the crop-growing area, being the basis for CAP reform and for milk production, roughly correspond to the production in the pre-EU period. The national subsidy scheme will result in a gradual lowering of national transfers. The taxation of agriculture will also be changed, as in the EU VAT will be applied, which will eliminate some of the present subsidies for certain products (see Alho and Widgrén, 1994, for more details). In addition, the EU will take responsibility for exporting the agricultural surplus to the European or world markets. This will result in a slight terms of trade gain for Finland.

2.4   Integration in the sheltered sector

An important issue is also the direct and indirect pressure to rationalise and increase competition elsewhere in the sheltered sector, such as in government services and the food industry existing partially under the umbrella of agricultural protection. International price differentials constitute an acid test of integration. It is common knowledge that the Nordic countries have been expensive; the overall price level in Sweden, Norway and Denmark was persistently at least 20 per cent higher than in Germany in the 1970s and 1980s. Finland in the 1970s was a notable exception, with roughly the same price level as Germany, but it came into line with the other Nordic countries in the 1980s. Price differentials tend to indicate that there are achievable gains from further integration of the Nordic countries with the EU. The equalisation of price and cost levels predicted by trade theory should also concern non-traded goods and services used as inputs for the traded goods, if identical technology is used in all countries (see Burgess, 1990).[2]

In Alho (1993) an analysis is presented of the various reasons behind the large price differentials between the Nordic countries and the EU. In this study, the aggregate price level of domestic final expenditure of the PPP calculations by the OECD is disaggregated into the value added price of the open sector in the home market and that of the sheltered sector, the import price and the level of indirect taxation. The 'open sector' is crudely defined to encompass manufacturing and the 'sheltered sector' is represented by the rest of the economy.

The price equations on unit labour costs (capital cost being proxied by a constant and a time trend) were estimated, producing estimates for the mark-up factors for both sectors in the economy. The mark-ups in the sheltered sector in Finland and Sweden are quite similar, of the order of 25 per cent, and higher than in Germany (with a mark-up factor of 13 per cent). This confirms the standard view of less aggressive competition in this sector in the Nordic countries.

Using available information on the relative import barriers,[3] we can solve for the relative price in the sheltered sector starting from the aggregate price ratio given by the PPP estimates for 1985. This is a suitable year for comparison, as it was not preceded by large changes in relative export prices and so the identification of the sectoral price differentials can be based on the assumption of equal competitiveness of exports in the countries of comparison (see Alho, 1993, for details). The implied price deviations for the sheltered sector are really quite significant: in Sweden sheltered sector prices were 25 per cent higher than in Germany in 1985, while in Finland they were as much as 40 per cent higher. The higher mark-ups in Finland and Sweden contribute roughly 10 percentage points to these higher sheltered sector prices. The relative wage level in the sheltered sector raises the price ratio by 5 per cent in Finland, and comparably in Sweden. The residual is explained by a gap in productivity. The results clearly suggest that the major factor behind the high Nordic price levels has been the high price level in the sheltered sector, due mainly to monopolistic competition and deficient productivity in this sector.[4]

The deficiency in productivity in the Nordic sheltered sectors may be caused by many factors. Agriculture is clearly one such factor in the Finnish and Norwegian case, see figure 10.1 (p. 253). The ever-expanding and large public sectors have not been obliged to keep track of their costs and raise their productivity. The region's small population sparsely distributed over a large area (supported by regional policies), the consequently limited use of scale economies in public and private service production, and an expensive distribution network have all contributed to the situation. Accordingly, an important explanation for the different price levels could be that Nordic technology is different from that in the EU. As shown by Burgess (1990), under such conditions free trade in goods does not lead to an equalisation of price levels.

2.5   EMU participation

A main element of EU membership entails participation in the Economic and Monetary Union (EMU) of the EU. Although it is still somewhat unclear when and whether the final stage of EMU will be completed, Finland did not negotiate an opt-out for EMU in the Accession Treaty. However, according to the statement of the Finnish Parliament, entering the third stage of EMU will require a new discussion of its own if and when Finland faces this decision.

The question is often raised, intensified by the recent turmoil in the European exchange markets and the large devaluations of two of the Nordic currencies, whether participation in EMU is too tight a macroeconomic environment for Finland and Sweden. The problems here are twofold. First, in macroeconomic stabilisation the Nordic countries clearly weigh the importance of employment more heavily than curbing inflation, as compared to the EU core. The efforts to get the non-inflationary stable currency policies of the late 1980s adopted in society at large have more or less failed, and have even been condemned as incorrect policies in a period of severe recession. Existing in EMU may thereby prove to be painful. A major problem of policy making and research is how the economy's structures and adjustment will change to find new ways of absorbing macroeconomic shocks, as these mechanisms are in reality endogenous and dependent on the exchange rate regime. It can be shown (Kotilainen, Alho and Erkkilä, 1994) that, as a rational reaction by the trade unions, an irrevocably fixed exchange rate mechanism will lead to more flexible wage adjustment through means of nominal wage adjustment than the current real wage flexibility achieved through a combination of nominal wage inflexibility and inflation (devaluations).

For Finland, the special case of a clearly smaller share of intra-industry trade with the EU 12 than is the normal case in Europe (see, for example, Baldwin, 1992), is a factor which has raised concerns related to asymmetric shocks. However, the actual asymmetries have not been so great for Finland as might be expected from the trade pattern. On the other hand, the recent extremely deep recession in the Finnish economy, caused by a number of simultaneous adverse demand and supply shocks, calls for caution in this respect.

2.6   Harmonisation of indirect taxes

In the EU, most of the decisions and operations of the public sector remain under national influence and decision making. Only the harmonisation of indirect taxes is carried out at EU level. As is well known, this harmonisation concerns only the lower bounds of indirect and excise taxes. After a transition period of 2 years, the very liberal import quotas of alcohol would also apply to Finland. This would make it hard, or impossible, to maintain the high national taxation of alcohol. There would be a pressure to compensate for this by raising direct taxation, with the consequence of increasing the excess burden of taxation even further. However, it cannot be too easily assessed quantitatively how big this adjustment will be, as there are also quite large deviations in the EU tax rates between neighbouring countries, such as Germany and Denmark. We shall therefore omit this item from the calculations.

2.7   Budgetary contributions

For the other EFTA applicant countries, the situation differs in some important respects from that outlined for Finland above. As to the budgetary items, Austria and Sweden will clearly be net payers to the EU budget, while the depression-hit Finland is likely to be roughly in balance with respect to EU funds in the first few years of membership.

In 1995, Finland will be a net receiver of EU funds, with a net sum of 0.5 billion FIM.[5] In the years to come, this is likely to change so that Finland will be a net contributor to the EU budget. This will depend on how vigorously the Finnish economy recovers from the extremely deep recession of the early 1990s and on the enlargement of the EU budget. In Alho, Kotilainen and Widgrén (1992), it was estimated that the net payment of Finland would be some 2.5 billion FIM, 0.5 per cent of GDP, at the end of the decade.

3 Quantification of membership effects

3.1 Foreign trade

The foreign trade changes are important, but quite small taken as a whole. The increase in EU export earnings will be 1.5 per cent. As Flam (1994) notes, non-EEA imports will face an average tariff of some 3.5 per cent in Finland, and 2.9 per cent in the EU-12 after the completion of the Uruguay Round. As the import barriers against the EU will be slightly reduced, the overall import cost will be reduced by some 0.5 per cent. When the loss in tariff revenues is taken into account in the estimates of the budgetary flows between Finland and the EU, the welfare gain in foreign trade is altogether some 0.3 per cent in relation to GDP.

3.2 FDI

The changes accruing in FDI are an important, but complicated, factor to estimate; their strategic role was also emphasised by the CEPR (1992). The experiences of the EU countries after joining the EU can be examined and contrasted to the EFTA experiences. For Finland, the average net outflow of some 5 billion FIM of FDI was estimated to decline by 1–2 billion on a per annum basis due to membership in the EU, because the incentive for domestic firms to invest inside EU borders would be eliminated and the attractiveness of Finland for foreign investors would be likely to rise, for example, through the simultaneous interaction between EU membership and access to the emerging markets in Russia and in the Baltic countries. This increase in manufacturing capital stock will in the long run be some 20 billion FIM, which will then result in an increase of 0.3 per cent in aggregate income using a standard elasticity of income with respect to capital stock.

3.3 Integration gains in the sheltered sector

Normally, integration should ultimately lead to an equalisation of price levels. But if there are natural reasons behind, and an efficient adjustment to, the situation of persistent price differentials, this equalisation can probably be achieved only to a limited degree. This is crucially linked to how the burden of sheltered sector in efficiency is borne in the Nordic countries. In the present conditions of internationally freely mobile financial and real capital, the rental rate on capital is in the long run given to both the open and sheltered sector from abroad. Capital cannot, therefore, bear the burden of sheltered sector inefficiency. If labour is in fixed supply in the economy and the labour market is competitive, the inefficiency is fully absorbed only by lowered real labour incomes. A potential rationalisation of the sheltered sector does not therefore have a multiplier effect on open sector production. If efficiency in the sheltered sector improves, this is cashed in on completely in the form of higher real-labour incomes, and equivalently in aggregate real incomes as well, but not in higher profits.

The above-mentioned monopolistic features of the EFTA economies in imperfectly competitive goods and labour markets can make things look quite different. Normally, a union is taken to have two goals, employment and the real (consumption) wage rate. If the real wage is low, due to an inefficient sheltered sector or agricultural protection, a union substitutes the real wage for employment by pushing up the nominal wage rate. This means that the open sector bears part of the burden through reduced profits and reduced output. So, if sheltered sector efficiency rises, both the open sector firms and labour benefit. The extent to which this happens is an empirical issue.[6]

Qualitatively, EU membership is likely to lead to a development along the above lines. However, it is not a straightforward task to fix quantitatively which changes in sheltered sector activities will be due to EU membership, because a number of potential but diverse channels will contribute to these changes. Part of them have taken place already under the EEA, such as opening of public procurement and financial services. Those more closely related to EU membership are harmonisation of indirect taxation, effects caused by the transparency of a common currency, intensified tax competition due to capital and labour mobility, the pressure created by EMU convergence leading to cost reductions and efficiency gains in the public sector, and the effects of reduced protection and increased competition in the foodstuffs industry closely linked to protected agriculture. However, the possibility argued above, that part or even all of the burden of inefficiency can be borne in a 'costless' way, creates a caveat about not rushing to excessive estimates of the gains. In Alho, Kotilainen and Widgrén (1992), an estimate of a reduction in the sheltered sector prices by 1.5 per cent in relation to wages was formed, which would contribute to a rise in aggregate real income by 1 per cent of GDP.[7]

The potential welfare increase in the sheltered sector is clearly greater than that to be achieved through open sector integration. This was also concluded by Victor Norman when he stated,

> There is room to expect EFTA countries to reap significant but modest gains from integration of European markets in manufactures, and to reap quite substantial gains from international competition in markets for services. Moreover, international competition might be a prerequisite for domestic deregulation of key service industries. (Norman, 1991, p. 128)

If labour also becomes internationally mobile, this would impose a dilemma for the Nordic countries as the burden of inefficiency could then no longer be shifted on to a domestic factor of production. The sheltered sector would have to be raised to the same level of productivity as that in neighbouring EU countries, which would probably impose significant adjustment pressures on the economy and society.

3.4   Restructuring of agriculture

On a global scale, the CAP of the EU is a policy of extensive agricultural protection, which generates a significant cost in the form of trade diversion to the more efficient producers outside the EU and to EU consumers (see, for example, Sapir, 1992). At the same time, it is also considered to be a very complicated and bureaucratic system of controlling production. The EFTA countries thus lose a potential welfare gain if they become members of the CAP, instead of adopting 'fully free trade' in agriculture, as was argued in the CEPR (1992) report on the enlargement of the EU. But there is even higher protection of agriculture in some EFTA countries, notably in Finland, Norway and Switzerland, and welfare gains can also be reaped from the opening of agriculture to EU markets.

As, in order to mitigate the adjustment process of agriculture, which is likely to result at least in temporary unemployment, the structural change will deliberately be slowed down by policies channelling direct income transfers to farmers, resources will remain in agriculture, the production structure will remain inefficient and, in the extreme case, the overall welfare gain will be significantly lower than its highest potential level. Permanent income-supporting systems should thus be applied with caution. EU membership will entail significant adjustment pressure in this sector and a loss of producer incomes for Finnish farmers. At the same time, it can bring a substantial welfare gain to consumers, and taxpayers (see, for example, chapter 9 in this volume). The welfare gains from adoption of the CAP depend on whether the current use of resources in the economy is efficient or not, and whether there will be a shift of resources from agriculture to other sectors of the economy, or whether the existing resources will continue to be tied to farming – by, for example, channelling national transfers which compensate the loss in producer incomes. Trade liberalisation in the case where the resources of an economy are not internally efficiently allocated (i.e. at current prices a higher national income could be produced), leads to a larger welfare gain if it can be combined with a more efficient internal allocation of resources. As we argue below, the current situation in Finland is likely to give such potential.

If there is a drop in agricultural production, the social cost of this must now be evaluated at EU prices rather than at high domestic prices. In Alho, Kotilainen and Widgrén (1992), we started from the prospect, normally accepted in Finland, that there will be a loss of one-third of agricultural output due to EU membership. The change will be more marked in grain production than in livestock, reflecting the different relative prices in Finland compared to those in the EU. We further assumed that one-quarter of the agricultural labour force could find a job in another industry with the same productivity as the average in the economy. This causes a welfare gain of around 1 per cent of GDP. This should be added to the consumer gain through reduced prices, to the reduced budgetary support in the longer term, and the support coming to the Finnish agriculture from the EU budget, which altogether appear to be of the order of almost 1 per cent of GDP.

As an additional evaluation of the change in agriculture, let us attempt to get a firmer analytical hold of what can be expected from an adjustment of agriculture to the CAP. The current pre-EU agricultural policies pursued in Finland could be described in the following way. There is a set of farms with fixed capital and labour endowments

$$\{K_i, L_i\}, \; i = 1, \ldots, n, \; Q_i = F_i(K_i, L_i),$$

being the production on farm i. Let P_A be the price of agricultural output, W the wage level and r the cost of capital in the economy. The goal of the previous agricultural policies has been to guarantee the same income for farmers as in corresponding occupations elsewhere in the economy. So, P_A is set in such a way that for each farm,

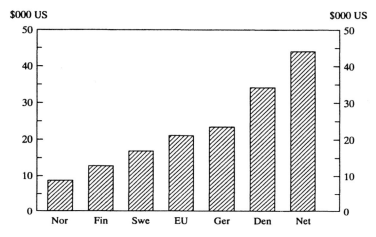

The average productivity shown by the national accounts has been corrected by the relative producer prices. The producer price in country i in relation to that in the EU has been estimated as $(1 - s_{EU}) / (1 - s_i)$, where s is the net percentage producer subsidy equivalent measured by the OECD.

Figure 10.1   Average productivity of labour in agriculture in relation to the EU, 1990

$$\frac{P_A Q_i - rK_i}{L_i} \geq W. \tag{1}$$

It is clearly evident that there are significant scale economies in agriculture, which are at present to a large extent underutilised in Finland, and also in those other EFTA countries having the highest agricultural support. For example, the average crop-growing farm in Finland is only 18 hectares, while that in Sweden is roughly 50 hectares, in France 63, and the UK 127 (Kola, Marttila and Niemi, 1991). Of the Finnish farms 69 per cent have an area less than 20 hectares and only 4 per cent are larger than 50 hectares (Kettunen, 1993). Measurements on costs and production as a function of farm size also clearly indicate that the average cost is reduced as farm size grows. Figure 10.1 demonstrates the productivity gap, which is due both to the inefficient internal production structure and to the inferior climatic conditions. As the climatic conditions for crop-growing in the Nordic countries are inferior to those in the more southerly-located EU areas with a longer annual growing season, striving towards a larger farm size here would have been a natural reaction, but the reality is quite the contrary. This is, of course, due to historical and political reasons, and the extensive protection against agricultural imports.[8]

Transition to the CAP would cut the price of agricultural products to a new level, which is roughly some 40–50 per cent lower than at present, denoted by P_A^1 as the price on agricultural value added. Now, for the least efficient farms the rental $P_A^1 Q_i - WL_i$ turns negative. According to normal economic principles these farms have to shut down. Let us assume that in such a case the market price of the farm is equal to its alternative use, for example, as forest land or in housing, and denoted by c per unit of capital, c being less than unity.

For the most efficient farms condition (1) holds in the new situation as well. As farm capital is financed by both loans and by net wealth (own capital), those farms for which the market value of equity remains positive, i.e. for which the rental is sufficient to pay the interest charges, can also continue. Let us denote this minimum efficient scale for the farm size in EU membership by K^*.

If the possibility of transforming to a larger farm size is simultaneously utilised as the current rent is eliminated, the outcome can be quite different from that predicting a lower output, reached above. Let us for simplicity imagine that all farms use the same amount of labour input, which does not limit the validity of the argument. A merger of farm j with farm i can, due to scale economies, generate a positive net profit, S_i, although for both of them it is negative, and the new farm can continue production. Let simply farm i be fully leveraged and farm j be unprofitable. The condition for a successful merger is then,

$$S_i = P_A^1 F(K_i + K_j, L_i) - WL_i \geq r(K_i + cK_j). \qquad (2)$$

It can be seen that as $c < 1$, all mergers of i and j for which $K_i K_j > K^*$ result in farms which can continue production. (In fact, this limit on the farm size through a merger is slightly less than K^*, because c is less than unity.) Imagine that all the N farms in the country are evenly distributed by size over the interval $(0, K_{max})$. The maximum number of mergers of two farms leading to a positive surplus in (2), where they both are initially located in the range $(0, K^*)$, is $\frac{1}{2} N(K^*/K_{max})$. This is also the loss of jobs in agriculture due to membership. However, this rationalisation through mergers would imply that none of the agricultural capital is lost from production, it is only used more efficiently, and agricultural output will on the contrary rise.[9] In agricultural reforms, this kind of output reaction has indeed been observed (see Koester, 1991, who also discusses the effects and problems of agricultural reforms, reaching similar conclusions as here).

However, it may be difficult in reality to reach this situation. The capital markets may not be efficient enough to facilitate the mergers of farms, in which case there will be a loss of agricultural capital and corresponding output. Of course, spatial considerations omitted here also dictate that the number of mergers will be less than suggested above, but not necessarily to a great extent if the farms are concentrated in large enough clusters.

There could thus be a need for public intervention to facilitate the restructuring of agriculture. This could take the form of financing investments leading to a larger farm size, and perhaps loan guarantees to those farmers expanding, and also training and assistance for those leaving the agricultural sector so that they can find new jobs. Capital losses can, of course, also be a severe problem and cause social unrest, as when any rent created by public policies is eliminated.

3.5   Participation in EMU

A main element of EU membership entails participation in EMU, the formation of which still remains uncertain. In the Accession negotiations the EFTA applicants nevertheless took EMU at full face value and expected it to be realised. The room for manoeuvering under floating or unilaterally pegged exchange rates should be contrasted with the cost of staying outside EMU. This would entail exacerbation of credibility problems in policy making, as there would be no possibility of borrowing credibility from abroad. Inflation control could easily be a problem, given the deep-rooted macroeconomic preferences favouring low unemployment. This would require devaluations from time to time, and consequently expectation of devaluation would be a common situation. This would probably lead to a permanent differential in real interest rates.

In the period 1987–92, after the liberalisation of the credit markets but admittedly in a phase of mounting imbalance in the economy, the average differential in the Finnish long-term nominal interest rates *vis-à-vis* Germany was 4.5 percentage points. The differential narrowed in mid-1993 to 2 percentage points, and later, at times, even lower. However, a positive differential in real interest rates still exists. In Alho, Kotilainen and Widgrén (1992), we assumed that the gap in real long-term interest rates would be $1\frac{1}{2}$ percentage points higher outside than inside EMU. Elimination of this differential could imply an increased capital accumulation, the estimates of which range from a very small figure, implied by empirical investment equations as a reaction to a reduction in the capital cost, to as much as a quarter if a Cobb–Douglas aggregative production function is used. We cautiously estimated the effect of a rise in the capital stock at some 5 per cent, leading to a long-term rise in the consumption potential of 0.8 per cent in relation to GDP. This gain would outweigh any gains to be reaped from elimination of transactions costs and currency risk with respect to the EU currencies, which are only 0.3 per cent in relation to GDP.

3.6   An overall assessment

The overall estimate of long-term welfare gain reached in Alho, Kotilainen and Widgrén (1992) is an increase of some 4 per cent in real income in relation to GDP. This follows from the above effects and allowing for their magnification through capital accumulation in those cases where there is also an initial rise in the marginal productivity of capital.

The changes in agriculture and in the restructuring of the sheltered sector require rationalisation of the industries concerned, labour-shedding and therefore some painful adjustments. If such an adjustment did not happen (see section 3.4), the gain from EU membership would clearly be reduced, say to the order of only 1 or 2 per cent of GDP, and comprising the improvements in the external trading conditions, the reduced national burden of subsidising agriculture and the gains related to EMU. In agriculture, structural change is likely to be lower than the highest potential level, as it has been accepted in the Accession negotiations that losses in farmers' income will ultimately be compensated by a national subsidy scheme.

4   Summary and conclusions

Full membership of the EU by the EFTA-3 countries is a deviation from their traditional policies of integration, which have been confined to free trade in manufactured goods, and have avoided commitment to supranational political or economic decision making arrangements. The major reasons behind this traditional strategy were twofold. First, most of the EFTA countries pursued neutrality in their foreign policies, which formerly dictated exclusion of membership in the EU. Second, the countries have had a model for social and economic management that has differed from, and which they themselves have considered to be superior to, that of the large European countries. The most prominent example depicting this is the coinage of the term the 'Nordic' or 'Swedish' model. It is easy to understand that a natural corollary of, and a prerequisite for, this is that a high level of national sovereignty should be preserved in economic, social and political decision making.

The accession of EFTA countries to the EU would probably resolve the 'influence deficit' of these countries in European – and their own – affairs prevailing under the EEA. The final social assessment of the diverse goals of sovereignty and autonomous social management, and the gains from European-level cooperation and commitment in the EFTA countries, were finally resolved in referendums after the negotiation stage, and led Austria, Finland and Sweden to become members of the EU, but Norway to be excluded.

Some improvements in trading relations with the EU will occur, but these are likely to be quite small. The main impact of the economic changes will be felt in new sectors of the economy included in the integration process. As these may involve changes of the inter-industry type, adjustment to them will not be easy and may create social problems as EU membership is aimed to be a Pareto-type of welfare improvement for society at large. A conflict between 'EU winners' and 'EU losers' may emerge, which a policy making approach based on national homogeneity would be hard pressed to reconcile. This would deviate from the intra-industry nature of European integration (found by Balassa, 1966), with the implication of little need for large structural changes, which has facilitated political acceptance of and commitment to integration (see Sapir, 1992, for an interesting discussion on this).

EU membership may mean a change in the equilibrium of vested interests of 'economy-wide rent-sharing' and lead to more competitive surroundings and, consequently, to reduced distortions linked to the existing structures of protectionism and monopolistic behaviour, and even to a pressure towards a revised kind of social model. However, one should refrain from drawing hasty conclusions in this respect. The EU is not 'a competitive heaven' and the EU countries are in most respects not much different from the EFTA countries and have similar problems – and strengths – in their societies.[10] If the Nordic countries are going to preserve their own model, this should be arranged in a costless way with respect to their participation in integration and, accordingly, the labour market should be transformed into a more competitive one. However, if the degree of labour mobility does not remain as small as it has been, a new pressure of adjustment arises.

NOTES

Financial support by the Yrjö Jahnsson Foundation and the Finnish Cultural foundation is gratefully acknowledged. I am grateful to Richard Baldwin and two anonymous referees for sharpening the analysis.
 1 On details of the EEA, see, for example, CEPR (1992).

2 The devaluations and flotations in 1991–2 have changed this situation markedly – at least temporarily. In 1993, the price level in Finland was even lower than in Germany. After the Swedish krona was allowed to float in November 1992, the Swedish price level was at the end of 1992 roughly the same as in Germany. The current situation would thus on the surface imply a convergence to parity from the earlier disparity. However, the devaluations should be contrasted with the simultaneous reduction in export market prices and the recession, which have been more severe for Finland and Sweden than for many other countries (see OECD, 1993). We should, therefore, not make too far-reaching long-term evaluations based on very recent experiences. As the excess supply in the export markets disappears and leads to a rise in export market prices and as the domestic economy recovers, a return towards the previous price situation is already under way.

3 The relative price differential in import goods is estimated mainly from Leamer (1990), who has analysed tariffs and non-tariff barriers in 14 countries, including Finland and Germany, but not Sweden, and also using evidence provided by Horwitz (1988) and Alho (1990). This information shows that tariffs do not differ significantly between these countries, and their effect on the possible difference in import prices can only be marginal. Non-tariff barriers may, however, play a more substantial role. On the basis of these estimates, we assume that import prices are 10 per cent higher in Finland than in Germany, while for Sweden this figure is 5 per cent.

4 A proper measure for relative efficiency can be reached by constructing a Malmquist productivity index (see on this, for example, Berg et al., 1991). The idea is to study the efficiency of a unit, here the sheltered sector in Germany, and compare it with that in Finland and Sweden. To do so, a scale factor is found such that German output is produced with German factor proportions, but using Finnish or Swedish production technology. In order to carry out this comparison we had to transform to the same currency, specify a production technology (CES) and use the above estimate on the sheltered sector price differential. The results suggest that the Finnish and Swedish efficiency was a third lower than German efficiency in 1985.

5 An estimate made by the Finnish Ministry of Finance.

6 The estimates derived from the wage equations do not produce unambiguous answers. For Sweden, Calmfors and Forslund (1991) estimate that 70 per cent of the wedge between the consumer and producer prices is reflected in the nominal wage.

7 This dilemma is symptomatic of a general problem in theoretical and empirical integration analysis, namely that quite extensive welfare gains can be achieved if a situation of uniform competitive pricing is reached in Europe, instead of the present oligopolistic pricing with market segmentation. However, it is quite difficult to predict whether this kind of ultimate market integration will take place in Europe even after completion of the Single Market programme, because such an outcome is assumed, rather than shown, to be a consequence of the programme, as is done in the seminal paper by Smith and Venables (1988). A researcher seeking to give an estimate of the magnitude of integration gains faces the daunting task of either taking a position on the gains related to a final equilibrium of complete integration, but without knowledge of the articulated steps leading to it, or of omitting them totally and sticking only to the smaller gains related to elimination of

trade barriers. In the empirical estimate, this kind of choice had to be made between full price and productivity parity and the situation remaining more or less unchanged as it has been in the past.

8 Of course, it can be questioned why the existing returns to scale in agriculture are not utilised, as they would result in higher aggregate profits for the industry. There are a number of reasons which can support the prevailing situation as a quasi-equilibrium and which prevent or slow down the process towards a more efficient structure of production. One of them is the very high prices on agricultural land (capital), coupled with the fact that, if a gain in efficiency were to take place, the policies would be likely to change endogenously to eliminate this gain by reducing the price P_A, as it would be socially difficult to accept the rent linked to agricultural production rising even further.

9 As an illustration, let $Q_i = K_i^a, a > 1$. If the farm size is uniformly distributed over $(0, K_{max})$ and the farms in the range $(0, K^*)$ are merged with each other so that all the resulting farms are of the size K^*, the change in output is $d\log Q = (K^*/K_{max})^{a+1}(a-1)/2 > 0$. The resulting reduction in agricultural employment is $d\log L = \frac{1}{2}(K^*/K_{max})$.

10 See Winters (1993) for a discussion on the success of the EU in terms of regional integration and its competitive aspects.

REFERENCES

Alho, K., 1990. 'Identification of the barriers in international trade under imperfect competition', ETLA, *Discussion Paper*, **348**
     1993. 'An evaluation of the high Nordic price levels', in J. Fagerberg and L. Lundberg (eds.), *Economic Integration – A Nordic Perspective*, London: Gower
Alho, K. and M. Widgrén, 1994. 'Finland: economics and politics of EU accession', *The World Economy*, **17(5)**, 701–9
Alho, K., M. Kotilainen and M. Widgrén, 1992. 'Finland in the European Community – an assessment of the economic impact' (in Finnish with English summary), The Research Institute of the Finnish Economy, ETLA, Series B, **81**, Helsinki
Balassa, B., 1966. 'Tariff reductions and trade in manufactures among industrial countries', *American Economic Review*, **56**, 466–73
Baldwin, R., 1992. 'An eastern enlargement of EFTA: why the East Europeans should join and the EFTAns should want them', CEPR, *Occasional Paper*, **10**, London: CEPR
Berg, S.A., F.R. Försund and E.S. Jansen, 1991. 'Malmquist indices of productivity growth during the deregulation of Norwegian banking, 1980–89', *Scandinavian Journal of Economics*, **94**, Supplement, 211–28
Burgess, D.F., 1990. 'Services as intermediate goods: the issue of trade liberalization', in R.W. Jones and A.P. Krueger (eds.), *The Political Economy of International Trade*, Oxford: Basil Blackwell, 127–39
Calmfors, L. and A. Forslund, 1991. 'Real-wage determination and labour market policies: the Swedish experience', *Economic Journal*, **101(408)** (September), 1130–48

CEPR, 1992. 'Is bigger better? The economics of EC enlargement', *Monitoring European Integration*, 3, London: CEPR

Flam, H., 1994. 'From EEA to EU: economic consequences for the EFTA countries', CEPR, *Occasional Paper*, 16: London: CEPR

Horwitz, E.C., 1988. 'Några aspekter av en svensk anpassning till EGs handelspolitik mot tredje land. Skillnader i tullar och tariffära handelshinder' (On the Swedish adjustment to the EC trade policy *vis-à-vis* third countries. Differences in tariffs) (in Swedish), in *The Nordic Countries and the EEC*, papers presented at a workshop in Lund (September 1988), FIEF, NEF and Institute of Economic Research at Lund University

Kettunen, L., 1993. 'Finnish agriculture in 1992', Agricultural Economics Research Institute, *Research Publication*, 70a

Koester, U., 1991. 'The experience with liberalization policies: the case of the agricultural sector', *European Economic Review*, 35(2/3) (April), 562–70

Kola, J., J. Marttila and J. Niemi, 1991. 'EY:n ja Suomen maatalouden ja maatalouspolitiikan vertailua' (Comparison of the EC and Finnish agricultural policies) (in Finnish), *Research Reports*, 179/1991, Helsinki: Agricultural Economics Research Institute

Kotilainen, M., K. Alho and M. Erkkilä, 1994. 'Suomen valmistautuminen EMU-jäsenyyteen' (Finland's preparation for EMU membership) (in Finnish with English summary), ETLA, Series B, 103

Leamer, E.E., 1990. 'The structure and effects of tariff and nontariff barriers in 1983', in R.W. Jones and A.O. Krueger (eds.), *The Political Economy of International Trade*, Oxford: Basil Blackwell

Norman, V.D., 1989. 'EFTA and the internal European market', *Economic Policy*, 9, 425–65

1991. '1992 and EFTA', in A.S. Venables and L.A. Winters (eds.), *European Integration: Trade and Industry*, Cambridge: Cambridge University Press

OECD, 1985. *Purchasing Power Parities and Real Expenditure in the OECD*, Paris: OECD

1993. *Economic Outlook* (June), Paris: OECD

Sapir, A., 1992. 'The regional integration in Europe', *Economic Journal*, 102(415), 1491–1506

Smith, A. and A. Venables, 1988. 'Completing the internal market in the European Community: some industry simulations', *European Economic Review*, 32(7) (September), 1501–25

Winters, L.A., 1993. 'The European community: successful integration?', CEPR, *Discussion Paper*, 755

Discussion

YNGVE LINDH

1 Introduction

In his chapter 10, Kari Alho points to important adjustment mechanisms and possible welfare effects following Finland's integration with the EU. Some empirical results for Sweden are also presented. In particular, Alho analyses the effects in the sheltered sector, including agriculture. The chapter ends with a brief discussion of the effects on Finland of adjusting towards, and later participating in EMU.

In my discussion, I will emphasise Alho's analysis of the sheltered sector and the effects of taking part in EMU. I will not discuss the effects on agriculture, since they are considered in great depth in chapter 9 in this volume.

2 The Nordic–Swedish model

Alho's point of departure is that the special adjustment problems which can be foreseen in the new Nordic EU countries are a consequence of the model for social and economic management in those countries, the Nordic or Swedish model. Alho characterises the model as reliance on a collective consensus type of agreement between government, trade unions, employers' organisations and farmers. He calls this kind of society one with an economy-wide rent-sharing by pressure groups. He claims that the consequences are low efficiency and high relative prices in the sheltered sectors.

I agree to some extent with Alho's description. However, in my interpretation the real core of the Nordic–Swedish model consists of the special features of the centralised wage formation process and labour market policies. I would call this type of policy centralised supply-side economics. These type of conditions successfully promoted high productivity growth, fast restructuring of industries and a small wage dispersion up to the early 1970s.

From the mid-1970s until the 1990s, the balance of power between pressure groups was disturbed. Wage increases became higher than the norm; productivity and growth weakened. The Nordic–Swedish model was undermined and in the economic policy debate in the Nordic countries the model, as a norm for wage formation, was questioned. My point is that it was after the core of the model had crumbled that the welfare state began to expand, especially as regards social security, other transfers and subsidies, and local government consumption.

3   Integration gains of the sheltered sector

In the main part of chapter 10 Alho analyses sheltered sector efficiency in Finland and to some extent in Sweden compared to that in Germany. This analysis is done by identifying the reasons why the sheltered sector price levels in Finland and Sweden differ from those in Germany. Alho's numbers on mark-ups and their components seem reasonable. In February 1995, little more than a month after Finland and Sweden joined the EU, prices for domestic food products had fallen significantly in Finland, but not to the same extent in Sweden. This is in accord with Alho's results. However, a somewhat clearer discussion of the relationships between, and definitions of, efficiency, monopolistic price behaviour and degree of integration, would have been desirable.

4   Participation in EMU

As Alho points out, net costs would be incurred by staying outside EMU. The credibility problem could to some extent be exacerbated. Also, the benefits of being in a position to manoeuvre under floating rates may be minor. We are well aware of the timing problem in economic policy. Information and reaction lags are significant problems.

For an assessment of how well a country fits into a monetary union, a comparison of that country's industrial structure with that of the union is crucial. It says something about how sensitive the country is to various shocks. According to studies carried out at the Riksbank (Alexius, 1994; Sardelis 1994), Sweden seems to belong, together with Great Britain, Austria and Spain, to the EU countries whose industrial structure is most similar to Germany. Finland's industrial structure is somewhat less similar, but not nearly as different as that of Norway. A diversified industry is preferable in this context. In this respect, Finland and Sweden seem to belong to an intermediate group in the EU area. The industrial structures of Germany and Great Britain are much more diversified, while Norway is at the other extreme. A conclusion is that, as members of a monetary union, Sweden might manage industry-specific shocks slightly better than Finland.

Finally, Alho claims that in Finland, high employment has a relatively high weight in preferences compared to curbing inflation. Alho's conclusion is that EMU could therefore be painful.

In the case of Sweden, preferences used to be similar. Since the early 1990s there has been a shift towards low inflation seen as a means for high employment. A vast majority of the political parties, measured by their strength in Parliament and other important organisations (for instance, trade unions and the employers' organisation), now support the Swedish monetary policy objective of price stability.

This change in attitude is based on hard-earned experience. Since the mid-1970s high inflation has been a recurrent problem. In repeated cycles export firms have lost market share by pricing themselves out of the market. Production and employment have been lost as a result of high inflation. An uncontrolled redistribution of income and wealth has also been a result of unstable prices. The observed change in preferences implies that Sweden in this respect now also fits into EMU.

REFERENCES

Alexius, A., 1994. 'EU- and EFTA-länderna som optimalt valutaomräde' (The EU and EFTA countries as an optimal currency area), *Arbetsrapport*, **21** (December), Sveriges Riksbank

Sardelis, C., 1994. 'EMU och svensk stabiliseringspolitik' (EMU and Swedish stabilisation policy), *Ekonomisk Debatt*, **1994:6**

Index

Printed in the United Kingdom
by Lightning Source UK Ltd.
132860UK00002B/41/A

9 780521 057851